The Approved Mental Health Professional's Guide to Mental Health Law

ROBERT BROWN

SAGE was founded in 1965 by Sara Miller McCune to support the dissemination of usable knowledge by publishing innovative and high-quality research and teaching content. Today, we publish over 900 journals, including those of more than 400 learned societies, more than 800 new books per year, and a growing range of library products including archives, data, case studies, reports, and video. SAGE remains majority-owned by our founder, and after Sara's lifetime will become owned by a charitable trust that secures our continued independence.

Los Angeles | London | New Delhi | Singapore | Washington DC | Melbourne

The Approved Mental Health Professional's Guide to Mental Health Law

ROBERT BROWN

4th Edition

$$SAGE$$

LearningMatters

Los Angeles | London | New Delhi
Singapore | Washington DC | Melbourne

Learning Matters
An imprint of SAGE Publications Ltd
1 Oliver's Yard
55 City Road
London EC1Y 1SP

SAGE Publications Inc.
2455 Teller Road
Thousand Oaks, California 91320

SAGE Publications India Pvt Ltd
B 1/I 1 Mohan Cooperative Industrial Area
Mathura Road
New Delhi 110 044

SAGE Publications Asia-Pacific Pte Ltd
3 Church Street
#10-04 Samsung Hub
Singapore 049483

First edition published 2006
Second edition published 2009
Third edition published 2013
Fourth edition published 2016

Editor: Kate Wharton
Development editor: Lauren Simpson
Production controller: Chris Marke
Project management: Swales & Willis Ltd, Exeter,
Devon
Marketing manager: Tamara Navaratnam
Cover design: Wendy Scott
Typeset by: C&M Digitals (P) Ltd, Chennai, India
Printed and bound by CPI Group (UK) Ltd,
Croydon, CR0 4YY

Library of Congress Control Number: 2016933143

British Library Cataloguing in Publication Data

A catalogue record for this book is available from the
British Library.

ISBN 978-1-4739-4829-7
ISBN 978-1-4739-4830-3 (pbk)

At SAGE we take sustainability seriously. Most of our products are printed in the UK using FSC papers and boards.
When we print overseas we ensure sustainable papers are used as measured by the PREPS grading system.
We undertake an annual audit to monitor our sustainability.

Contents

List of abbreviations

AA	Appropriate Adult
AC	Approved Clinician
AMHP	Approved Mental Health Professional
ASW	Approved Social Worker
AWOL	Absent Without Leave
BIA	Best Interests Assessor
CCfW	Care Council for Wales
CCG	Clinical Commissioning Group
CPA	Care Programme Approach
CPN	Community Psychiatric Nurse
CQC	Care Quality Commission
CTO	Community Treatment Order
DH	Department of Health
DHSS	Department of Health and Social Security
DoLS	Deprivation of Liberty Safeguards
DRO	Disablement Resettlement Officer
ECHR	European Convention on Human Rights
ECT	Electro-Convulsive Therapy
ECtHR	European Court of Human Rights
GSCC	General Social Care Council
HA	Health Authority
HPC	Health and Care Professions Council
IMCA	Independent Mental Capacity Advocate
IMHA	Independent Mental Health Advocate
LA	Local Authority
LPA	Lasting Power of Attorney
LSSA	Local Social Services Authority
MCA	Mental Capacity Act 2005
MHA	Mental Health Act 1983
MHRT	Mental Health Review Tribunal
MHT	Mental Health Tribunal
NHS	National Health Service
NIMHE	National Institute for Mental Health in England
NR	Nearest Relative
PACE	Police and Criminal Evidence Act 1984
PCT	Primary Care Trust
RC	Responsible Clinician

RMO	Responsible Medical Officer
SCT	Supervised Community Treatment
SI	Statutory Instrument
SOAD	Second Opinion Appointed Doctor
SSD	Social Services Department

About the author

Rob Brown is a social worker and trainer. He was a founding director of Edge Training and Consultancy Ltd. He runs refresher courses for approved mental health professionals (AMHPs) and teaches s12 doctors and approved clinicians in England and Wales. He provides consultation and supervision for the AMHPs/BIAs in the Deprivation of Liberty Team in Cornwall. He also provides consultation for lead AMHPs in Hampshire, West Berkshire and Lambeth. He was a Mental Health Act Commissioner from 1993 to 2010. Rob is a Visiting Fellow at Bournemouth University. He has published widely in the field of mental health and mental capacity law.

Foreword from the Series Editor

This new edition of *The Approved Mental Health Professional's Guide to Mental Health Law* has been expertly produced by Rob Brown. Those of us who have been fortunate to know Rob personally know him to be a person of great wisdom and insight in this area and of course we are all aware of his wit and humour. The sector really has benefited from his expertise over the years and his contribution to mental health care and services has been simply remarkable.

The role of the approved mental health professional (AMHP) is very similar to that of its predecessor, the approved social worker (ASW), but it may now be undertaken by nurses, occupational therapists and psychologists, as well as social workers. The training is now overseen and quality-assured by the Health and Care Professions Council but otherwise currently remains the same as per the previous outcomes specified by the General Social Care Council.

Of note has been the fact that the number of assessments being carried out by AMHPs has increased considerably in the past few years, making this guide's various checklists even more useful when AMHPs are under such pressure.

I warmly recommend this text to all budding AMHPs as well as others who are interested in the operation of the Mental Health Act 1983. It sits alongside other texts in the Post-Qualifying Social Work Practice series such as *The Approved Mental Health Professional's Guide to Psychiatry and Medication* and *The Mental Capacity Act 2005: A Guide for Mental Health Professionals*. Readers will also find this book useful to read in conjunction with another Sage/Learning Matters text – *Mental Health Law in England and Wales* – as this contains the full text of the Mental Health Act 1983 as well as relevant regulations.

Professor Keith Brown
Series Editor
Director of the National Centre for Post-Qualifying
Social Work, Bournemouth University

Preface to the 2016 edition

Welcome to *The Approved Mental Health Professional's Guide to Mental Health Law*. This has been designed primarily for mental health professionals who are on an AMHP course or for those helping to provide placement opportunities for such an AMHP trainee. The book should also be useful for practising AMHPs, other mental health professionals, service users, carers and others interested in the field of mental health law. The law covered here is that which covers England and Wales. Note that mental health law is significantly different in Scotland, Northern Ireland, the Isle of Man, Guernsey and Jersey. References to the Code of Practice to the Mental Health Act are for the English Code (Department of Health, 2015). Unfortunately at the time of going to print the new Welsh Code was only available in draft form. Any use of the Act in Wales needs to be compliant with the Welsh Code.

The companion volume *Mental Health Law in England and Wales* will provide readers with a copy of the Mental Health Act 1983 itself (as amended by the 2007 Act) together with relevant Regulations. The specific competences required of approved mental health professionals are set out in separate Regulations for England and for Wales. These are included in this text at Appendices 4A and 4B respectively. There are minor differences between the English and Welsh versions. This book cross-refers to these competences at the beginning of each chapter (using the English numbering system). Typical assignment questions are also included at the end of each chapter, together with a number of multiple choice questions to aid learning.

The assessment examples are based on the Bournemouth University Postgraduate Diploma in Advanced Mental Health Practice, a course delivered in partnership with a number of local authorities. The course meets the Health and Care Professions Council (HPC) standards and requirements for the role of approved mental health professional and the Department of Health requirements for the role of best interests assessor (BIA) (Mental Capacity Act 2005). The course is at Master's level and many students will continue with their studies to complete an MA in Advanced Mental Health Practice. Not all AMHP courses in England or Wales will be linked so directly to the BIA role. This role is part of the Deprivation of Liberty Safeguards (DOLS) and even AMHPs who do not complete BIA training will need to be aware of how these safeguards operate. More detailed information is included in the companion volume *The Mental Capacity Act 2005: A Guide for Mental Health Professionals*.

Mental health law has been changing rapidly in recent years. Apart from the statutory changes, there have been several important developments in case law. This book is up to date as at the beginning of April 2016. Readers may wish to check that there has been no major recent case law which alters the position as stated here. A good source is **www.mentalhealthlaw.co.uk**. There is also mental health material on the Department of Health's website **www.dh.gov.uk**, which covers England, and on the Welsh Government website at **www.wales.gov.uk**, which covers the position in Wales.

Recent changes which are covered in this book include:

- the revised English Code of Practice to the Mental Health Act;
- the revised Reference Guide to the Mental Health Act;
- a number of cases concerning the nearest relative;
- clarification on personal accountability of the AMHP;
- revisions to the tribunal report requirements in England;
- the impact of the *Cheshire West* case decisions in the Supreme Court.

The number of assessments requiring AMHPs has increased greatly in the last few years. In the first full year of operation of the amended Act (2009–10) in England there were 44,343 applications for detention under section 2 or 3 or where there was a revocation of a CTO. In 2014–15 this number had risen to 66,921. These figures do not include assessments where detention was not the outcome and they also exclude the use of section 4 as well as cases where an application was made after a patient had been taken to hospital under section 135. Community treatment orders also require an AMHP assessment. Completed CTOs have been running at about 4000 per year for the last five years. At the same time the number of AMHPs has fallen and availability of beds has become a considerable problem. Pressure on AMHPs has never been so high.

This guide should be read in conjunction with the Mental Health Act 1983, as amended, and the relevant Code of Practice for England or Wales. These are issued to most trainee AMHPs. The Code referred to in this text is the English version. Many trainees also find the *Reference Guide to the Mental Health Act* helpful as it is written in accessible English.

Readers may note that, in terms of personal pronouns, 'he' is used rather than 'he/she'. This is consistent with the approach taken in Acts of Parliament and is used in a non-gender-specific way. Occasionally the Code of Practice uses 'they' in the singular sense, though this has been known to confuse judges.

Inevitably, there will be changes to the law during the life of this volume but we hope it will help in keeping you reasonably well informed on current mental health law. There is a list of legal references at the end of the guide.

I would like to thank Neil Allen, Paul Barber, Anthony Harbour and Debbie Martin who have all made helpful comments on this new edition. Their views, based on their experience and knowledge of how the law operates in practice, have been very helpful. However, I accept responsibility for any inaccuracies which remain within the text.

Finally I would like to thank my wife Pamela who once again has supported me in producing this fourth edition, and who encouraged me to persevere when I was struggling with the implications of the Supreme Court decision and some of the changes in the revised English Code of Practice. Her support has been invaluable.

Robert Brown
Edge Training and Consultancy, Office 706,
c/o Scott-Moncrieff and Associates Ltd,
88 Kingsway, London, WC2B 6AA

Chapter 1

Introduction and definitions of mental disorder

BECOMING AN APPROVED MENTAL HEALTH PROFESSIONAL

This chapter should help candidates to achieve the following competences:

Application of knowledge: the legal and policy framework

Applied knowledge of:

2(1)(a)(i)   *mental health legislation, related codes of practice, national and local policy guidance.*

Application of knowledge: mental disorder

Critical understanding of:

3(a)   *a range of models of mental disorder, including the contribution of social, physical and developmental factors;*

3(b)   *the social perspective on mental disorder and mental health needs in working with patients, their relatives, carers and other professionals;*

3(c)   *the implications of mental disorder for patients, their relatives and carers.*

Common law

Although the role of the approved mental health professional (AMHP) is rooted firmly in statute there are sometimes overlaps with the common law. The *Oxford Dictionary of Law* (Law, 2015, p122) gives three basic definitions of common law:

1. *The part of English law based on rules developed by the royal courts during the first three centuries after the Norman Conquest (1066) as a system applicable to the whole country, as opposed to local customs . . .*

2. *Rules of law developed by the courts as opposed to those created by statute.*

3. *A general system of law deriving exclusively from court decisions.*

Montgomery (2002, p7) has described common law as:

> *The rules which are extrapolated from the practice of the judges in deciding cases. Judges should take a consistent approach to recurring issues and are obliged to follow the decisions of earlier cases, at least when they have been given by the higher courts. Once a matter has been resolved by a judge it therefore sets a precedent which enshrines the legal rule.*

Some practitioners have referred to this as 'common sense under a wig'.

An example of an area covered by common law rather than statute is intervention in an emergency for an informal patient. Even if the patient lacks capacity they may be an immediate risk to others and relying on the Mental Capacity Act may not be possible in terms of treatment or restraint. See Chapter 6 for a more detailed discussion of this area of law.

Civil liberties vs welfarism

Before considering models and definitions of mental disorder in depth it is important to think of the consequences which might flow from being seen as mentally disordered. This depends to some extent on the prevailing ideology as reflected in law and practice. One way of looking at the effects of different ideologies on mental health law is to contrast the views of those with 'civil libertarian' leanings such as Thomas Szasz with those of a more 'welfarist' persuasion represented by the Zito Trust until its closure in 2009. If one were to adopt Szasz's views (disputing the notion of 'mental illness' but, if conceding that it might exist, adopting the view that people should make their own decisions about their treatment, as with physical illness), then presumably there would be no need for mental health law at all. There might be a case to consider law relating to mental incapacity linked to brain injury, dementia, demonstrable learning disability, etc., but this would not allow for the detention of people who psychiatrists consider to be suffering from schizophrenia, depression, etc.

A welfarist approach might make an assumption that mental illness is linked to a degree of mental incapacity (as in the term 'lack of insight') but whether or not this is the case, a welfarist view would be that it is sometimes necessary to intervene against someone's will to protect a person from themselves or for the protection of others. The rapid growth in the numbers of community treatment orders could be seen as a victory for welfarism, especially as there is no reduction in the number of detained patients.

The contrast between these competing ideologies is illustrated in Figure 1.1. The Mental Health Act 1983 can be seen as positioned somewhere in the middle of the upper continuum illustrated. AMHPs, doctors, tribunals and courts are left to make decisions as to when the circumstances justify intervention. With the exception of ECT treatment, however, mental capacity is not the relevant test used in the Mental Health Act. The criteria needed are a mental disorder of a nature or degree to warrant intervention plus an appropriate level of risk.

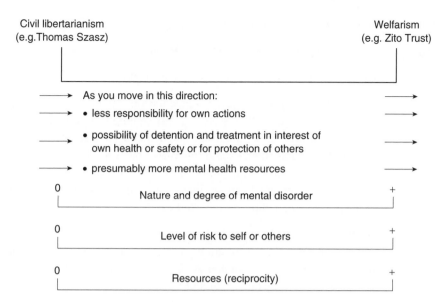

Figure 1.1   Different perspectives on mental health law

Gostin (1975) made the ethical point that, if you deprive someone of liberty, you should have a duty to provide a good quality service. One part of the Mental Health Act which addresses this issue is section 117 relating to after-care. Consistent guidance that section 117 services should not incur charges could be seen to reflect the link between the positive end of the resource continuum with the welfarist intervention point. Similarly the Richardson Committee on the Reform of the Mental Health Act considered the principle of 'reciprocity'. Free after-care services have been retained in the reformed Mental Health Act despite the controversy on this subject. The same is not true, however, for the new Deprivation of Liberty Safeguards (DoLS) or indeed where guardianship is used.

Another way of using Figure 1.1 is to imagine a point in the middle of the upper continuum where detention would be justified if there was:

- mental disorder of a nature or degree to justify this;

- a level of risk to self or others which also justified detention.

Mental health terminology and the law

Common law distinguished 'idiots' from 'lunatics' before the first of the Acts. These terms correspond with the distinction between people with a learning disability and those who are mentally ill. Historically, the groups have sometimes been dealt with in separate legislation and sometimes together, as in the Mental Health Act 1983.

1713/44	Vagrancy Acts allowed detention of 'Lunaticks or mad persons'.
1774	Act for regulating private madhouses.

3

1845   Lunatics Act included 'Persons of unsound mind'.

1886   Idiots Act provided separately for idiots and imbeciles.

1890   Lunacy (Consolidation) Act ignored the distinction.

1913   Mental Deficiency Act favoured segregation of 'mental defectives': *idiots* were unable to guard themselves against common physical dangers such as fire, water or traffic; *imbeciles* could guard against physical dangers but were incapable of managing themselves or their affairs; *feeble-minded* needed care or control for protection of self or others; *moral defectives* had vicious or criminal propensities (use of this category later included many poor women with unsupported babies).

1927   Mental Deficiency Act emphasised care outside institutions. Mental deficiency was defined as 'a condition of arrested or incomplete development of mind existing before the age of 18 years whether arising from inherent causes or induced by disease or injury'.

1930   Mental Treatment Act allowed for voluntary admissions.

1946   NHS Act ended distinction between paying and non-paying patients.

1948   National Assistance Act made provision for those in need.

1959   Mental Health Act. Mental disorder means: 'mental illness; arrested or incomplete development of mind, psychopathic disorder, and any other disorder or disability of mind'. Further classifications for long-term compulsion were: mental illness, severe subnormality, subnormality, psychopathic disorder, with a kind of treatability test for the last two.

1970   LA Social Services Act created Social Services Departments (SSDs).

1983   Mental Health Act. The broad definition is exactly the same as in the 1959 Act. However, the classifications were changed to: *mental illness* (undefined); *severe mental impairment*: 'a state of arrested or incomplete development of mind which includes severe impairment of intelligence and social functioning and is associated with abnormally aggressive or seriously irresponsible conduct on the part of the person concerned'; *mental impairment*: 'a state of arrested or incomplete development of mind (not amounting to severe mental impairment) which includes significant impairment of intelligence and social functioning and is associated with abnormally aggressive or seriously irresponsible conduct on the part of the person concerned'; *psychopathic disorder*: 'a persistent disorder or disability of mind (whether or not including significant impairment of intelligence) which results in abnormally aggressive or seriously irresponsible conduct on the part of the person concerned'.

1984   Police and Criminal Evidence Act (plus its Codes of Practice) uses the term 'mental disorder' as per the Mental Health Act and the revised PACE Codes use the concept of the mentally vulnerable adult.

2002	Draft Mental Health Bill definition: 'any disability or disorder of mind or brain which results in an impairment or disturbance of mental functioning'.
2003	Mental Capacity Bill. Provides for people unable to make a decision 'because of an impairment of, or a disturbance in the functioning of, the mind or brain'.
2004	Revised Draft Mental Health Bill definition of mental disorder was: 'an impairment of or a disturbance in the functioning of mind or brain resulting from any disability or disorder of the mind or brain'.
2005	Parliamentary Scrutiny Committee accepted the above definition but stated: 'that a broad definition of mental disorder in the draft Bill must be accompanied by explicit and specific exclusions which safeguard against the legislation being used inappropriately as a means of social control'. However, the final version as a result of reforms is . . .
2007	'Any disorder or disability of the mind'. The word 'brain' is removed, which gives at least some potential space between the Mental Health Act definition and that of the test for incapacity in the Mental Capacity Act. However, it is still a very broad definition and the removal of most of the exclusions has potentially broadened it still further. There are no longer any separate classifications of mental disorder.

The Scottish Mental Health Act 2003 defines mental disorder as mental illness, personality disorder or learning disability. This is probably more in line with current mental health practice than the definition for England and Wales, especially as Scotland retained exclusions for sexual orientation, sexual deviancy, transsexualism and transvestism.

Models of mental disorder

There are many theoretical approaches to mental disorder. In the *Journal of Mental Health* Pilgrim (2002) traces the history of the biopsychosocial model. There is also a chapter by Dallos in the Open University text, *Mental Health Matters* (Heller *et al.*, 2000). This is rather light on social explanations so the bio-social model is outlined below and a few other approaches are considered. Dallos identified three levels of analysis: societal, interpersonal and individual. He described what he saw as the most influential psychological frameworks under these headings: biological and medical, behavioural, psychodynamic, humanistic and systemic. They share important features (e.g. in terms of the importance of empathy, the therapeutic relationship and clear communication) but they can lead to different approaches to intervention.

Biological and medical frameworks

These would see problems stemming from physical causes including illness, accident and hereditary factors. Some theorists suggest that schizophrenia and depression are linked to brain defects such as neurotransmitter problems. Medical frameworks see mental health problems as similar to physical illness. This leads to classification of mental disorders and a regime of treatment which relies heavily on the use of medication. Psycho-educational approaches often have a biological view of causation but also recognise that, as with physical illness, social and environmental factors interact with the illness. Some approaches emphasise the importance of stress and lead to treatments which include work with the emotional atmosphere in families (see Leff and Vaughn, 1985).

Behavioural frameworks

These suggest psychological problems are acquired through learning experiences and are then affected by various punishments and rewards from social interaction. Treatments might include systematic desensitisation (e.g. with phobias), behaviour modification (e.g. to remove rewards which are maintaining problem behaviour) or cognitive-behavioural approaches (which would include helping people to modify immediate cognitive response to potentially upsetting situations). Cognitive-behavioural techniques have recently gained some ground within psychiatric practice in Britain.

Psychodynamic approaches

An individual's emotional experiences (especially in early childhood) are seen as the primary cause of later problems. Treatment often focuses on bringing memories of these early experiences into consciousness and thereby enabling the person to deal with them in a way that empowers them to be more autonomous. Some theorists (such as Freud) emphasised the importance of sexuality and an inability to resolve sexual feelings within a family. Treatment often focuses on the therapeutic relationship and the concept of transference (e.g. the patient transfers feelings from earlier relationships onto the therapist). Psychoanalysis is an expensive and time-intensive therapy but briefer psychodynamic techniques have also been developed.

Humanistic frameworks

These also consider unconscious processes but see people as essentially creative and motivated by a need to grow and develop. Conscious and unconscious states can be integrated, leading to more autonomy and freedom. Use is made of art, music, writing, drama, etc. The emphasis is on self-direction rather than interpretation and may lead to support groups being formed or self-help groups with no therapist involvement.

Systemic frameworks

These see problems as being rooted in communications within relationships and in patterns of action rather than within the individual. Systemic family therapy focuses on communication within the family and uses feedback to look at how people's actions relate to the effects of previous actions. Repetitive relationship patterns are seen to arise partly from shared beliefs and understandings.

Social models

There are various versions of a social model of mental disorder. At one level, mental illness would be seen as a consequence of social disadvantage, the symptom of a sick society. The solution would lie in improving social and physical conditions. In 1992 David Goldberg and Peter Huxley published an influential text entitled *Common Mental Disorders: A Bio-Social Model* which sought to link some social factors in mental disorder with biological aspects. Their model looks at susceptibility to mental disorder in terms of social, psychological and biological factors. Their work is based on three key concepts:

- *vulnerability* – factors which make some people more susceptible to episodes of mental disorder: a vulnerable individual may experience symptoms after a relatively minor stress;
- *destabilisation* – the process of beginning to experience symptoms;
- *restitution* – the process of losing symptoms: factors which determine how long an episode of illness will last in a given individual.

In summarising key features of the model, Goldberg and Huxley (1992, p144) state:

> *The development of different types of symptom is seen as being determined by early childhood events, the present social circumstances and the kind of provoking event, and not at all by genetic factors. Genetic factors are seen as being very important in determining overall vulnerability towards common mental disorders and are responsible for some of the specific vulnerability to major mental disorders such as schizophrenia and bipolar illness, but they do not determine why one person will become depressed and another anxious.*

Another helpful text which gives some different perspectives on mental disorder is *Mental Health in a Multi-ethnic Society* edited by Suman Fernando and Frank Keating (2008).

Other models

Historically and culturally there have been wide-ranging explanations for mental disorder. Some of those not included above are:

- *The moral model.* The person's behaviour is seen as bad on the basis of judgements made on their observed behaviour and that they need moral treatment.
- *The impaired model.* The person is seen as handicapped and unlikely to be restored to normality by treatment.

- *The psychedelic model.* The mad have been chosen by society to act out its prob-lems. They can reveal themselves as particularly gifted members of society and must be allowed to develop their potential for inner exploration and to change the world through their insights.

- *The conspiratorial model.* Madness stems from the way mentally ill people are labelled. See the work of Thomas Scheff, Szasz and Laing.

Recent texts focus on development in biological sciences and on philosophical issues. See Gelder *et al.* (2012).

Models of mental disorder and the law

People's understanding of how the mind works together with their views on mental capacity, free will, determinism and social responsibility combine to influence how they think the law should operate in this field. The law will sometimes make assump-tions and reflect some models of mental disorder more strongly than others. It helps to have a grasp of these models in order to consider how the law will affect service users and carers, and how it might constrain their ability to choose an approach that matches their own preferred explanations of mental disorder.

Definitions of mental disorder (section 1)

Introduction

Definitions of mental disorder are of central importance as the Act applies only to those believed to be mentally disordered. Section 1 states: *The provisions of this Act shall have effect with respect to the reception, care and treatment of mentally disordered patients.* Judgements on mental disorder may be made by a range of peo-ple, e.g. doctors, police, magistrates, mental health tribunal members. In each case, judgements must be made within the framework of the definitions given in section 1. Coming within the definition of mental disorder is not sufficient, by itself, to warrant detention in hospital. The disorder must be of a nature or degree to warrant the use of compulsion. Unless the person is seen as mentally disordered, the Act does not apply. Problems arising from including people with learning disabilities are considered below.

Broad definition of 'mental disorder'

The Mental Health Act 1983 as amended gives a broad definition of the generic term 'mental disorder' and there are no longer any specific classifications.

'Mental disorder' is described in section 1(2) as:

> *any disorder or disability of the mind.*

This is a significant broadening of the definition that had previously been used, espe-cially in relation to the longer-term forms of compulsion and court-related orders.

A list of possible examples of mental disorder is set out in para 2.5 of the Code of Practice (Department of Health, 2015):

- *affective disorders, such as depression and bipolar disorder*
- *schizophrenia and delusional disorders*
- *neurotic, stress-related and somatoform disorders, such as anxiety, phobic disorders, obsessive compulsive disorders, post-traumatic stress disorder and hypochondriacal disorders*
- *organic mental disorders such as dementia and delirium (however caused)*
- *personality and behavioural changes caused by brain injury or damage (however acquired)*
- *personality disorders . . .*
- *mental and behavioural disorders caused by psychoactive substance use . . .*
- *eating disorders, non-organic sleep disorders and non-organic sexual disorders*
- *learning disabilities . . .*
- *autistic spectrum disorders (including Asperger's syndrome) . . .*
- *behavioural and emotional disorders of children and adolescents.*

There is no longer a specific reference to 'mental illness' although this would clearly be included within the broader definition. In the Mental Health (Northern Ireland) Order 1986 mental disorder is defined as *mental illness, mental handicap and any other disorder or disability of mind.* Mental illness is defined as a *state of mind which affects a person's thinking, perceiving, emotion or judgement to the extent that he requires care or medical treatment in his own interests or in the interest of other persons.*

Exclusions

Section 1(3) used to exclude a range of behaviours from being seen in themselves as mental disorders. These were: *promiscuity or other immoral conduct, sexual deviancy or dependence on alcohol or drugs.* The DHSS in the *Review of the Mental Health Act 1959* (1978) saw these as 'social and behavioural problems' rather than mental disorders. The revised Act has removed the exclusions (apart from dependence on alcohol or drugs) and this has led to concerns about mental health law being used to control social problems. In general, Hale (2010) argues that the distinction in law between social or behavioural problems on the one hand and mental disorder on the other is still far from clear. The current discussions on how to deal with people who have a severe personality disorder are a good illustration of her argument. In Northern Ireland the response to this issue was to make personality disorder an exclusion (together with promiscuity or other immoral conduct, sexual deviancy or dependence on alcohol or drugs). It is therefore not possible to treat someone as mentally disordered in Northern Ireland by reason only of personality disorder.

There was some heated debate around the proposed removal of the exclusions from mental disorder as the 2007 Bill was passing through Parliament. The House of Lords wanted the addition of further exclusions while the government wished to remove all of them. As we have noted, the conclusion was that only the exclusion relating to dependence on alcohol or drugs was retained. This means that it will still not be possible to use the Act's compulsory powers on the basis of drug or alcohol dependence alone. However, as the Code of Practice notes at 2.11:

> Alcohol or drug dependence may be accompanied by, or associated with, a mental disorder which does fall within the Act's definition. If the relevant criteria are met, it is therefore possible, for example, to detain people who are suffering from mental disorder, even though they are also dependent on alcohol or drugs. This is true even if the mental disorder in question results from the person's alcohol or drug dependence.

As a result, a related or consequential mental disorder could lead to detention. The removal of the exclusions relating to promiscuity, other immoral conduct and sexual deviancy are undoubtedly controversial.

The Explanatory Notes to the Mental Health Act 2007 state at para. 24:

> Clinically, neither promiscuity nor 'other immoral conduct' by itself is regarded as a mental disorder, so the deletion of that exclusion makes no practical difference. Similarly, sexual orientation (homo-, hetero- and bi-sexuality) alone is not regarded as a mental disorder. However, there are disorders of sexual preference which are recognised clinically as mental disorders. Some of these disorders might be considered 'sexual deviance' in the terms of the current exclusion (for example paraphilias like fetishism or paedophilia). On that basis, the amendment would bring such disorders within the scope of the 1983 Act.

Barber *et al.* (2012) comment:

> Clearly the government intends (so long as the other criteria are met) that paedophilia, for example, should be capable of being regarded as a mental disorder for the purposes of using the compulsory powers of the Act. If paedophilia could be considered a symptom of a personality disorder it would not have been excluded from consideration in any event under the unamended Act. The question is whether without being such a symptom, the removal of sexual deviancy as an exclusion makes it easier to argue that such conditions constitute mental disorders eligible for consideration for use of the compulsory powers. Of course all other criteria would have to be met (e.g. as to risk), but an argument can be anticipated that rather than being true mental disorders they are behaviours deviating from society's norms and therefore falling foul of the Winterwerp criteria for what constitutes lawful detention on the basis of unsoundness of mind . . . As Fennell (2007, pp49–50) points out the mere presence of such conditions in manuals such as ICD-10 or DSM IV does not establish them as mental disorders for legal purposes. Nor does the non-appearance of a condition in the manuals mean that it cannot legally be considered a mental disorder.

If an AMHP is asked to assess a person at a police station (where they have been taken following an arrest for an alleged offence or under section 136 of the Mental Health Act) and the person is an alleged paedophile, any decision would need to be especially well recorded in terms of any judgement on the nature or degree of any possible mental disorder. Fortunately even the section 2 medical recommendations now require the doctors to give a clinical description of the mental disorder. This is an area where there may be some legal challenge.

Learning disability

There is a school of thought which believes that people with learning disabilities should be excluded from mental health legislation. Some groups consider that such people should either be dealt with under separate legislation (e.g. based on mental incapacity) or should not be subject to any form of compulsion. The counter view is that people with learning disabilities should be included for all aspects of the Mental Health Act. The compromise position adopted in 1982 has been preserved in the revised Act. This means that at least a minority of people with learning disabilities are covered by the Mental Health Act in general, and that an even smaller group, who are abnormally aggressive or seriously irresponsible, are liable to longer-term compulsion in some circumstances. There was some confusion generated by this compromise. Even after publication in 1983 of the consolidated Mental Health Act, some people believed that the Act stated that people with learning disabilities could be detained only if they were also abnormally aggressive or seriously irresponsible. In fact, this restriction applies only to some longer-term sections (e.g. sections 3, 7 and 37). A look at the Parliamentary Scrutiny Committee report (House of Lords, 2005, p33) shows that confusion continued to exist after 2000, as their explanation of the 1983 Act contained errors, e.g. stating that arrested or incomplete development of mind must be associated with abnormally aggressive or seriously irresponsible conduct before someone can be detained under section 2.

One by-product of the compromise in the 1983 Act was the exclusion of some people from the provisions of guardianship where they might have benefited from it. These are people who have arrested or incomplete development of mind, who are subject to exploitation or neglect, but would not be seen as abnormally aggressive or seriously irresponsible, thereby excluding them from the definition of mental impairment. Apart from a change in behaviour, the only way such individuals could be received into guardianship was where the relevant professionals took a liberal interpretation of the definition. However, some doctors and others, understandably, were not willing to see someone who was exploited or neglected as 'seriously irresponsible' just because they have failed to rectify the position for themselves. The death of Beverley Lewis drew this problem to people's attention. In a Court of Appeal case (*Re F* (Mental Health Act: Guardianship (2000)) the court overturned a county court judge's decision (when displacing her father as nearest relative) that a 17-year-old with learning disability, who wished to return home where she would be at risk of abuse, was acting in a 'seriously irresponsible' manner. The Appeal Court preferred a more restrictive interpretation of this phrase. Subsequent court decisions have followed this line. However, for those people with learning disabilities who exhibit more active risky behaviour the decision in *R (GC)* v *Kingswood* (2008) means that this may be seen as 'seriously irresponsible conduct' on a case-by-case basis.

The position since November 2008 is that learning disability can be seen as a mental disorder and needs specific consideration only when looking at long-term compulsion. At this point the definition of learning disability is defined in section 1(4) as:

> *a state of arrested or incomplete development of the mind which includes significant impairment of intelligence and social functioning.*

For longer-term compulsion learning disability will not constitute a mental disorder unless 'associated with abnormally aggressive or seriously irresponsible conduct' on the part of the patient. It follows that, for example, neither section 3 nor section 7 can be invoked without this qualification being met. This in effect recreates the previous position when the term 'mental impairment' was used to cover such patients.

Particular care will need to be taken by AMHPs and doctors when completing the relevant forms as those used for applications and medical recommendations do not make this behavioural requirement explicit. AMHPs should be alert so that as soon as they see a reference to learning disability in a recommendation for section 3 or 7 they check to see that the behavioural issue is included in the doctor's description. The additional behavioural test will not be an issue where the patient also has another form of mental disorder. It may be of some interest to note that the Code of Practice suggests that autistic spectrum disorders should be seen as mental disorders in their own right.

> *2.17 The learning disability qualification does not apply to autistic spectrum disorders (including Asperger's syndrome). It is possible for someone with an autistic spectrum disorder to meet the criteria for compulsory measures under the Act without having any other form of mental disorder, even if it is not associated with abnormally aggressive or seriously irresponsible behaviour. While experience suggests that this is likely to be necessary only very rarely, the possibility should never automatically be discounted.*

In conclusion we are left with a situation where some very vulnerable patients with learning disabilities could be detained under section 2 but, at the end of the 28 days, unless there was evidence of abnormally aggressive or seriously irresponsible conduct, the Mental Health Act could no longer be used. The Mental Capacity Act might provide some protection but whether the safeguards are as appropriate as with the Mental Health Act is open to question.

The 'appropriate medical treatment' test

The government was determined to remove the 'treatability' test contained in the unamended Act. It was seen as a bar to admitting certain patients (especially those with personality disorders who posed a risk to others) whom the government did not wish to see excluded from compulsory admission. There was a counter-argument that some therapeutic purpose should be required before a person could be admitted and treated compulsorily. A compromise was reached whereby for section 3 there is a requirement that 'appropriate medical treatment' is available. Of some significance is that the medical recommendations now require the doctors to specify the hospital where a bed is available offering the appropriate treatment. The AMHP could apply only to a hospital listed on the medical recommendations. This, combined with changes in the Code's guidance on the use of section 2 and section 3, has led to a decline in the number of section 3 admissions from the community and a corresponding increase for section 2 where there is no such appropriate treatment test.

'Medical treatment' itself is defined in section 145 of the Mental Health Act 1983:

> *Any reference in this Act to medical treatment in relation to mental disorder shall be construed as a reference to medical treatment the purpose of which is to alleviate, or prevent a worsening of, the disorder or one or more of its symptoms or manifestations.*

This introduces a therapeutic purpose test but no requirement that treatment is 'likely' to achieve its aims as was the case with the old 'treatability test'. The definition of medical treatment is very broad. Section 145(1) states:

> *'Medical treatment' includes nursing, psychological intervention and specialist mental health habilitation, rehabilitation and care.*

The Code of Practice states at para. 23.19:

> *An indication of unwillingness to co-operate with treatment generally, or with a specific aspect of treatment, does not make such treatment inappropriate.*

The test will require some consideration by the professionals involved with assessments for section 3 detention but it is unlikely to act as a barrier to admission in many cases. The key for staff will be to look at the nature and degree of the mental disorder and consider how the proposed treatment relates to these aspects. Given the broad definition of mental disorder and of medical treatment the availability of a hospital bed is likely to be a far more crucial factor, and the revisions to the Act have done nothing to pressurise health authorities into ensuring that beds are available for patients where professionals consider admission is necessary.

Summary of 'mental disorder' as defined in section 1 of the MHA 1983

For all detentions up to 28 days (e.g. sections 2, 4, 136):

- 'any disorder or disability of the mind' – but a person should not be seen as suffering from a mental disorder by reason only of dependence on alcohol or drugs.

For compulsion under longer-terms sections (e.g. sections 3, 7 or 37):

As above with two additional restrictions:

- appropriate medical treatment must be available, and the doctors must identify on their recommendations where this would be located;

- where the patient is identified as having a learning disability (defined in section 1(4) as: a *state of arrested or incomplete development of the mind which includes significant impairment of intelligence and social functioning*) then this must also be *associated with abnormally aggressive or seriously irresponsible conduct.*

ACTIVITY *1.1*

Sample questions on definitions
(Questions are typical AMHP examination questions and are usually in three parts.)

1a *What is the relevant definition of 'mental disorder' as per section 1 of the Mental Health Act 1983 when considering a possible compulsory admission under section 2?*

1b *List anything which, by itself, would be excluded from being a mental disorder under section 1.*

1c *Using one of these as an example, identify why the exclusion might be a problem for those considering the use of section 2.*

2a *What are the essential elements of the definition of 'learning disability' as given in section 1 of the Mental Health Act 1983? When does the definition become relevant?*

2b *What relevance does this issue have to the protection of a vulnerable adult with a learning disability?*

2c *What alternatives to the Mental Health Act might be considered for such a patient, and what are some of the advantages and disadvantages of these?*

Multiple choice questions

(Answers in Appendix 9)

1. *For the purposes of an admission under section 3 which of the following could, by themselves, be considered as a form of 'mental disorder'?*

(a) *Learning disability* ☐

(b) *Dependence on alcohol* ☐

(c) *Disorder of mind* ☐

(d) *Dependence on drugs* ☐

(e) *Disability of mind* ☐

(f) *Learning disability associated with abnormally aggressive or seriously irresponsible conduct* ☐

2. *Psychopathic disorder does not appear in the Mental Health Act 1983 as amended.*

    (a) *True* ☐
    (b) *False* ☐

3. *Learning disability is defined in the Act as 'a state of arrested or incomplete development of mind which includes significant impairment of intelligence and social functioning'.*

    (a) *True* ☐
    (b) *False* ☐

15

Chapter 2

Civil admissions, guardianship and community treatment orders

Compulsory admission to hospital and detention under sections 2, 3, 4, 5 or 135 of the MHA 1983

Introduction

This chapter concentrates on civil admissions (as opposed to those involving the courts – see Chapter 5). There are variations in the criteria for admissions to hospital between the different sections and these are set out below. Before looking at each of the sections in turn, however, it should be stressed that the need for the AMHP to seek the 'least restrictive alternative' is common to all of them (see Chapter 4). Careful attention should be paid to the grounds for detention. In practice, the expression 'a danger to himself or others' is often used erroneously for section 2 in place of the actual grounds, i.e. that detention is necessary for the patient *in the interests of his own health or safety or with a view to the protection of other persons.* The 'danger' grounds come into play only where the nearest relative intends to

Table 2.1   Periods of compulsion for Part 2 patients (including access to mental health tribunals and whether Part 4 consent to treatment rules apply)

Section number and purpose	Maximum duration	Can patient apply to the tribunal?	Can nearest relative apply to the tribunal?	Automatic tribunal hearing?	Consent to treatment rules?*
2 Admission for assessment	**28 days** Not renewable	Yes. Within first 14 days	No – s23 gives discharge power but see s25	No	Yes
3 Admission for treatment	**6 months** Renewable for 6 months and then yearly	Yes. Within first 6 months and then in each period	No – s23 gives discharge power but see s25	Yes. At 6 months and then every 3 years (yearly if under 18)	Yes
4 Admission for assessment in an emergency	**72 hours** Not renewable but second doctor can change to s2	Yes. Only relevant if s4 converted to an s2	No	No	No
5(2) Doctor or AC's holding power	**72 hours** Not renewable	No	No	No	No
5(4) Nurse's holding power	**6 hours** Not renewable but doctor or AC can change to s5(2)	No	No	No	No
7 Reception into guardianship	**6 months** Renewable for 6 months and then yearly	Yes. Within first 6 months and then in each period	No – s23 gives them power to discharge	No	No
17A Community treatment order (CTO)	**6 months** Extendable by 6 months and then yearly	Yes. Within first 6 months and then in each period	No – s23 gives them power to discharge but see s25	Yes – at 6 months or if CTO is revoked	Yes Part 4A
19 Transfer between guardianship and hospital	**6 months** Renewable for 6 months and then yearly	Yes. In first 6 months and then in each period	No – s23 gives them power to discharge, but see s25	Yes – at 6 months and every 3 years; yearly if under 16	Yes
25 Restriction by RC of discharge by NR	Variable	No	Yes. Within 28 days of being informed. (No appeal if s2)	No	N/A
29 Appointment of acting NR by court	Variable	No	Yes. Within one year and then yearly	No	N/A
135 Warrant to search for and remove patient	**72 hours** Not renewable	No	No	No	No
136 Police power in public places	**72 hours** Not renewable	No	No	No	No

* Where consent to treatment rules do not apply, a patient is in the same position as an informal patient and should not be treated without their consent except where covered by the Mental Capacity Act or in an emergency under common law. Chapter 6 has fuller information on consent to treatment.

discharge the patient (see the last paragraph on section 2 beginning 'Section 11(3)' on p19 below).

Similarly, mistakes are made by people not concentrating on whether it is an 'or' or an 'and' in the text. Note, for example, that it could be either the nature *or* degree of mental disorder which makes an admission appropriate. Again, an admission may be necessary for the health *or* safety of the patient *or* with a view to the protection of others. All three conditions do not need to be met, so health grounds alone could suffice. In contrast, note the importance of the *and* between section 2(2)(a) and (b) below. The requirements of (a) *and* (b) must be met before detention is possible.

Section 131 promotes the use of informal admission wherever possible. The philosophy of the Act is to seek the least restrictive alternative and this should be borne in mind when considering the use of any of the following sections. However, note the effect of the European Court's decision in *HL* v *UK* (the *Bournewood* case), and more recently the Supreme Court's decision in the cases known as *Cheshire West*, described after the discussion on section 5 later in this chapter. Informal admission is not appropriate if the patient is in effect deprived of his liberty and the Supreme Court's lowering of the threshold for what amounts to a deprivation of liberty has had the effect of increasing the number of patients who would fit this category. A further case (*A PCT* v *LDV*, 2013) has then set a high level for the amount of information a patient needs to take in and retain before making a decision whether to be a voluntary patient. With the reduction of the number of psychiatric beds these cases have led to a situation where the number of informal patients in psychiatric hospitals is very low.

Admission for assessment: section 2

Section 2 allows for a patient who meets certain criteria to be compulsorily admitted to hospital and to be detained there for up to 28 days. The admission is for assessment (or for assessment followed by medical treatment) rather than for observation as was the case with the 1959 Act because, in the words of the 1981 White Paper, *it implies more active intervention to form a diagnosis and to plan treatment* (DHSS, 1981).

Two doctors need to sign recommendations (singly or jointly) based on their examinations of the patient. Section 12 requires at least one doctor to have special experience in the diagnosis or treatment of mental disorder and one should preferably have previous acquaintance with the patient. What amounts to 'previous acquaintance' was dealt with in *Reed (Trainer)* v *Bronglais Hospital* (2001).

In this case the doctor in question:

- attended a case conference which gave much background information on the patient and included the minutes of two previous case conferences;
- following the case conference, saw the patient for about five minutes;

- 'scanned' the medical records received from the family health authority;
- then saw the patient again to make his recommendation.

The court held the words should be given their ordinary meaning and that the reference in the Code to 'personal' knowledge did not import any greater requirement. The doctor had sufficient 'previous acquaintance', and any doctor would have who had some previous knowledge of the patient and was not coming to him or her 'cold'.

The recommendations will state as per section 2(2):

(a) *he is suffering from mental disorder of a nature or degree which warrants the detention of the patient in a hospital for assessment (or for assessment followed by medical treatment) for at least a limited period; and*

(b) *he ought to be so detained in the interests of his own health or safety or with a view to the protection of other persons.*

An application to hospital must be based on these two medical recommendations and may be made by either an AMHP or the patient's nearest relative (NR). The Code of Practice states at para. 14.30:

An AMHP is usually a more appropriate applicant than a patient's nearest relative, given an AMHP's professional training and knowledge of the legislation and local resources. This also removes the risk that an application by the nearest relative might have an adverse effect on their relationship with the patient.

Then at para. 14.32 the Code states:

Doctors who are approached directly by a nearest relative about the possibility of an application being made should advise the nearest relative of their right to require a local authority to arrange for an AMHP to consider the patient's case.

If the nearest relative makes an application for detention, section 14 requires an AMHP to provide a social circumstances report to the hospital. If an AMHP had been bypassed or had earlier refused to make an application, their report should include an account of the reasons for this. The Code recommends that AMHPs provide assistance with conveyance where the nearest relative has made an application but only where they believe detention is justified. At para. 17.11 it states:

If the nearest relative is the applicant, any AMHP and other professionals involved in the assessment of the patient should give advice and assistance. However, they should not assist in a patient's detention unless they believe it is justified and lawful.

Section 11(3) requires the AMHP, when applying for a section 2 detention, to inform the nearest relative of their rights to discharge the patient under section 23. This, together with section 25, allows the nearest relative to discharge the patient if they have given 72 hours' written notice to the hospital managers of their intention to discharge the patient. The responsible clinician (RC) may block this only if they are able to produce within the 72 hours a *report certifying that, in the opinion of that clinician, the patient, if discharged, would be likely to act in a manner dangerous to other persons or to himself.*

The next section illustrates the various risk levels set out in the Mental Health Act.

Risk levels and the Mental Health Act

Two-stage approach to a Mental Health Act assessment

1. The first important step in any intervention is to assess a person's mental health. If they have a mental disorder of a nature or degree which warrants compulsory intervention one can then move to the chart below.

2. Check Figure 2.1 to note significance of different risk criteria for detention and guardianship.

(The illustration is of an imagined scale from no risk at the bottom to extremely high at the top.)

There is particular significance where a person is seen to be within the lightly shaded area between 'high' and 'very high' risk levels. The nearest relative would be able to order the patient's discharge (giving 72 hours' notice) but the RC would be unable to block this as they do not perceive the patient as dangerous. If the RC and the AMHP

100%	**(For example, certain death if person not detained)**
	In any case where a person was seen by the RC to be above this line, the RC would bar any attempt by the NR to discharge the patient.
Very high	**Patient, if discharged, would be likely to act in a manner dangerous to others or self**
	In any case where a person was seen to be above this line they could be detained under section 2 or 3 but could be discharged by the nearest relative giving 72 hours' notice unless RC blocks as above.
High	**Detention necessary for health or safety of patient or for the protection of other persons**
	In any case where a person was seen to be above this line they could be received into guardianship under s7 but could be discharged by the NR at any time.
Less	**Guardianship necessary in interest of welfare of patient or the protection of others**
	On this scale, there can be no compulsory intervention until at least the grounds for guardianship are met.
0%	**No perceived risk**

Figure 2.1   Differential risk criteria for detention and guardianship

nevertheless consider that the patient should still be detained (i.e. the nearest relative's intervention has not altered the situation to drop the risk level below the middle heavily shaded line marked 'high'), the AMHP should consider making an application to the county court for the displacement of the nearest relative under section 29.

Admission for treatment: section 3

This allows a patient to be compulsorily admitted to hospital and detained there for up to six months in the first instance. If the grounds are still met, detention may be renewed for six months and after that for a year at a time. The renewal process involves the RC examining the patient within the last two months of the period of detention, consulting with another professional and obtaining the agreement of another professional who has been professionally concerned with the patient that the grounds for section 3 are met, and submitting a report to the hospital managers. If the patient has not had an MHT hearing during the first six months, there will be an automatic one if detention is renewed.

An admission under section 3 is for treatment and two doctors sign recommendations (singly or jointly) based on their examinations of the patient. As with section 2, at least one doctor must be approved under section 12 and one should preferably have previous acquaintance with the patient. Para. 14.5 says that the recommendations will state that:

- *he is suffering from mental disorder of a nature or degree which makes it appropriate for him to receive medical treatment in a hospital; and*

- *it is necessary for the health or safety of the patient or for the protection of other persons that he should receive such treatment and it cannot be provided unless he is detained under this section; and*

- *appropriate medical treatment is available for him.*

An application to a hospital must be based on these two medical recommendations and may be made by either an AMHP or the patient's nearest relative. If the AMHP intends to apply, they must contact the nearest relative unless this is not reasonably practicable or would involve unreasonable delay. If the nearest relative objects to the application, it may not be made. If the AMHP thinks the nearest relative is acting unreasonably they may make an application to the county court under section 29 for the displacement of the nearest relative. It would be unusual not to be able to contact the nearest relative for section 3 unless the AMHP was unable to trace where they were.

Para. 14.60 of the Code states that circumstances in which the nearest relative need not be informed or consulted would include situations where:

- *it is not practicable for the AMHP to obtain sufficient information to establish the identity or location of the nearest relative, or where to do so would require an excessive amount of investigation involving unreasonable delay; and*

- *consultation is not possible because of the nearest relative's own health or mental incapacity.*

The Code also refers to the case of *TW* v *Enfield Borough Council* (2014) which is explored in more detail in Chapter 3 on relatives. The effect of the *Enfield* case on the Code is the statement at para. 14.61 that:

> There may also be cases where, although physically possible, it would not be reasonably practicable to inform or consult the nearest relative because the detrimental impact of this on the patient would interfere with the patient's right to respect for their privacy and family life under article 8 of the European Convention on Human Rights to an extent that would not be justified and proportionate in the particular circumstances of the case. Detrimental impact may include cases where patients are likely to suffer emotional distress, deterioration in their mental health, physical harm, or financial or other exploitation as a result of the consultation. Consultation with the nearest relative that interferes with the patient's article 8 rights may be justified to protect the patient's article 5 right to liberty.

However, there is an appropriate warning at para. 14.62 that:

> Consulting and notifying the nearest relative is a significant safeguard for patients. Therefore decisions not to do so on these grounds should not be taken lightly. AMHPs should consider all the circumstances of the case, including:

> • the benefit to the patient of the involvement of their nearest relative, including to protect their article 5 rights;

> • the patient's wishes including taking into account whether they have the capacity to decide whether they would want their nearest relative involved and any statement of their wishes they have made in advance. However, a patient's wishes will not be determinative of whether it is reasonably practicable to consult the nearest relative;

> • any detrimental effect that involving the nearest relative would have on the patient's health and wellbeing; and

> • whether there is any good reason to think that the patient's objection may be intended to prevent information relevant to the assessment being discovered.

There is further useful guidance for AMHPs in the Code at para. 14.63:

> If they do not consult or inform the nearest relative, AMHPs should record their reasons. Consultation must not be avoided purely because it is thought that the nearest relative might object to the application.

At para. 14.64 advice is given that when they are consulting nearest relatives, AMHPs should, where possible:

> • ascertain the nearest relative's views about both the patient's needs and the nearest relative's own needs in relation to the patient;

- *inform the nearest relative of the reasons for considering an application for detention and what the effects of such an application would be; and*

- *inform the nearest relative of their role and rights under the Act.*

Chapter 3 of this book includes further discussion on nearest relative issues and the impact of recent case law on the importance of full and proper consultation before signing an application for section 3.

The choice between section 2 and section 3

This is a matter for professional judgement of the criteria involved. The guidance in the new Code is a little different from the previous edition. It appears to be giving a nudge towards more use of section 3. Combined with the effects of the 'appropriate medical treatment' test and the requirement to name the relevant hospital in the medical recommendation for a section 3 detention, it was no surprise that, after the changes in 2008, the number of section 3 applications from the community fell whereas the number of section 2 applications rose. It remains to be seen whether the minor revisions to the Code will affect these figures.

The use of section 2 rose from 15,508 in 2007–8 to a total of 20,931 in 2011–12. In the same period the use of section 3 fell from 9,763 to 7,701. Even if you add in all the revocations of CTOs this only lifts the figure to 9,170 so there is still a fall.

The Code now states (changes in bold print) at para. 14.27 that:

*Section 2 should **only** be used if:*

- *the full extent of the nature and degree of a patient's condition is unclear;*

- *there is a need to carry out an initial in-patient assessment in order to formulate a treatment plan, or to reach a judgement about whether the patient will accept treatment on a voluntary basis following admission; or*

- *there is a need to carry out a new in-patient assessment in order to reformulate a treatment plan, or to reach a judgement about whether the patient will accept treatment on a voluntary basis.*

Section 3 should be used where the following criteria are met:

- *the patient is already detained under section 2 (detention under section 2 cannot be renewed by a new section 2 application); or*

- *the nature and current degree of the patient's mental disorder, the essential elements of the treatment plan to be followed and the likelihood of the patient accepting treatment as an informal patient are already sufficiently established to make it unnecessary to undertake a new assessment under section 2.*

Jones (2015) is a strong advocate of using section 2 before going on to look at section 3 later. Certainly many well-known patients would still come under the list of factors indicating a section 2 application. In his general note (Jones, 2015, after section 2) states that a *patient whose current mental health and circumstances require him to be subject to the very significant procedure of compulsory detention surely needs to be assessed however well known he might be to the mental health service*. Hale (2012, p122) notes that a *short-term intervention is more consistent with the 'least restrictive' principle* and this point may also be relevant in the increased use of section 2.

AMHPs would be well advised, except where a patient is already detained under section 2, not to accept referrals 'for a section 3' just because the patient is known. They should agree to assess but with an open mind as to the outcome, including the possibility, even where detention is indicated, of a section 2 or section 3. If they accept from the outset that there is no need for assessment in hospital and that it is appropriate just to look at section 3, the implications of *R v Wilson ex parte Williamson* (1996) may prove problematic. The case has been widely quoted to support the view that using a section 2 as a stopgap measure because a section 3 has been blocked would be unlawful. Thus an AMHP who agrees that a section 3 is appropriate and who is then prevented by a nearest relative objection from making such an application would need to apply to the county court for a displacement of the nearest relative and would not be able to fall back on a section 2 as an interim measure. This problem has not disappeared but it may be less frequent if the decline in the number of patients going straight on to a section 3 before they are in hospital continues. On the other hand, even though there are fewer section 3 applications from the community, they have become more problematic because of the recent case law concerning the nearest relative, and this is considered in Chapter 3.

Short-term detentions and holding powers: sections 4, 135 and 5

These are second-best solutions compared with detention under sections 2 or 3. They are temporary responses to crises where circumstances do not allow a full assessment before invoking compulsory powers. Section 5 should not be used just to demonstrate to patients that they cannot leave hospital when they wish to. Each use of the section should be followed as soon as possible by an assessment of the need for further detention. The sections last for a maximum of 72 hours (for sections 4 and 135 this is timed from the moment when the patient is admitted to hospital or arrives at the place of safety) or until the assessment is completed, whichever is the sooner. They are not renewable, although a section 4 can be converted to a section 2 by the addition of a second medical recommendation and section 5(4) can be changed to a section 5(2) if the doctor or approved clinician in charge of the patient's treatment deems this appropriate. None of the sections allows for an appeal to the MHT (because of the short time period involved) and patients are not covered by consent to treatment procedures set out in Part 4 of the Act. Therefore these patients have the same right to refuse treatment as any informal patient.

Admission for assessment in cases of emergency: section 4

Where only one doctor is available and waiting for a second doctor would involve 'undesirable delay', it is possible to effect an admission under section 4. An application may be made by either an AMHP or the nearest relative. Para. 15.8 of the Code states:

> An emergency may arise where the patient's mental state or behaviour presents problems which those involved cannot reasonably be expected to manage while waiting for a second doctor. To be satisfied that an emergency has arisen, the person making the application and the doctor making the supporting recommendation should have evidence of:
>
> - an immediate and significant risk of mental or physical harm to the patient or to others;
> - danger of serious harm to property; or
> - a need for the use of restrictive interventions on a patient.

Apart from the urgent necessity for admission, the grounds are basically the same as for section 2. The doctor providing the recommendation does not need to be section 12 approved and may not have previous acquaintance with the patient. This significantly reduces the safeguards for the patient and should be avoided if possible. It is important to remind the hospital to let the AMHP know if the section is converted to a section 2 so that the AMHP can inform the nearest relative as required by section 11(3).

AMHP reports for applications under sections 2, 3 or 4

Para. 14.93 of the Code states that the AMHP should:

> provide an outline report for the hospital at the time the patient is first admitted or detained, giving reasons for the application and any practical matters about the patient's circumstances which the hospital should know. Where possible, the report should include the name and telephone number of the AMHP or a care co-ordinator who can give further information. Local authorities should use a standard form on which AMHPs can make this outline report.

Where there are any children involved with the patient, local authority circular LAC(99)32 contains a helpful approach at para. 9.1:

> (a) In those instances where a compulsory admission is being considered, the needs of and arrangements for children involved with the patient should be considered by the [AMHP] as an integral element within the assessment. This information

should be recorded by the [AMHP] and communicated to the hospital in the event of admission. The [AMHP] should alert their colleagues in children's services if they have any concerns about child care arrangements for dependent children of the patient. It would assist this process if documents were designed to incorporate information from this element of the assessment.

(b) Similarly, the [AMHP] should provide the hospital with information about the views of other person(s) with parental responsibility for the children of the patient, where it is appropriate to do so and if these can be ascertained. [AMHPs] should be sensitive to situations where the relationship between parents has broken down so that any decision about child visiting is not used inappropriately in residence or contact disputes.

(c) In the vast majority of cases where no concerns are identified, arrangements should be made to support the patient and child and to facilitate contact.

AMHPs should give the provision of the outline report a very high priority. In the case of *BB* v *Cygnet Health Care and Lewisham* (2008) the judge stated that the failure of the ASW to leave an outline report at the hospital with the admission papers *did not give me any confidence in his overall ability properly to discharge his responsibilities under the Act*.

Warrant to search for and remove patients: section 135

This section covers two main sets of circumstances where an AMHP, constable or other person might need to enter premises and remove a patient. Section 135(1) states:

If it appears to a justice of the peace, on information on oath laid by an Approved Mental Health Professional, that there is reasonable cause to suspect that a person believed to be suffering from mental disorder –

(a) *has been, or is being, ill-treated, neglected or kept otherwise than under proper control, in any place within the jurisdiction of the justice, or*

(b) *being unable to care for himself, is living alone in any such place,*

the justice may issue a warrant authorising any constable [. . .] to enter, if need be by force, any premises specified in the warrant in which that person is believed to be, and, if thought fit, to remove him to a place of safety with a view to the making of an application in respect of him under Part II of this Act, or of other arrangements for his treatment or care.

In using the warrant, the constable needs to be accompanied by an AMHP and by a doctor. As a result of a House of Lords decision in *Ward* v *Commissioner of Police* (2005), magistrates may not apply additional requirements, e.g. naming the AMHP, doctor or police officer who would have to then attend. Any AMHP, doctor or police officer may attend.

The 'place of safety' to which the patient is taken could be a hospital, a police station, social services premises or any suitable place where the occupier is willing to receive the patient. The patient may be kept there for up to 72 hours or until the assessment is completed, whichever is the sooner.

Para. 16.38 of the Code states:

> *A police station should not be used as a place of safety except in exceptional circumstances, for example it may be necessary to do so because the person's behaviour would pose an unmanageably high risk to other patients, staff or other users if the person were to be detained in a healthcare setting. A police station should not be used as the automatic second choice if there is no local health-based place of safety immediately available.*

Despite this advice there are parts of the country where a police station is still the usual place of safety. The National Policing Improvement Agency states:

> *The existence of a warrant does not mean that it must be executed, either immediately or at all. Where officers assess that the warrant does not need to be executed on arrival, the decision is theirs. If officers later assess that lawful access to the premises is required (perhaps because permission to be there has been withdrawn) they can decide to execute the warrant at that point.*

> (2010, p121)

There has been some controversy in recent years over whether it is lawful, having obtained entry, for an AMHP and doctors to assess the patient with a view to detention under Part 2 of the Act. The revised Code states (at para 16.8):

> *The AMHP and the doctor may convene a mental health assessment in the person's home if it is safe and appropriate to do so and the person consents to this. In taking this decision, consideration should be given as to who else is present, particularly if a person might be distressed by the assessment taking place in these circumstances.*

This would suggest that in the majority of cases the person should be taken to the place of safety for assessment. If the patient lets the police and mental health assessors in without use of the warrant there would be nothing to prevent an assessment from taking place. The patient could of course ask people to leave at any point but the police could then decide to exercise the warrant.

Section 135(2) covers circumstances where a patient liable to be taken to hospital or elsewhere under the Act appears to be on premises where entry has been refused or is likely to be refused. A constable (or other authorised person) may apply for a warrant which will authorise a constable to enter the premises and remove the patient. This might be used for a patient who has refused to return to hospital after a period of leave or who has absconded from hospital or from the place in which they are required to reside when subject to guardianship, or a community patient who is refusing to go to a hospital despite having been recalled.

Application in respect of patient already in hospital: section 5

Section 5 allows for the detention of a person under section 2 or 3 even if they are already an in-patient. It also contains provisions for preventing in-patients from leaving hospital where an assessment for detention under one of these sections is incomplete.

Under section 5(2) the doctor or approved clinician in charge of a patient's treatment (or, if they are absent, one nominee) may sign Form H1 (or HO12 in Wales) stating that the patient should be detained under Part 2 of the Act. They pass the form to the hospital managers who may detain the patient for up to 72 hours to enable a full assessment of the need for a section 2 or 3 to take place. The patient could at this point be in any hospital, not necessarily a psychiatric unit. The power cannot be used to extend a section 2 or 3 which is about to expire.

For patients already receiving psychiatric treatment, there is provision under section 5(4) for specified nurses to detain them for up to six hours if they sign Form H2 (or HO13 in Wales) indicating that:

(a) *this patient, who is receiving treatment for mental disorder as an inpatient of this hospital, is suffering from mental disorder to such a degree that it is necessary for the patient's health or safety or protection of others for this patient to be immediately restrained from leaving the hospital; and*

(b) *it is not practicable to secure the immediate attendance of a registered medical practitioner or an approved clinician (who is not a registered practitioner) for the purposes of furnishing a report under section 5(2) of the Mental Health Act 1983.*

Informal or 'voluntary'?

With its advice relating to section 5 of the Act the 1993 version of the Code of Practice led to an interesting debate concerning the definition of an informal patient. In a critique of the 1999 version of the Code, Brown (1999) identified some of the issues arising from a lack of clarity and noted that the Code did not require hospitals to have written statements on what would amount to an admission procedure. There is still a lack of understanding about the distinction between informal and voluntary (and recent case law has made it harder to be voluntary for reasons we shall explore below). For example, the 2008 version of the Code made a fairly common mistake when in its Annex A it stated on p361 that an informal patient is also sometimes known as a voluntary patient. In current law all voluntary patients should be informal but not all informal patients will be voluntary as some will lack the capacity to have agreed to admission. For public hospitals the voluntary patient was a creation of the 1930 Mental Treatment Act. The classification disappeared in 1959 but, with the lowering of the threshold for what amounts to a deprivation of liberty, it has become an important issue again.

From the Percy Commission, which led to the 1959 Act, there was a presumption that a 'non-objecting' patient should be grouped with those consenting rather than those dissenting. This meant that professionals involved in the admission procedure tended not to use compulsion where there was an absence of dissent. For many experienced AMHPs and doctors it has been hard to adjust to the current position where incapacitated informal patients are a rarity in psychiatric hospitals because the bar for what amounts to a deprivation of liberty has been set so low.

The *Bournewood* case (1993–1998)

The definition of an informal patient became a key issue in the *Bournewood* case which led in turn to *HL* v *UK*. The definition given in para. 8.4 of the 1993 Code for the purposes of a section 5 suggested that there should have been active consent:

> *An informal in-patient, for the purposes of this Section, is one who has understood and accepted the offer of a bed, who has freely appeared on the ward and who has co-operated in the admission procedure. The Section, for example, cannot be used for an out-patient attending a hospital's accident and emergency department.*

The last sentence may give an indication of the area this advice was supposed to clarify. In December 1997, the Appeal Court ruled (in overturning the judgement of *R* v *Bournewood Community and Mental Health Trust ex p. L* (1993)) that where a hospital had the intention and the ability to prevent a patient from leaving, then the patient was, in effect, detained and should therefore be so detained by the Mental Health Act if they were to be kept in hospital and treated. This ruling gave such patients the protection offered by the Act (e.g. consent to treatment rules and the role of the Mental Health Act Commission). In June 1998, however, the House of Lords ruled that a compliant mentally incapacitated patient could effectively be detained and treated in hospital. If the patient subsequently showed signs of being unwilling to remain in hospital, they should be assessed with a view to possible detention.

The revised form of words which was used in para. 8.4 of the third edition of the Code of Practice was as follows:

> *For the purposes of s.5(2), informal patients are usually voluntary patients, that is, those who have the capacity to consent and who consent to enter hospital for in-patient treatment. Patients who lack the capacity to consent but do not object to admission for treatment may also be informal patients (see para. 2.8). The section cannot be used for an out-patient attending a hospital's accident and emergency department. Admission procedures should not be implemented with the sole intention of then using the power in section 5(2).*

Para. 2.8 referred to here stated:

> *If at the time of admission, the patient is mentally incapable of consent, but does not object to entering hospital and receiving care or treatment, admission should be informal . . . The decision to admit a mentally incapacitated patient informally should be made by the doctor in charge of the patient's treatment in accordance*

with what is in the patient's best interest and is justifiable on the basis of the common law doctrine of necessity . . . If a patient lacks capacity at the time of an assessment or review, it is particularly important that both clinical and social care requirements are considered, and that account is taken of the patient's ascertainable wishes and feelings and the views of their immediate relatives and carers on what would be in the patient's best interests.

HL v UK (2004)

This final court stage of the *Bournewood* saga has had profound implications for English mental health law. Extracts from the judgement are reproduced below.

The applicant was born in 1949 and lives in Surrey. He has suffered from autism since birth. He is unable to speak and his level of understanding is limited. He is frequently agitated and has a history of self-harming behaviour. He lacks the capacity to consent or object to medical treatment. For over 30 years he was cared for in Bournewood Hospital . . . He was an in-patient at the Intensive Behavioural Unit (IBU) from 1987. The applicant's responsible medical officer (who had cared for him since 1977) was Dr M . . . In March 1994 he was discharged on a trial basis to paid carers, Mr and Mrs E, with whom he successfully resided until 22 July 1997 [when] he was at the day centre when he became particularly agitated, hitting himself on the head with his fists and banging his head against the wall. Staff could not contact Mr and Mrs E and got in touch with a local doctor who administered a sedative.

HL remained agitated and on the recommendation of the local authority care services manager (AF) with overall responsibility for the applicant, he was taken to the A & E unit at the hospital. He was seen by a psychiatrist (Dr P) and transferred to the IBU. It was recorded that he made no attempt to leave. 'Dr P and Dr M considered that the best interests of the applicant required his admission for in-patient treatment.' Dr M considered detention under the 1983 Act but concluded it 'was not necessary as the applicant was compliant and did not resist admission'. Dr M later confirmed that she would have recommended HL's detention if he had resisted admission. The carers were discouraged from visiting at this point. In a report on August 18th Dr M concluded that HL suffered from a mood disorder as well as autism and that his discharge would be against medical opinion.

On 29 October 1997 the Court of Appeal indicated it would decide the appeal in the applicant's favour. HL was then held on section 5(2) and on 31 October an application for section 3 was made. On 2 November he was seen by his carers for the first time since July.

Application was made to the MHRT in November and independent psychiatric reports were obtained recommending HL's discharge. Before an MHRT hearing application was also made for a managers' hearing. On 5 December HL was allowed home on section 17 leave and on 12 December the managers discharged him from the section 3.

The European Court noted that the following safeguards were available to those detained under the Mental Health Act 1983:

- statutory criteria need to be met and applied by two doctors and an applicant;
- Part 4 consent to treatment procedures;
- applications and automatic referrals to mental health review tribunals;
- nearest relative powers (including discharge powers);
- section 117 after-care;
- the Code of Practice and the Mental Health Act Commission;
- section 132 rights to information.

The key to the decision of the European Court is Article 5 of the European Convention on Human Rights, i.e. the right to liberty and security of person:

> *No one shall be deprived of their liberty except for specific cases and in accordance with procedure prescribed by law, e.g. after conviction, lawful arrest on suspicion of having committed an offence, lawful detention of person of unsound mind, to prevent spread of infectious diseases. Everyone deprived of liberty by arrest or detention shall be entitled to take proceedings by which the lawfulness of the detention shall be decided speedily by a Court and release ordered if the detention is not lawful.*

The court concluded that HL was 'deprived of his liberty' within the meaning of Article 5.1 of the European Convention on Human Rights. It was not crucial that the door was locked or lockable.

> *The Court considers the key factor in the present case to be that the health care professionals treating and managing the applicant exercised complete and effective control over his care and movements from the moment he presented acute behavioural problems on 22 July 1997 to the date he was compulsorily detained on 29 October 1997.*

It was clear that *the applicant would only be released from the hospital to the care of Mr and Mrs E as and when those professionals considered it appropriate*. HL *was under continuous supervision and control and was not free to leave*.

The court accepted that HL was suffering from a mental disorder of a kind or degree warranting compulsory confinement. However, the court found that there had been a breach of Article 5.1 in that there was an absence of procedural safeguards to protect against arbitrary deprivation of liberty in the reliance on the common law doctrine of necessity. Article 5.4 was also breached in that the applicant had no right to have the lawfulness of his detention reviewed speedily by a court. Judicial review and habeas corpus proceedings were not adequate. The court did not find there had been a breach of Article 14 which covers discrimination.

Implications

In a case similar to HL's circumstances, an AMHP would have to decide whether to apply for detention or to allow him to return to Mr and Mrs E. If the patient (unlike HL who is autistic) suffered only from a learning disability and a section 2 was expiring, DoLS might become an option (see Chapter 11). This issue has become an even bigger one because of the *Cheshire West* and related cases.

Cheshire West (2014)

This title is shorthand for three cases which were determined by the Supreme Court in 2014. In each of these cases a key question was 'when do living arrangements for a mentally incapacitated person amount to a deprivation of liberty?' Where they do, then unless the person is detained under the MHA the deprivation would need to be authorised by DoLS or a court. Without these safeguards the court noted that there would be no independent check of the arrangements. The court also concluded that disabled people have the same right to liberty as everyone else. This put paid to the 'comparator' approach which had been adopted by the Appeal Court, i.e. comparing each individual with those with similar disabilities rather than the 'ordinary person on the bus'. The judgement re-emphasised that the distinction between a deprivation and a restriction of liberty is one of degree and intensity and not one of nature or substance.

What came as a surprise to many was how low the bar was set for what would amount to a deprivation of liberty. All three individuals that were considered had some degree of learning disability. MIG had moderate to severe learning disability as well as hearing and sight problems. She was living in foster care. MEG had mild to moderate learning disabilities and better communication skills than her sister; she had quite sophisticated emotional understanding but autistic traits and exhibited challenging behaviour. She was in an NHS residential setting. In 2011 the Court of Appeal laid stress on the relative normality of the sisters' lives when compared with living with their family together. In the *Cheshire West* case P was living in Z House, a spacious staffed bungalow close to the family home. He needed a lot of help including coping with challenging behaviour. In all three cases the Appeal Court had considered that the circumstances fell short of deprivation of liberty.

However in all three cases (albeit with a narrow 4:3 majority in the cases of MIG and MEG) the Supreme Court concluded there was a deprivation of liberty. All three individuals lacked capacity to agree to the living arrangements, would have been prevented from leaving, and were under continuous supervision and control in circumstances that were attributable to the state. This formula is referred to as 'the acid test'. The fact that living arrangements may be comfortable and indeed making life as enjoyable as possible made no difference. Lady Hale used a simple phrase to sum this up: 'a gilded cage is still a cage' (para. 46).

So the essential characteristics of a deprivation of liberty are:

- the objective component of confinement in a particular restricted place for a not negligible length of time; and

- the subjective component of a lack of valid consent; and

- the attribution of responsibility to the state.

Where a person is under continuous supervision and control and not free to leave then, unless they are able to give valid consent to the restrictions, they are likely to be seen as deprived of their liberty. What would not be relevant would be: their compliance or lack of objection; the relative normality of the placement; the reason or purpose for the particular placement. This has meant that thousands of people in hospital or care homes who would previously have been seen as informal with a degree of restriction would now be seen as deprived of their liberty and in need of a procedure prescribed by law to meet the requirements of Article 5 of the ECHR. Chapter 11 will look at the impact on DoLS.

In psychiatric hospitals people will often consider whether the person has given valid consent to the regime, therefore meaning that they are not in effect deprived of their liberty. However, another recent case has proved to be problematic here.

A PCT v *LDV, CC and B Healthcare Group* (2013)

As well as providing an example of what would amount to a deprivation of liberty, this case addressed the question of how much a patient would need to understand of a hospital admission plan before they could be seen to have capacity to agree to it. L was a 33-year-old former Winterbourne View patient who suffered from a mild learning disability and an emotionally unstable personality disorder. In April 2011 L was detained on a section 3 in a medium secure facility. In May 2012 the tribunal ordered her discharge to take effect in September 2012 (which should have given time to find a more appropriate residential placement nearer to home). Although L was transferred to a hospital nearer to home she was still detained when the discharge date arrived. An AMHP identified 15 separate restrictions on L's liberty and concluded that these amounted to a deprivation of liberty. She had previously stated that she was unable to sign a new section 3 as, on the basis of *R (von Brandenburg)* v *East London*, there was no significant new information since the tribunal decision.

L remained on the ward as an informal patient. The hospital argued that the restrictions did not amount to a deprivation of liberty but, if they did, then L had given valid consent to the arrangements. The judge ruled that was clearly a deprivation of liberty and that, in order to give valid consent, L would need to understand the key features of their concrete situation. *The information which must be understood, retained, used and weighed extends to some information about the context in which deprivation is being imposed* (para. 40). Whilst there is still no clear definition of a 'voluntary' patient (or indeed of when a patient is actually admitted to a hospital) any agreement to admission is subject to a higher level of understanding than mere compliance. Most psychiatric wards (and many general hospital wards) will have regimes where most patients are under continuous supervision and control and many will not be free to leave. There are probably many patients who are compliant but lack the capacity to be voluntary and who should, therefore, be subject to a procedure prescribed by law. Should this be under the Mental Health Act or via DoLS?

AM v *SLAM* (2013)

This case concerned a tribunal decision regarding a section 2 patient. In making their decision the First-tier Tribunal had failed to consider DoLS as an alternative to the MHA. Where a patient needs to be in hospital for their mental disorder, lacks capacity to make the decision, and is not objecting, but where the regime is likely to amount to a deprivation of liberty, then the decision-makers should consider DoLS as a possible alternative to detention under the MHA. They would have to consider whether the DoLS regime is actually available and whether it would provide less restrictions than the MHA. This is not an easy issue as the two regimes are very different and the following would all be potentially relevant:

- the role of the nearest relative under the MHA compared with the person's representative under DoLS;
- access to advocacy (IMHA vs IMCA);
- access to a hearing in court (MHT vs Court of Protection) including automatic hearings;
- the role of the hospital managers vs the supervisory body;
- consent to treatment issues;
- the cost of any subsequent care (s117 – 'the section that dare not speak its name' – a highly contentious issue for the professionals to handle);
- arrangements if a patient were to abscond from the hospital;
- might the patient be a risk to others even if they are compliant with the regime?

The revised English Code of Practice provides helpful and clear guidance (as long as the reader ignores the misleading case example which follows para. 13.70 of the Code; fortunately the case does not formally count as part of the Code and can be discounted). The Code begins at para. 13.49 by identifying the target group, i.e. an individual who:

a. *is suffering from a mental disorder (within the meaning of the Act)*
b. *needs to be assessed and/or treated in a hospital setting for that disorder or for physical conditions related to that disorder (and meets the criteria for an application for admission under sections 2 or 3 of the Act)*

c. has a care treatment package that may or will amount to a deprivation of liberty

d. lacks capacity to consent to being accommodated in the relevant hospital for the purpose of treatment, and

e. does not object to being admitted to hospital, or to some or all the treatment they will receive there for mental disorder.

Having identified the target group the Code gives guidance which AMHPs should find helpful when determining which route to take:

13.58 The choice of legal regime should never be based on a general preference for one regime or the other, or because one regime is more familiar to the decision-maker than the other. Such considerations are not legally relevant and lead to arbitrary decision-making. In addition decision-makers should not proceed on the basis that one regime is generally less restrictive than the other. Both regimes are based on the need to impose as few restrictions on the liberty and autonomy of patients as possible. In the particular circumstances of an individual case, it may be apparent that one regime is likely to prove less restrictive. If so, this should be balanced against any potential benefits associated with the other regime.

13.59 Both regimes provide appropriate procedural safeguards to ensure the rights of the person concerned are protected during their detention. Decision-makers should not therefore proceed on the basis that one regime generally provides greater safeguards than the other. However, the nature of the safeguards provided under the two regimes are different and decision-makers will wish to exercise their professional judgement in determining which safeguards are more likely to best protect the interests of the patient in the particular circumstances of each individual case.

13.60 In the relatively small number of cases where detention under the Act and a DoLS authorisation or Court of Protection order are available, this Code of Practice does not seek to preferentially orientate the decision-maker in any given direction. Such a decision should always be made depending on the unique circumstances of each case. Clearly recording the reasons for the final decision made will be important. The most pressing concern should always be that if an individual lacks capacity to consent to the matter in question and is deprived of their liberty they should receive the safeguards afforded under either the Act or through a DoLS authorisation or a Court of Protection order.

13.61 Part 9 of the DoLS Code of Practice details steps to be taken if someone thinks a person is being deprived of their liberty without authorisation. These steps include raising the matter with the responsible person at the managing authority (the provider) and if necessary with the supervisory body (the local authority). Hospitals should have policies in place to deal with circumstances where disagreement results in an inability to take a decision as to whether the Act or DoLS should be used to give legal authorisation to a deprivation of liberty – to ensure that one is selected.

Despite this fairly clear guidance the situation where professionals have to choose between two very different regimes is far from perfect. At the end of Chapter 11 there is a comparison of the key features and safeguards of the MHA and the MCA which may be of some assistance to AMHPs in those cases where there is a choice to be made between DoLS and the MHA (i.e. the compliant mentally disordered person in hospital where the regime will amount to a deprivation of liberty). For some years the author has advocated a reform of guardianship to simplify matters in this area. The issue will be addressed at the end of the following part of this chapter.

Guardianship: section 7

Guardianship is a form of community compulsion which is used in a limited way and in comparatively small numbers in England and Wales. It was introduced in the Mental Deficiency Act 1913 where the guardian had all the powers of a father of a child under the age of 14. Between 1930 and 1947 the use of guardianship went from 1,591 cases to 4,798. After 1948, guardianship status was not necessary for the guardian to receive financial support, and its use declined. It has received some attention recently for three main reasons: the introduction of the community treatment order has focused attention on the issue of compulsion in the community; it has a new power to convey to a place in the first instance; the introduction of DoLS has raised the question of whether guardianship is an alternative approach.

The Code of Practice (at para. 30.4) states that guardianship:

> *provides an authoritative framework for working with a patient, with a minimum of constraint, to achieve as independent a life as possible within the community. Where it is used, it should be part of the patient's overall care plan.*

Guardianship may be applied through a civil route (s7) or, very infrequently, via the courts (s37). For civil admissions, the applicant may be an approved mental health professional or the nearest relative as defined in section 26. The application is based on two medical recommendations and is made to the local authority. Social services departments vary in their procedures for making decisions on guardianship applications and some are negative in their attitude to this piece of legislation. The relevant local authority is the one where the patient lives unless the guardian is a private individual when their address determines the relevant authority. Guardianship lasts up to six months, is renewable for a further six months and then yearly.

The guardian may be the local authority or a private individual approved by the local authority. However, private individuals hardly ever act as guardians. For example, in 2014–15 there were 212 new cases in England where the local authority was the guardian and only one where the guardian was a private individual or other organisation. This is perhaps surprising as many private citizens caring for relatives who lack capacity to make important decisions might benefit from having a clear legal status as decision-maker.

The grounds for using guardianship

No one under the age of 16 can be received into guardianship. For a mentally disordered child under 16 who requires some supervision in the community, childcare law (including the rights of parents and the local authority) is available.

The grounds for guardianship under section 7 or section 37 are similar. Section 7(2) states:

A guardianship application may be made in respect of a patient on the grounds that –

(a) *he is suffering from mental disorder of a nature or degree which warrants his reception into guardianship under this section; and*

(b) *it is necessary in the interests of the welfare of the patient or for the protection of other persons that the patient should be so received.*

Note that if the mental disorder is learning disability this must be associated with abnormally aggressive or seriously irresponsible conduct. The forms do not raise this point so AMHPs need to be alert to the issue. This was discussed in Chapter 1 and readers may recall the significance of the case law which reduces the occasions where guardianship can be used to protect vulnerable adults with learning disabilities. The Mental Capacity Act may need to be relied on for this group of patients and many would consider that this lacks the robust safeguards of the Mental Health Act for someone who is detained in a psychiatric hospital.

There is no such problem in using guardianship for other vulnerable patients such as those with dementia as there is no secondary behavioural test. This is an unhappy situation which could be rectified by removing the behavioural requirement for guardianship in learning disability cases.

The guardian's powers are set out in section 8(1) and give the guardian:

- *the power to require the patient to reside at a place specified by the authority or person named as guardian;*

- *the power to require the patient to attend at places and times so specified for the purpose of medical treatment, occupation, education or training;*

- *the power to require access to the patient to be given, at any place where the patient is residing, to any medical practitioner, approved mental health professional or other person so specified.*

The changes to the legislation resulting from the Mental Health (Amendment) Act 2007 included the power to convey in the first instance (as well as retaining the old power to return the person when they have absconded from the place of residence). Note that Parts 4 and 4A of the Act on consent to treatment do not apply to guardianship. Thus there is no statutory route to make a patient accept treatment, such as medication, against their will. If the patient lacks capacity the Mental Capacity Act may provide some limited ability to treat without the valid consent of the patient.

Guardianship does not give any powers in relation to property and affairs. For these reasons there may sometimes be occasions where the powers of a deputy or the donee of a financial lasting power of attorney (LPA) become relevant. Equally an LPA may have granted powers to an attorney to make certain health or welfare decisions on behalf of the patient. The donee would not, however, be able to override decisions made by the guardian which fell within their powers, such as where the patient should live. The relationship between the role of attorney and the nearest relative could clearly be important.

There is a myth that guardianship cannot be used to place people into residential care. The Code of Practice (at para. 30.12) starts by stating:

> *Where a patient aged 16 or over is assessed as requiring residential care but lacks the capacity to make a decision about whether they wish to be placed there, guardianship is unlikely to be necessary where the move can properly, quickly and efficiently be carried out on the basis of:*
>
> - *section 5 of the MCA or the decision of an attorney or deputy; or*
>
> - *(where relevant) a deprivation of liberty authorisation (a DoL authorisation) (in relation to a patient aged 18 or over) or deprivation of liberty order (Court of Protection order) under the MCA.*

But the Code then continues at 30.13 to state:

> *But guardianship may still be appropriate in such cases if:*
>
> - *there are other reasons – unconnected to the move to residential care – to think that the patient might benefit from the attention and authority of a guardian;*
>
> - *there is a particular need to have explicit statutory authority for the patient to be returned to the place where the patient is to live should they go absent; or*
>
> - *it is thought to be important that decisions about where the patient is to live are placed in the hands of a single person or authority – e.g. where there have been long-running or particularly difficult disputes about where the person should live.*

The third situation is far from uncommon and the identification of a clear decision-maker will often be important.

The Code of Practice at para. 30.16 introduces a list of responsibilities that fall to local authorities and this provides a useful checklist. It states that each local authority should have a policy setting out the arrangements for:

> - *receiving, scrutinising and accepting or refusing applications for guardianship. Such arrangements should ensure that applications are properly but quickly dealt with;*
>
> - *monitoring the progress of each patient's guardianship, including steps to be taken to fulfil the authority's statutory obligations in relation to private guardians and to arrange visits to the patient;*

- *ensuring the suitability of any proposed private guardian, and that they are able to understand and carry out their duties under the Act;*

- *ensuring that patients under guardianship receive, both orally and in writing, information in accordance with regulations under the Act, including their right to have access to an independent mental health advocate (IMHA);*

- *ensuring that patients are aware of their right to apply to the Tribunal and that they are given the name of someone who will give them the necessary assistance, on behalf of the local authority, in making such an application;*

- *authorising an approved clinician to be the patient's responsible clinician;*

- *maintaining detailed records relating to guardianship patients;*

- *ensuring that the need to continue guardianship is reviewed in the last two months of each period of guardianship in accordance with the Act; and*

- *discharging patients from guardianship as soon as it is no longer required.*

AMHPs may wish to check that their approving authority has covered all of these areas in their policy documents.

Frequency of the use of guardianship

The use of guardianship varies considerably in different areas. Overall its use has declined since 2000 after significant increases in the 1990s. From a very low base of 60 new guardianships in England in 1983–4, the numbers increased to 672 new cases in 1999–2000. The number of new cases then declined to 427 new cases in 2007–8. In 2014–15 there were only 212 new cases.

It is also possible to look at guardianship in terms of continuing cases on a given date. Here the numbers are a little more stable but still declining. On 31 March 2005, there were 948 people in guardianship compared with 161 in 1984. The number dropped to 522 in 2015. Table 2.2 illustrates the significant variations around the country (England only).

Supervised after-care was introduced in 1996. It provided similar powers to guardianship but was available only to patients who had been detained on long-term sections. The publicity around its introduction may have contributed to increased use of guardianship in the late 1990s. The community treatment order which replaced supervised after-care in 2008 has different implications and the relationship with guardianship is considered later in the chapter.

The use of guardianship varies considerably between local authorities as Table 2.2 shows. There appears to be no satisfactory explanation for these differences apart from the preferences of staff and the willingness of local authority managers to support the use of guardianship. There are also significant changes even within

Table 2.2 Continuing guardianships at 31 March 2015 for 29 English local authorities

Local authority	Total	Population	Per 100,000
Herefordshire	14	186,087	7.52
Middlesbrough	6	138,744	4.32
Plymouth	9	258,026	3.49
Cumbria	17	499,900	3.40
Liverpool	14	469,690	2.98
Poole	4	148,615	2.69
Bath	4	177,643	2.25
Westminster	5	226,841	2.20
Southampton	5	239,428	2.09
Gloucestershire	12	597,000	2.01
Cornwall	10	537,914	1.86
Lancashire	21	1,450,000	1.45
Nottinghamshire	11	796,216	1.38
Devon	10	744,282	1.34
Somerset	7	530,100	1.32
Wiltshire	5	476,816	1.05
Birmingham	11	1,085,417	1.01
Hampshire	13	1,344,610	0.97
Swindon	2	211,934	0.94
Lewisham	2	281,556	0.71
Bournemouth	1	186,744	0.54
Portsmouth	1	206,836	0.48
Bexley	1	234,271	0.43
Buckinghamshire	2	506,600	0.40
Surrey	4	1,132,390	0.35
Lambeth	1	310,200	0.32
Oxfordshire	2	653,800	0.31
Dorset	1	414,900	0.24
Torbay	0	131,492	0.00
Totals from sample	**195**	**14,178,052**	**1.38**
Total England	**522**	**54,316,600**	**0.96**

Sources: Office for National Statistics and Health and Social Care Information Service.

local authorities over time. For example, Herefordshire jumped from one guardianship in 2012 to 14 in 2015. Bath and North East Somerset fell from 10 to 4 in the same period.

Guardianship and deprivation of liberty

With the Supreme Court having set a low threshold for what amounts to a deprivation of liberty (see *P* v *Cheshire West and Chester Council* [2014]) a number of patients who have been received into guardianship have been subject to care plans where the question has arisen as to whether they are in fact being deprived of their liberty.

This first question was dealt with by Jacobs J. (*NL* v *Hampshire County Council* [2014]) when he said of the case in question that it was not the guardianship that caused a deprivation of liberty but the care plan. DoLS or a section 16 order from the Court of Protection could authorise the deprivation of liberty. So should the whole plan then be authorised via the MCA or could guardianship sit alongside?

In a subsequent case (*NM* v *Kent County Council* [2015]) the same judge looked at the differences between the MHA and the MCA. The MCA deals with the person's best interests, whereas the MHA deals with the protection of the patient and the public. Each is subject to different adjudication procedures before different judicial bodies. In the case in question one advantage of having guardianship sitting alongside the MCA authorisation of a deprivation of liberty was that if the person absconded section 18(3) of the MHA gave explicit authority for their return.

Finally in *KD* v *Walsall MBC and Others* (2015) Charles J. gave some support to the idea of using guardianship alongside DoLS. KD was required to live in a care home with 24-hour supervision and support. He was not free to leave and not permitted to go out unless accompanied by a member of the care staff. He sought to be discharged from his guardianship on the basis that it was not necessary because DoLS was less restrictive and guardianship could not authorise his deprivation of liberty. He lost this argument. Charles J. stated (at paras 30 and 31):

> *Albeit that the MCA does not confer on the Guardian an express power equivalent to an injunction to prevent the person leaving his place of residence or to dictate the terms of the care plan, in my view, the combination of the express powers conferred on a Guardian and s. 18(3) of the MHA have the practical effects that:*
>
> i) *in choosing the place that the relevant person (P) is to live the Guardian will have regard to, and may require a commitment from the provider of the placement in respect of, the terms of the care plan and so the restrictions it is to contain,*
>
> ii) *if the care plan is changed the Guardian can require P to live elsewhere, and so*

iii) *the relevant person (P) is required to live at a certain place under a care regime and so certain conditions and restrictions,*

iv) *so by requiring P to live at a given place a Guardian is at least indirectly requiring him to live there under those conditions and restrictions, albeit that the Guardian cannot impose them on the provider of the care or treatment and they are based on agreement and the performance by the provider of its functions, and in NL v Hampshire CC [2014] UKUT 0475 (AAC) the Upper Tribunal decided that it was the care plan and not the guardianship that was the basis of a deprivation of liberty,*

v) *the power to return P to his place of residence has the effect of a requirement or an injunction preventing P from leaving.*

Further, and importantly the power mentioned in (v) is a more readily available, effective and sensible means of enforcing the result that P lives at a certain place than an injunction against a person who lacks capacity to decide where he should live that either restrains him from leaving or which also has a mandatory element that requires him to go to, or to return to, the placement. This is because enforcement of such an injunction against the patient is problematic as it engages issues of contempt against a person who lacks capacity, the issue of a warrant by the court and often a consideration of whether third parties who have assisted the patient are in contempt and should be ordered to take defined steps to return the patient to his placement.

The future of guardianship

It remains to be seen whether these cases will have any impact on the use of guardianship. It would be ironic if guardianship numbers all but disappeared only to find that an equivalent measure is seen as the solution to the expense and procedural difficulties currently facing the MCA approach to deprivation of liberty.

Relatively minor amendments could allow guardianship to authorise deprivation of liberty within care homes and other community settings. However, it would require reform in terms of: removing the behavioural qualifications for patients with learning difficulties; introducing automatic tribunals; reversing the burden of proof at tribunals; and extending all of section 13 to cover guardianship in terms of the AMHP's duties. Finally, in a Court of Protection case when guardianship was under consideration (*C v Darwen and Blackburn*, 2011), the judge stated that the Mental Health Act should have primacy over the Mental Capacity Act:

In my view, there are good reasons why the provisions of the Mental Health Act should prevail when they apply. It is a self-contained system with inbuilt checks and balances and it is well understood by professionals working in the field. It is cheaper than the Court of Protection.

Herein may lie its attraction.

Leave of absence and absence without leave

Section 17 leave under the MHA 1983

The main features of section 17 leave are as follows:

- The RC may grant leave to any patient liable to be detained under Part 2 of the Act to enable them to be absent from the hospital.

- Hospital order (section 37 – see Chapter 5) patients may be granted leave by the RC but restricted patients may be granted leave only with the permission of the Secretary of State for Justice.

- The Code (para. 27.4) states that patients subject to sections 35, 36 or 38 may not be granted leave by the RC.

- Leave may be subject to any conditions the RC thinks necessary in the interests of the patient or for the protection of others.

- It may be granted indefinitely, on specified occasions or for a specific period. It may not go beyond the renewal date for the section.

- A patient could be granted leave to another hospital (e.g. nearer home or where physical treatment is needed) and could later be transferred under section 19.

- If a patient is placed on section 17 leave in a hospital or care home in conditions that amount to a deprivation of liberty, Schedule A1 of the Mental Capacity Act 2005 requires a DoLS authorisation for eligible patients.

- The RC may direct the patient should remain in custody when on leave.

- The RC may revoke leave in writing and recall the patient to hospital if they consider it necessary in the interest of the patient's health or safety or for the protection of others.

- A patient may not be recalled to hospital for the sole purpose of renewing the detention.

- A patient on leave is still liable to be detained and therefore is still subject to the consent to treatment provisions of Part 4 of the Act.

- The duty to provide section 117 after-care applies when a patient is on leave (Code para. 27.26).

- A community treatment order could be made while a patient is on section 17 leave.

In terms of recording there is no statutory form but para. 27.22 of the Code states:

> *Hospital managers should establish a standardised system by which responsible clinicians can record the leave they authorise and specify the conditions attached to it. Copies of the authorisation should be given to the patient and to any carers, professionals and other people in the community who need to know. A copy should also be kept in the patient's notes. In case they fail to return from leave, an up-to-date description of the patient should be available in their notes.*

The Code of Practice includes two important statements:

> *27.8 Only the patient's responsible clinician can grant leave of absence to a patient detained under the Act. Responsible clinicians cannot delegate the decision to grant leave of absence to anyone else. In the absence of the usual responsible clinician (e.g. if they are on leave), permission can be granted only by the approved clinician who is for the time being acting as the patient's responsible clinician.*

> *27.9 Responsible clinicians may grant leave for specific occasions or for specific or indefinite periods of time. They may make leave subject to any conditions which they consider necessary in the interests of the patient or for the protection of other people.*

A patient liable to be detained under section 3 may have this renewed, even if on leave, if there is a significant hospital element to the treatment plan: *B* v *Barking, Havering and Brentwood Community Healthcare NHS Trust* (1999), together with *R (on the application of DR)* v *Mersey Care NHS Trust* (2002) and *R (CS)* v *MHRT* (2004).

The last case involved a patient who had been on section 17 leave for three months. Hospital attendance was limited to a four-weekly ward round and weekly sessions with a ward psychologist. The judge noted that it was:

> *clear to me the RMO was engaged in a delicate balancing exercise by which she was, with as light a touch as she could, encouraging progress to discharge. Her purpose was to break the persistent historical cycle of admission, serious relapse and readmission. It may be that in the closing stages of the treatment in hospital her grasp on the claimant was gossamer thin, but to view that grasp as insignificant is, in my view, to misunderstand the evidence.*

With a broad definition of what amounts to a hospital, section 17 leave in some cases is virtually a community treatment order (CTO). As the new requirement is just for the RC to consider the use of section 17A when granting leave for more than seven consecutive days, many RCs may have wished to continue to rely on section 17 to maintain patients in the community. However, indications are that CTOs are far more numerous than expected and a range of pressures push RCs to use CTOs.

Absence without leave (section 18)

When a detained patient is absent without leave he or she may be taken into custody and returned to hospital. Changes in 1996 extended the period during which patients on long-term sections may be so taken. This is six months or the end of the period of detention, whichever is longer. If the detention section has lapsed, the patient may be detained for a week for the RC to examine the patient and consider a possible renewal of detention.

If the power of entry is needed but refused, consideration should be given to the use of section 135(2) (see p27). When a patient in guardianship absents themselves without permission from any place where they are required to reside, they may be taken into custody and returned to that place (*KD* v *Walsall MBC and Others* (2015)).

Community treatment orders: section 17A

Community treatment orders were introduced as an essential part of the Mental Health Act 2007 reforms. They provide a new framework for ensuring that certain patients receive compulsory care and treatment within the community.

The government's main aim in replacing supervised after-care with the community treatment order was to ensure that patients would not be left untreated in the community. However, they had to make a number of compromises as the Bill went through Parliament. In particular, the House of Lords obtained a number of concessions on the issue of compulsory treatment. CTOs have been used about ten times more than expected and with significant geographical variations. See Table 2.3.

Table 2.3   Detentions and patients subject to CTOs in 2014–15 for 21 English NHS providers

NHS provider	All detentions during year	CTOs on 31.03.15	CTO as a % of detentions
North East London NHS Foundation Trust	575	140	24.35
Camden and Islington NHS Foundation Trust	630	145	23.02
Coventry & Warwickshire Partnership NHS Trust	435	100	22.99
Birmingham & Solihull MH NHS Foundation Trust	1,190	210	17.65
Greater Manchester West MH NHS Foundation Trust	545	95	17.43
Cheshire and Wirral Partnership NHS Foundation Trust	870	145	16.67
SW London & St George's Mental Health NHS Trust	970	160	16.49
Oxleas NHS Foundation Trust	700	110	15.71
Nottinghamshire Healthcare NHS Foundation Trust	955	130	13.61
Tees, Esk and Wear Valleys NHS Foundation Trust	1,580	210	13.29
Bradford District Care Trust	530	70	13.21
East London NHS Foundation Trust	1,340	175	13.06
Lancashire Care NHS Foundation Trust	1200	140	11.67
Norfolk and Suffolk NHS Foundation Trust	1,065	120	11.27
Dorset Healthcare University NHS Foundation Trust	670	70	10.45
Barnet, Enfield & Haringey Mental Health NHS Trust	970	100	10.31
Surrey & Borders Partnership NHS Foundation Trust	565	55	09.73
Central and NW London NHS Foundation Trust	1,690	160	09.47
Oxford Health NHS Foundation Trust	735	60	08.16
5 Boroughs Partnership NHS Foundation Trust	910	60	06.59
South London and Maudsley NHS Foundation Trust	1,850	45	02.43
Totals from sample*	19,975	2500	12.52

*CTO numbers for individual providers are rounded to the nearest 5 in the published statistics, and those with less than 5 are not included. Total for England is 5,340 – this is not rounded and includes all providers.

Source: Health & Social Care Information Service.

Table 2.4   Use of CTOs, recalls, revocations and discharges in England

	2009–10	2010–11	2011–12	2012–13	2013–14	2014–15
Total use of CTOs	4,107	3,834	4,220	4,647	4,434	4,564
CTO recalls	1,217	1,601	2,082	2,272	2,316	2,389
CTO revocations	779	1,018	1,469	1,509	1,401	1,427
Discharges from CTOs	1,010	1,167	1,712	2,162	2,230	2,491
CTOs on March 31	3,325	4,291	4,764	5,218	5,365	5,461

Ideally one would look at the numbers of CTOs compared with the overall number of patients discharged on to section 117 after-care, but such figures are not yet available at a national level. What is clear is that, as with guardianship, the use of CTOs varies considerably between areas. The reasons for these variations may become clearer as more research findings on the use of CTOs are published. The implications for AMHPs of having over 5,000 CTOs are considerable as they are so involved in the making of CTOs. Similarly, each revocation involves an AMHP.

With the increase in the use of section 2 compared with section 3, the general increase in the number of patients detained, the number of new CTOs and nearly 1,500 revocations, it is clear that the number of AMHP assessments has increased dramatically in the years since the Act was changed in 2008. No doubt this has contributed to the stress reported in a recent study (Hudson and Webber, 2012).

The OCTET Study

Community orders were introduced as a central part of the reforms to the MHA which came into effect in November 2008. There was nothing significant in the way of international research to suggest that they would be effective but the government was convinced that they were needed and that research would support this. Their expectations were given a jolt by the publication of the OCTET study in 2013 (Burns *et al.*). The results were summarised as follows:

> *In well coordinated mental health services the imposition of compulsory supervision does not reduce the rate of readmission of psychotic patients. We found no support in terms of any reduction in overall hospital admission to justify the significant curtailment of patients' personal liberty.*

The study was fairly large and looked at the circumstances of 333 patients who were placed on CTOs (166 patients) or on section 17 leave (167 patients). The first group were subject to compulsion for an average of six months while those on section 17 leave were only subject to compulsion for an average of eight days. Not only were there no significant differences in terms of readmission rate (one of the major arguments for introducing CTOs), the study found no other benefits for those patients whose liberty was curtailed.

Two years on from the study there are few signs that responsible clinicians or indeed AMHPs are less enthusiastic about the use of CTOs. Further studies on why this should be so would be interesting as professionals often claim to follow 'evidence based practice'.

Grounds for a CTO

Section 17(2A) requires the RC to consider the use of a CTO in any case where he is granting section 17 leave that will exceed seven consecutive days.

A CTO can be made only when a patient is liable to be detained in a hospital for treatment. Patients of any age who are liable to be detained under sections 3, 37, 45A, 47 and 48 can be made subject to a CTO by their RC, if they obtain the agreement of an AMHP and if the criteria set out in section 17A(5) are met:

(a) *the patient is suffering from mental disorder of a nature or degree which makes it appropriate for him to receive medical treatment;*

(b) *it is necessary for his health or safety or for the protection of other persons that he should receive such treatment;*

(c) *subject to his being liable to be recalled as mentioned in paragraph (d) below, such treatment can be provided without his continuing to be detained in a hospital;*

(d) *it is necessary that the responsible clinician should be able to exercise the power under section 17E(1) below to recall the patient to hospital;*

(e) *appropriate medical treatment is available for him.*

The relevant form (CTO1 in England) requires that the RC and the AMHP both state that these criteria are met. The AMHP also needs to state that it is appropriate to make the CTO, and where discretionary conditions are set, that they agree that they are necessary or appropriate. So both the RC and the AMHP must address all five of the criteria so the AMHP must form a clear view of the nature and degree of the mental disorder. Given that the RC may not be medically trained it is perhaps surprising that there has been no challenge to the 'medical expertise' of the assessors. The form (in Wales as well as England) is far from ideal as there is no space for the AMHP to give their reasons for their opinion. Many will choose therefore to record their assessment of the five criteria in other documentation.

A patient who is made subject to a CTO will have two conditions attached to the order and these are set out on the form itself. Section 17B(3) states:

The order shall specify –

(a) *a condition that the patient make himself available for examination under section 20A below; and*

(b) *a condition that, if it is proposed to give a certificate under Part 4A of this Act in his case, he make himself available for examination so as to enable the certificate to be given.*

Section 17B(2) states that the RC may also specify discretionary conditions if they obtain the agreement of the AMHP. Any discretionary conditions must be considered:

> *necessary or appropriate for one or more of the following purposes –*
>
> *(a) ensuring that the patient receives medical treatment;*
> *(b) preventing risk of harm to the patient's health or safety;*
> *(c) protecting other persons.*

Although the RC needs the agreement of the AMHP before making these conditions, they can subsequently be varied or suspended by the RC at any time without the agreement of an AMHP. The Code notes this at para. 29.40 but states:

> *The responsible clinician has the power to vary the conditions of the patient's CTO, or to suspend any of them. The responsible clinician does not need to agree any variation or suspension with the AMHP. However, it would not be good practice to vary conditions which had recently been agreed with an AMHP without discussion with that AMHP.*

This is an area that may need to be monitored.

Failure by the patient to comply with a mandatory condition provides grounds to recall a patient but this is not true of failure to comply with a discretionary condition. In this case the RC would need to believe that the patient required treatment in hospital and that there would be a risk of harm to the health or safety of the patient or to others if they were not recalled to hospital for treatment of their mental disorder.

The Code of Practice at para. 29.32 gives some guidance about the sorts of conditions that might be attached to a patient's CTO:

> *They might cover matters such as where and when the patient is to receive treatment in the community; where the patient is to live; and avoidance of known risk factors or high-risk situations relevant to the patient's mental disorder.*

It is generally accepted that the cumulative effect of the conditions imposed on a patient should not amount to a deprivation of liberty. The Code (para 31.9) states that an incapacitated patient whose care and treatment amounts to a deprivation of liberty may be subject to DoLS which could co-exist with a CTO. The community order would have certain conditions but the deprivation of liberty would need to be covered by the DoLS procedure being followed.

Recall

A patient who is subject to a CTO may be recalled to hospital by the RC. Notice of recall must be in writing and can take place only if either the patient has failed to comply with a mandatory condition or they require medical treatment in hospital for their mental disorder and there would be a risk of harm to the health or safety of the patient or to others if they were not recalled to hospital for treatment of their mental disorder. In deciding whether to recall a patient to hospital the RC may take into account any failure to comply with a discretionary condition.

The Code gives some guidance on recall (para. 29.49):

> *The responsible clinician should consider in each case whether recalling the patient to hospital is justified in all the circumstances. For example, it might be sufficient to monitor a patient who has failed to comply with a condition to attend for treatment, before deciding whether the lack of treatment means that recall is necessary. Failure to comply with a condition (apart from those relating to availability for medical examination, as above) does not in itself trigger recall. Only if the breach of a condition results in an increased risk of harm to the patient or to anyone else will recall be justified.*

If a patient is served with a notice of recall but does not comply with this then they can be returned under the authority of section 18 of the Act. This may require obtaining a warrant under section 135(2).

A patient who has been recalled can be detained in hospital for up to 72 hours, during which time the RC may do one of the following:

- treat the patient and then allow them to return home within 72 hours from the time of recall (this course of action may be quite common after recall because the patient is subject to Part 4 on recall instead of Part 4A and this makes it much easier to compel the patient to have medication), or

- revoke the CTO (which has the effect of making the patient subject to section 3 again), with the agreement of an AMHP, if the grounds for detention are met, or

- discharge the CTO completely.

Revocation

The RC together with an AMHP may revoke a CTO in writing if the criteria for detention under section 3 are met, i.e.:

- *the patient is suffering from a mental disorder of a nature or degree which makes it appropriate for him to receive medical treatment in a hospital; and*

- *it is necessary for the health or safety of the patient or for the protection of other persons that he should receive such treatment and it cannot be provided unless he is detained under this section; and*

- *appropriate medical treatment is available for him.*

The effect of revocation is that the patient remains in hospital under their original detention section but the patient will start a new detention period of six months from the time of revocation. However, for consent to treatment purposes, the protection of

Part 4 is preserved (e.g. the patient does not have to restart a period of three months before being eligible for a second opinion appointed doctor (SOAD)).

Revocation triggers an automatic mental health tribunal reference by the managers.

Extending a CTO

Section 20A of the Act sets out the provisions and criteria for the extension of CTOs. A CTO lasts for six months in the first instance but can be extended for a further six months and then yearly. The RC, with the agreement of an AMHP, needs to be satisfied that the criteria for a CTO are still met.

Discharging a CTO

The RC can discharge a CTO at any time. The patient can apply for a mental health tribunal hearing once in each period. The tribunal can discharge the CTO but it does not have the power to vary the conditions. The hospital managers also have the power of discharge so the patient may request a hearing. Finally the nearest relative can discharge the patient (giving 72 hours' written notice) unless the patient had formerly been on a Part 3 section (e.g. s37) rather than subject to section 3. The RC can block the NR discharge if they believe the patient might behave in a manner dangerous to themselves or others. Discharge from a CTO has the effect of discharging the initial liability for detention.

CTO, section 17 leave or guardianship?

The Code of Practice offers some guidance regarding which might be the most appropriate community provision in situations where any of the three would be possible (i.e. where the patient is detained in hospital for treatment). Para. 31.3 states that guardianship:

> *is social care-led and is primarily focused on patients with welfare needs. Its purpose is to enable patients to receive care in the community where it cannot be provided without the use of compulsory powers.*

Para. 31.4 continues by stating that section 17 leave:

> *is primarily intended to allow a patient detained under the Act to be temporarily absent from hospital where further in-patient treatment as a detained patient is still thought to be necessary. It is clearly suitable for short-term absences for a fixed period or specific purpose, e.g. to allow visits to family and to trial living more independently.*

The limitations on longer-term section 17 leave really arise from the case law requirement that there be some hospital element as a significant part of the care plan. Where patients are required to attend clinics in buildings that are designated as hospitals this is unlikely to be much of an obstacle. Para. 31.6 states that the CTO:

seeks to prevent the 'revolving door' scenario and the harm which could arise from relapse. It is a more structured system than leave of absence and has more safeguards for patients. A key feature of the CTO framework is that it is suitable only where there is no reason to think that the patient will need further treatment as a detained in-patient for the time being, but where the responsible clinician needs to be able to recall the patient to hospital if necessary.

One aspect of the CTO which limits its effectiveness is the lack of any legal sanction whereby a patient who is required to live somewhere can be returned there if they abscond. The CTO looks as though it may be most effective for the patient who is 'on the edge of compliance' with medical treatment but would not voluntarily accept it. A CTO and guardianship cannot co-exist because of sections 6(4) and 8(5).

Discharge and after-care of patients under section 117

The purpose of after-care is stated in para 33.5 of the Code of Practice as follows:

After-care is a vital component in patients' overall treatment and care. As well as meeting their immediate needs for health and social care, after-care should aim to support them in regaining or enhancing their skills, or learning new skills, in order to cope with life outside hospital.

Section 117 places a specific duty on health and social services authorities (in co-operation with relevant voluntary agencies) to provide (or arrange for the provision of) after-care to a patient who has been detained under sections 3, 37, 45A, 47 or 48 and is discharged and leaves hospital.

- The requirement still applies even if there is a gap between the date when the section is lifted and the date when the patient leaves hospital.

- There is a need to assess the needs of each individual to whom this section applies.

- The services should continue to be provided until both the health and social services authorities are satisfied that the person concerned no longer needs the services.

- Supervised after-care first introduced the possibility of requiring the patient to accept the services and this is now possible with a community treatment order.

- If a need for a service is then identified it must be provided but there is probably discretion as to the level and precise nature of the service.

Proper implementation of the Care Programme Approach (CPA) should ensure that the legal requirements of section 117 are met. Authorities should be able to identify clearly which patients are covered by section 117. What amounts to 'after-care services' is now defined in the Act as *services which have both of the following purposes*:

(a) *meeting a need arising from or related to the person's mental disorder; and*

(b) *reducing the risk of a deterioration of the person's mental condition (and, accordingly, reducing the risk of the person requiring admission to a hospital again for treatment of mental disorder).*

Charging for services

This has been a contentious area for some years. Essentially section 117 services should be free to the service user. The *Bournewood* case also drew attention to the fact that there are some benefits of being detained on section 3 in that residential and domiciliary services can be very expensive and may become free for someone who has been detained. From a family's point of view this would be one of the reasons for using the Mental Health Act to detain a patient in hospital rather than the DoLS procedure where both would be possible.

In *R v Manchester City Council ex parte Stennett* (2002) the House of Lords ruled that section 117 imposes a freestanding duty to provide after-care services rather than being a passport to services provided under other legislation. There is no power to charge people for section 117 services and therefore they must be provided free. This would include any medication which was part of the patient's psychiatric treatment. A number of authorities have had to reimburse people as a result of the *Stennett* judgement.

From an AMHP's perspective it is worth noting that it makes no difference who the AMHP is acting for in making an application for section 3. The key issue is the patient's ordinary place of residence when they become subject to section 3. Unfortunately there are changes within the Care Act that so far do not seem to be entirely clear when seeking to determine the patient's 'ordinary place of residence' at the time that they are made subject to section 3. This is not strictly an area for the AMHP to determine so they may seek relief by asking managers to resolve any disputes.

When planning for a patient's after-care it is important that health and social services staff are aware that section 133 of the Mental Health Act requires hospital managers to give the nearest relative notice of intention to discharge a detained patient (except if the patient or nearest relative has requested otherwise). If practicable, this notice should be given at least seven days before the intended date of discharge. This provision applies to all discharges from detention and not just to section 3. It is an especially important provision when a CTO is being considered and AMHPs may wish to ensure this notice is given where it applies. It may serve the purpose of slowing down the CTO process but section 17 could be used in the meantime. Carers have suggested that this provision is frequently ignored by hospitals (see Chapter 3). Hospital managers must take reasonable steps to identify the patient's nearest relative.

ACTIVITY **2.1**

Sample questions on Part 2 of the Mental Health Act 1983

1a What are the main grounds which need to exist before a doctor can recommend that a person should be detained in hospital for assessment under section 2 of the Act?

1b How does the expression 'dangerous to other persons or himself' compare with these grounds and what is its significance?

1c If the dangerousness test was considered to apply, how might an AMHP then become involved?

2a Who can apply to a magistrate for a warrant to be issued under section 135(1) so that a person believed to be suffering from mental disorder can be searched for and removed to a place of safety?

2b Who is required to be involved in the execution of a section 135(1) warrant and what issues might this raise in practice?

2c Identify any human rights issues associated with the use of section 135(1).

3a Who may grant leave to a patient detained on section 3?

3b What should this person do in granting leave and what conditions can be imposed?

3c When do you think it might be seen as justifiable for a patient to be kept subject to section 17 leave for a long period rather than being made subject to a community treatment order?

Multiple choice questions

(Answers in Appendix 9)

1. Which of the following criteria are necessary before a doctor can recommend compulsory admission on section 3?

   (a) The patient is suffering from a mental disorder of a nature or degree which makes it appropriate for him to receive medical treatment in a hospital. ☐

   (b) The patient is a danger to himself or others. ☐

   (c) Appropriate medical treatment is available to him. ☐

   (d) Treatment is likely to alleviate or prevent a deterioration of his condition. ☐

   (e) Treatment cannot be provided unless the patient is detained. ☐

   (f) Admission is necessary for the health or safety of the patient or for the protection of other persons. ☐

2. Sections 135 and 136 allow people to be moved from one place of safety to another.

   (a) True ☐

   (b) False ☐

3. A duly completed application form combined with the necessary medical recommendations provides sufficient authority for the applicant to force their way into the patient's home.

   (a) True ☐

   (b) False ☐

53

Chapter 3
Relatives and carers

The nearest relative under the MHA 1983

Introduction

The nearest relative has a number of important rights and functions under the Act. These are discussed later and include the right to:

- insist on an AMHP's assessment of the need for a person's detention in hospital;
- be consulted where practicable* before a section 3 is applied for (and in effect block it);
- apply for a person's detention in hospital;
- order the patient's discharge.

* See the discussion in Chapter 2 in the paragraphs covering section 3.

The first problem is to identify who exactly is the nearest relative. It will not necessarily be the person identified by the patient as their next of kin and, indeed, the patient has little control over who will be seen in law as the nearest relative. It is worth noting that in *Re D* (Mental patient: Habeas corpus) (2000) the judge stated:

> *The question the court had to consider in deciding whether the application for detention had been validly made was not whether the social worker consulted with the legally correct nearest relative, but whether the patient's daughter appeared to him to be the correct relative.*

This is important because as long as the AMHP follows a logical process which reflects the law, any application should not be ruled unlawful just because it emerges later, when new facts are available, that they have in fact identified the wrong person as nearest relative.

Section 26 provides a list of people considered to be relatives under the Act. Being a relative is of itself important as AMHPs should have regard to any wishes they express (see s13(1)); it may enable them to apply to the county court for a ruling on a nearest relative issue (see later in the chapter) and being such a relative is a prerequisite to being nearest relative (apart from where the court intervenes or where powers are transferred under Regulation 24; see p60).

Complications concerning children and 'the five-year rule' (whereby people in some settings find another resident may become their nearest relative) are discussed later. What follows here is a quick guide to enable an AMHP to make a reasonable decision in identifying the nearest relative.

Disagreements or mistakes in identifying a nearest relative

As noted above, there can be problems where the AMHP or the hospital managers decide after an admission that the wrong person has been identified as the nearest relative. There are different views as to the correct way to respond to this situation and in such a case staff would be well advised to seek legal advice from their local authority.

Another important point before actually identifying the nearest relative is that in a judicial review (*R v MHRT for West Midlands and North West ex parte H,* 2000) it was held that restricted patients do not have a nearest relative. This is because there is no legal function for a nearest relative for such a patient. When compiling reports for mental health tribunals it is important, therefore, not to refer to anyone as the nearest relative of a restricted patient.

How to identify the nearest relative

To identify a person's nearest relative go through the following four stages:

1. *Make a list* of any of the following who are ordinarily resident in the UK, the Channel Islands or the Isle of Man (*this assumes the patient is ordinarily so resident; if not, then the nearest relative may be someone who is, similarly, not so resident), i.e. list the patient's:

    *   husband, wife or civil partner

        (a) unless permanently separated from the patient by agreement or by a court order, or where one partner has deserted the other;

        (b) may be someone who has lived as husband, wife or civil partner for the last six months or more if patient not legally married, or patient is married or has civil partner but (a) applies;

- son or daughter
- father or mother
- brother or sister
- grandparent
- grandchild
- uncle or aunt
- nephew or niece
- any other person with whom the patient has ordinarily resided for five years or more.

In compiling the list, include half-blood relationships, treat illegitimate children as the legitimate children of their mothers (and of their fathers if they have parental responsibility) and do not include in-law relationships. You now have a list of people to be treated as relatives. To identify the nearest relative

2. *Cross out* anyone under the age of 18 unless they are the patient's husband, wife, civil partner or parent.

3. *Highlight* (with a highlighter pen) anyone on the list who ordinarily resides with *or* cares for the patient (or did so before the patient was admitted to hospital).

'Caring for'** is a matter of judgement and could include shopping, cooking or providing other care. If only one person is highlighted they are the nearest relative. There is no extra priority given to someone who both ordinarily resides with and cares for the patient. They are either highlighted or not; there are no bonus points for being highlighted twice although Jones (2015) advises (in his footnote to s26(7)) that this would be the case in a residential home. If in doubt AMHPs should seek advice.

If more than one person is highlighted (or no one) then go to:

4. *Rank* in order of priority. If more than one person was highlighted above under (3) then rank only those who were highlighted. If no one was highlighted the ranking applies to everyone on the list. The person highest in the list under (1) is the nearest relative. If there is more than one person in the same category, then whole-blood relatives are preferred to half-blood and elder is preferred to younger.

Patients not ordinarily resident in the UK. Some parts of the country with airports and seaports are used to contacting people in various parts of the world if the person is identified as having a mental disorder at the point of entry. The same situation applies whenever the patient is not ordinarily resident in the UK or listed areas. This may include students, holidaymakers, etc.

** In *Re D* (Mental Patient: Habeas corpus) (2000) the judge stated the words 'cared for' were not defined in the Act but they were clear everyday words set in the context where a social worker had to act in a common-sense manner. The word 'ordinarily' in section 4 applied to 'residing with' and not to 'caring', so a person may only recently have started providing the care.

Discussion points

1. *Listing relatives.* 'Illegitimate' is an old-fashioned word that has somehow survived in this legislation. Given the number of parents who are not married it immediately poses a problem in identifying relatives. AMHPs are often the first people who have to identify the nearest relative and it is a difficult area to approach. If the parents were not married, the father will only be a relative if he obtained parental responsibility at some point. As you cannot obtain parental responsibility once the child reaches 18 many apparent fathers will not be so for the purposes of this Act, even where the patient is now an adult. This is another difficult issue to explain to families in a crisis. The problem is best summed up by Brenda Hale (2010, p83) who appears at first to sit on the fence but on closer scrutiny seems to suggest that unless the parents were married the father is not a relative once the patient reaches 18.

   People whose parents were not married to one another are regarded as related only to their mother's side of the family and not to their father unless he 'has' parental responsibility for them (s26(2)). Parental responsibility comes to an end when the child reaches 18, so does this mean that the relationship also comes to an end for this purpose? This is an outdated exception to the general rule (in the Family Law Reform Act 1987, s1(1)) that relationships are to be traced without regard to whether or not a person's parents were married to one another. It is surprising that the opportunity was not taken to correct it in the 2007 amendments.

   Richard Jones in his footnote to s26(2) takes the same line as Hale (Jones, 2015). One unfortunate conclusion is that even where a father had parental responsibility, as soon as the child reaches the age of 18 the father only counts as a relative if he is, or was, married to the mother. Hewitt (2013) however has said: *On any careful interpretation, the position seems clear: as far as the role of nearest relative is concerned, the father ceases to be illegitimate once the child has come of age.* There has been no clarification of this argument in court so AMHPs will need to be clear on the opinion of their own legal representatives. At the time of writing the majority view of lawyers consulted by this author favoured the Jones view whilst recognising that this is an anomaly that should ideally be rectified through legal amendment.

2. Another strange question that has been identified is: 'When aren't aunts aunts?' It would seem that only blood relationships would count here, so that your mother's brother is your uncle, but this uncle's wife is not your aunt for the purposes of the MHA 1983. This is a recipe for confusion (Barber *et al.*, 2012, p105).

3. In the case of husband, wife or civil partner, what amounts to permanent separation and what is desertion? If there is no court order it is possible that the spouses or civil partners have agreed that their separation is permanent. This may not be enough if they are still in the same household and sharing meals or rooms. Desertion can be difficult to establish with confidence especially as it requires a lack of any justification for the separation as well as the mental capacity to form the intent.

4. Living together as if husband and wife or civil partners. This is a tricky one to deal with in practice as it is an odd piece of law, very personal and difficult to explain to those involved. In *Kimber* v *Kimber* (2000) the judge identified a number of factors which would indicate cohabitation. AMHPs should demonstrate that they have considered these in reaching a conclusion.

    (a) Are the parties living together in the same household?

    (b) Do they share daily household tasks and duties?

    (c) Is there stability and a degree of permanence in the relationship?

    (d) Is the way in which financial matters are being handled an indication of the cohabitation?

    (e) Do the parties have a sexual relationship with each other?

    (f) Are there children of the relationship?

    (g) What is the intention and motivation of the parties?

    (h) Would a reasonable person of normal perceptions consider that the parties were cohabiting?

These questions are not complete or comprehensive but are the main factors which should be considered. Any period spent in prison or detained in hospital should be deducted from the period spent together. The couple must have been living together at the point one of them was admitted to hospital.

5. *The Children Act 1989.* It is unusual for children under 18 to be detained under the Mental Health Act. In 2014–15 there were eight children aged 15 or under who were detained under the MHA in England and 71 young persons of 16 or 17. There is a lower age limit of 16 for guardianship but there is no lower age limit for detention. In cases where admission is considered, the nearest relative will usually be the older parent unless the father is unmarried or does not have parental responsibility. If a child is living with a person under a child arrangements order within the meaning of the Children Act, or if there is a special guardian, then that person will be the nearest relative (s28, MHA). If there are two people then they will share the role. If a child is subject to a care order (including interim care orders) then the local authority will be the nearest relative (s27, MHA). Chapter 19 of the Code of Practice to the Mental Health Act 1983 gives some specific advice on children and young people under the age of 18.

6. 'The five-year rule'. The Act introduced a new category of persons to be treated as if they are relatives. These are defined in section 26(7) as persons with whom the patient has been 'ordinarily residing for a period of not less than five years'. Together with the preference in section 26(4) for making the nearest relative the person whom 'the patient ordinarily resides with or is cared for by', this has created some strange situations in practice. Consider the situation of a patient who has lived in an old people's home with the same group of people for more than five years. If they eat together and share common facilities, they could be included within the meaning of

'the patient ordinarily resides with'. Assuming none of the other residents is a blood relative, the eldest of them will probably be nearest relative. This will apply even if the patient has blood relatives elsewhere, unless one of them is 'caring for' the patient. Each case would need to be determined on its own facts and the degree and kind of contact with other residents would clearly be significant.

7. *Patient objects to nearest relative.* The Act requires an AMHP to consult with the nearest relative where practicable but this poses a problem where the patient objects to contact (e.g. where there has been abuse) on the grounds that it violates their human rights. Article 8 of the European Convention on Human Rights states everyone has a right to respect for their private and family life, their home and correspondence.

    In the case of *JT* v *UK* (2000) JT was detained under section 3. She was moved to a secure unit in November 1984 and to a special hospital in 1987. Her detention was subject to periodic review by MHRTs and she was discharged in January 1996. JT complained to the Commission that she had been unable to change her nearest relative in violation of Article 8. Her nearest relative was her mother with whom she had had a difficult relationship. JT had wanted to nominate another person so personal information, mainly in relation to MHRTs, was not released to her mother or to her stepfather (against whom the applicant had made allegations of sexual abuse). The Commission declared admissible the complaint under Article 8, para. 1 concerning her inability to change her nearest relative during her period of detention. The case was struck out by the European Court of Human Rights after a friendly settlement was reached: the UK government agreed to amend the law to allow a detainee to apply to the county court to have a nearest relative replaced if the patient reasonably objected to that person acting in that capacity (Times Law Report 0504-2000). There was a long delay before this was addressed in the Mental Health Act 2007, and in the meantime the High Court provided some relief in the *R* v *Bristol* case (2005). The judge ruled that the ASW (now AMHP) had discretion to decide not to consult the nearest relative of a competent patient who objected and whose psychiatrist said such consultation would be detrimental to the patient's health. However this position was modified in the case of *TW* v *Enfield Borough Council* (2014). This case emphasised the important role of the nearest relative in protecting the patient's Article 5 rights. AMHPs would need to show an awareness of this protective role and we will see shortly that where they are not consulting the nearest relative they would usually be expected to apply to the county court for someone else to take on this function.

The Code reflects this new position:

> *14.61 There may also be cases where, although physically possible, it would not be reasonably practicable to inform or consult the nearest relative because the detrimental impact of this on the patient would interfere with the patient's right to respect for their privacy and family life under Article 8 of the European Convention on Human Rights to an extent that would not be justified and proportionate in the particular circumstances of the case. Detrimental impact may include cases where*

patients are likely to suffer emotional distress, deterioration in their mental health, physical harm, or financial or other exploitation as a result of the consultation. Consultation with the nearest relative that interferes with the patient's Article 8 rights may be justified to protect the patient's Article 5 right to liberty.

14.62 Consulting and notifying the nearest relative is a significant safeguard for patients. Therefore decisions not to do so on these grounds should not be taken lightly. AMHPs should consider all the circumstances of the case, including:

- *the benefit to the patient of the involvement of their nearest relative, including to protect the patient's Article 5 rights;*

- *the patient's wishes, including taking into account whether they have the capacity to decide whether they would want their nearest relative involved and any statement of their wishes they have made in advance. However a patient's wishes will not be determinative of whether it is reasonably practicable to consult the nearest relative;*

- *any detrimental effect that involving the nearest relative would have on the patient's health and wellbeing; and*

- *whether there is any good reason to think that the patient's objection may be intended to prevent information relevant to the assessment being discovered.*

Changing or displacing the nearest relative

If mentally competent, a nearest relative may authorise someone else to perform their functions under Regulation 24 of the Mental Health (Hospital, Guardianship and Treatment) (England) Regulations 2008. (In Wales the equivalent is Regulation 33.) This other person need not be a relative as defined by the Act but they must not be in one of the categories (such as persons under the age of 18) excluded under section 26(5). The authorisation needs to be in writing (or can be in electronic form if the recipient agrees) and copies lodged with the person authorised and with the hospital managers (for detained or community patients) or the local authority (for guardianship). The donor should also notify the patient. The authorisation begins when it is received by the person authorised and cannot be relied on until that point. This procedure may be useful in the circumstances outlined above concerning the five-year rule (where the eldest resident could authorise a suitable relative) or in any other cases where both parties are agreeable. This might be where those involved do not feel that the legal nearest relative is the right person to carry out that function. There is no requirement to obtain the patient's agreement but see the note below on 'suitability'. (Also see Appendix 11 for a sample form – the regulation number would need to be changed to 33 for Wales but the content could be the same.) The nearest relative can revoke this at any time in writing (or electronically if the recipient agrees).

There will be some circumstances (e.g. where the nearest relative of the patient is not capable of acting as such by reason of mental disorder) where use of the regulations would not be the appropriate action and where an application to the county court is needed. The court may direct someone to carry out nearest relative's functions on application from (s29(2)):

(za) *the patient;*

(a) *any relative of the patient;*

(b) *any other person with whom the patient is residing (or, if the patient is then an in-patient in a hospital, was last residing before he was admitted);*

(c) *an Approved Mental Health Professional.*

The grounds for an application are set out in section 29(3):

(a) *that the patient has no nearest relative within the meaning of this Act, or that it is not reasonably practicable to ascertain whether he has such a relative, or who that relative is;*

(b) *that the nearest relative of the patient is incapable of acting as such by reason of mental disorder or other illness;*

(c) *that the nearest relative of the patient unreasonably objects to the making of an application for admission for treatment or a guardianship application in respect of the patient;*

(d) *that the nearest relative of the patient has exercised without due regard to the welfare of the patient or the interests of the public his power to discharge the patient under this Part of this Act, or is likely to do so; or*

(e) *that the nearest relative of the patient is otherwise not a suitable person to act as such.*

Where (c) or (d) apply, and the patient is already detained under section 2, the detention will last until the court reaches a decision. If the court's decision is to make an order giving someone else the functions of the nearest relative, there is a further seven-day period which would allow a section 3 assessment form to be completed. Where (a), (b) or (e) are the grounds the court can specify a time limit for the order. If (c) or (d) obtain, or where no time limit is set under (a) or (b), the order lasts until the patient is no longer liable to detention or subject to guardianship or a CTO.

The important changes brought about by the Mental Health Act 2007 reforms are that the patient can now make an application and that the ground of 'unsuitability' is introduced. The ability for the patient to apply to the court was not as radical a response as had been considered at one stage. There were proposals to introduce a 'nominated person' to be chosen by the patient but these were dropped before the final version of the Bill went to parliament.

Where the patient or the AMHP makes application to displace on the new ground that *the nearest relative of the patient is otherwise not a suitable person to act as such* the question will arise as to what would amount to unsuitability. It will be for the court to decide in the final analysis. Even if the AMHP does not make the application it may be that the court will ask their opinion. The Code (at para. 5.14) gives advice on factors that might lead an AMHP to consider that a nearest relative is unsuitable to act as such:

> *any reason to think that the patient has suffered, or is suspected to have suffered, abuse at the hands of the nearest relative (or someone with whom the nearest relative is in a relationship), or is at risk of suffering such abuse;*
>
> *any evidence that the patient is afraid of the nearest relative or seriously distressed by the possibility of the nearest relative being involved in their life or their care; and*
>
> *whether the patient and nearest relative are unknown to each other, there is only a distant relationship between them, or their relationship has broken down irretrievably.*

Whatever the grounds might be for applying to the county court for the appointment of a nearest relative an AMHP needs to plan ahead with regard to who might take the role on. Para. 5.19 of the Code states:

> *When applying to displace a nearest relative, AMHPs should nominate someone to become the acting nearest relative in the event that the application is successful. Wherever practicable, they should first consult the patient about the patient's own preferences and any concerns they have about the person the AMHP proposes to nominate. AMHPs should also seek the agreement of the proposed nominee prior to an application being made, although this is not a legal requirement.*

The AMHP's local authority should provide help and guidance on the issue of who should be nominated. It will rarely make sense for this person to be the AMHP because of the potential conflict in roles. The court will need evidence that the nominated person is willing to take on the function.

Where there is no nearest relative

A significant addition to the revised Code of Practice is to be found in para. 5.6:

> *Where an approved mental health professional (AMHP) discovers, when assessing a patient for possible detention or guardianship under the Act (or at any other time), that the patient appears to have no nearest relative, the AMHP should advise the patient of their right to apply to the county court for the appointment of a person to act as their nearest relative. If the patient lacks capacity to decide to apply themselves, the AMHP should apply to the county court.*

This addition to the Code, if followed in every case, could lead to a considerable volume of new work and early indications are that not every local authority's legal team is keen for AMHPs to make application to court in every single case where an incapacitated patient has no nearest relative. In the absence of someone such as a friend who is willing to take on such a role applications could lead to the local authority ending up carrying out the function of nearest relative to a large number of patients. In the absence of any schemes to make this a robust, genuinely protective system for the patient, AMHPs might have a cogent reason for departing from the Code. The nearest relative role is overdue a serious review and overhaul. In the meantime lead AMHPs may be well advised to discuss this issue with their legal section staff.

Further new guidance of particular interest to AMHPs is contained in para. 5.15 which makes it clear that the decision whether or not to apply to the court 'lies with the AMHP personally'. Para. 5.17 states:

> All local authorities should provide clear practical guidance to help the AMHP decide whether to make an application and how to proceed. Before producing such guidance, local authorities should consult with the county court. Local authorities should ensure that they have access to the necessary legal advice and support.

The courts have clearly been seeing the nearest relative role as a significant protection of the patient's Article 5 rights. Thus another area where practice may need to change is in those rare cases where the AMHP decides it is not practicable to consult the nearest relative over a possible section 3 application or to inform them of a section 2 application because of the detrimental effect on the patient. In these cases it would seem wise now for the AMHP to make an application to the court on the grounds of unsuitability. Here there is some very helpful new advice in the Code at para. 5.21:

> If the patient has any concerns that any information given to the court on their views on the suitability of the nearest relative may have implications for their own safety, an application can be made to the court seeking its permission not to make the current nearest relative a party to the proceedings. The reasons for the patient's concerns should be set out clearly in the application.

Rights and functions of the nearest relative

The nearest relative is able to be the applicant

The nearest relative is able to be the applicant for detentions in hospital under sections 2, 3 and 4 and for guardianship under section 7. Para. 14.30 of the Code of Practice states:

> An application for detention may be made by an AMHP or the patient's nearest relative. An AMHP is usually a more appropriate applicant than a patient's nearest relative, given their professional training and knowledge of the legislation and local resources. This also reduces the risk that an application by the nearest relative might have an adverse effect on their relationship with the patient.

Then at para. 14.32 there is a further statement:

> Doctors who are approached directly by a nearest relative about the possibility of an application being made should advise the nearest relative of their right to require a local social services authority to arrange for an AMHP to consider the patient's case.

The number of nearest relative applications has fallen to such a low figure that statistics are no longer kept by the Department of Health.

Where the nearest relative is the applicant

Where the nearest relative makes an application for detention, section 14 requires an AMHP to provide a social circumstances report to the hospital. The Code of Practice recommends that AMHPs provide assistance with conveyance where the nearest relative is the applicant but the advice is given in a guarded way. Para. 17.11 states:

> If the nearest relative is the applicant, any AMHP and other professionals involved in the assessment of the patient should give advice and assistance. However, they should not assist in a patient's detention unless they believe it is justified and lawful.

If the AMHP had earlier refused to make an application, their report would no doubt include an account of the reasons for this. Experience suggests that in most circumstances hospitals would not wish to admit a patient where an AMHP had made a decision not to apply, unless the circumstances had changed. The Code, however, still gives the following advice at para. 14.101:

> An AMHP should, when informing the nearest relative that they do not intend to make an application, advise the nearest relative of their right to do so instead. If the nearest relative wishes to pursue this, the AMHP should suggest that they consult with the doctors to see if they would be prepared to provide recommendations.

Depending on the reasons for the AMHP declining to make an application this advice might be seen as rather contentious and in some circumstances, e.g. based on human rights reasons, the AMHP may consider that they have cogent reasons for departing from the Code of Practice.

Section 11(3) requires the AMHP to 'take such steps as are practicable' to inform the nearest relative

Section 11(3) requires the AMHP to take such steps as are practicable to inform the nearest relative before or within a reasonable time after an application for the admission of a patient for assessment that an application is being, or has been, made and of their rights to discharge a patient under section 23. If they choose to exercise this power, the nearest relative must give the hospital managers 72 hours' written notice of their intention. It would be advisable for the AMHP to explain that the responsible clinician (RC) may block this discharge if able to produce within the 72 hours a report certifying that in the opinion of that clinician, the patient, if discharged, would be likely to act in a manner dangerous to other persons or to himself. (See Figure 2.1 on p20 which illustrates these risk criteria.)

Where an AMHP is unable to meet the above requirement

Where an AMHP is unable to meet the above requirement to notify the nearest relative before an admission for assessment (under section 2) they should ensure that they persist with efforts to contact the nearest relative after an admission because the Act is worded as follows at section 11(3):

> *Before or within a reasonable time after an application for the admission of a patient for assessment is made by an approved mental health professional, that professional shall take such steps as are practicable to inform the person (if any) appearing to be the nearest relative of the patient that the application is to be or has been made and of the power of the nearest relative under section 23(2)(a) below.*

Strangely there is no statutory duty to follow up a section 3 application in the same way and there is no longer a reference in the Code of Practice to this issue. It would therefore be left to the judgement of the AMHP whether to pursue this issue, especially in cases where, after admission, the patient has asked the hospital not to contact the nearest relative.

The right to object

The AMHP must not make an application for the detention of a patient under section 3 or for guardianship under section 7 if the nearest relative objects. Under the provisions of section 11(4) the AMHP must consult with the nearest relative before making such an application unless it appears to them that in the circumstances such consultation is not reasonably practicable or would involve unreasonable delay. 'Not reasonably practicable' would include cases where the nearest relative was not capable of acting as such because of mental disorder or other illness (see also the discussion on Article 8 above).

Where a nearest relative is consulted, para. 14.64 of the Code states that the AMHP should, where possible:

- *ascertain the nearest relative's views about both the patient's needs and the nearest relative's own needs in relation to the patient;*
- *inform the nearest relative of the reasons for considering an application for detention and what the effects of such an application would be; and*
- *inform the nearest relative of their role and rights under the Act.*

CX v *LA* (2011) was decided against the AMHP who could not demonstrate that this function had been performed adequately. With an increasing number of legal actions based on allegations that AMHPs have not adequately consulted nearest relatives before applying for detention under section 3, considerable care needs to be taken in this regard and detailed records kept of any consultation.

The right to discharge the patient

The power of the nearest relative to discharge a patient from detention by way of section 23 is an intriguing piece of law which Bartlett and Sandland (2014, p30) use as an example of history's impact on current law. They state that it

> originates in the nineteenth-century statutes. If the confinement was in the private sector, the relative was responsible for paying the patient's upkeep, and therefore was perceived to have the right to demand the release of the patient, to limit their own financial exposure. If instead the patient was confined in a county asylum, the right to order release was conditional on an undertaking by the person ordering the release that the individual would no longer be chargeable on the poor law. The right to release was thus a way to enforce public economy in care provision, and to limit the shame of the family at receiving poor relief.

Perhaps a more thorough review of the Act might have led to a more logical overhaul of the role of the nearest relative under the Mental Health Act.

The power of discharge from guardianship is immediate (i.e. no 72-hour notice is required) and the RC has no barring powers. The power for the nearest relative to discharge a patient from a community treatment order requires 72 hours' notice and, as with discharge from detention, the RC can bar this if they think the patient is likely to be dangerous to themselves or others.

Where the nearest relative chooses to exercise their power of discharge from hospital there is no longer a statutory form which can be used. Instead para. 32.25 of the Code states:

> Hospital managers should offer nearest relatives any help they require, such as providing them with a standard letter to complete.

The letter on the next page illustrates what a standard letter might look like.

The right to an assessment

Under section 13(4) it is

> the duty of a local social services authority, if so required by the nearest relative of a patient residing in their area, to make arrangements under subsection (1) above for an approved mental health professional to consider the patient's case with a view to making an application for his admission to hospital; and if in any such case that professional decides not to make an application he shall inform the nearest relative of his reasons in writing.

The phrase 'as soon as practicable' was removed from the previous version of this section in terms of requiring the local authority to direct an AMHP to consider the case but it is hard to see this effectively reducing the pressure to make an assessment. It would be sensible for each case to be passed to an AMHP immediately and they would then consider how best to respond. Jones (2015, footnote to section 13(4)) states that this duty 'to consider the patient's case':

does not necessarily mean that the AMHP undertakes an assessment of the patient or even interviews the patient. The effect of a nearest relative's request under this provision is to require an AMHP to consider whether an application under this Act should be made in respect of the patient. The extent and nature of the inquiries made by the AMHP would depend upon the knowledge that the local mental health service has about the patient. If the patient has been the subject of a recent mental health assessment, the AMHP's obligation would be confined to identifying whether there has been a change in the patient's situation that would justify a reassessment.

To the managers of
[insert name and address of hospital in which the patient is detained, or (for a patient on a community treatment order) the responsible hospital.]

Order for discharge under section 23 of the Mental Health Act 1983
My name is [give your name]

and my address is [give your address]

[Complete A, B or C below]

A. To the best of my knowledge and belief, I am the nearest relative (within the meaning of the Mental Health Act 1983) of [name of patient].

or
B. I have been authorised to exercise the functions of the nearest relative of [name of patient]

by the county court.

or
C. I have been authorised to exercise the functions of the nearest relative of [name of patient]

by that person's nearest relative.

I give you notice of my intention to discharge the person named above, and I order their discharge from [say when you want the patient discharged from detention or a community treatment order].

[Please note: you must leave at least 72 hours between when the hospital managers get this letter and when you want the patient discharged].

The time when:

- the notice is received by the hospital manager or an authorised person; or
- if the notice is sent by pre-paid post, the day service is deemed to have taken place [for first-class post, service is deemed on the second business day following posting, and for second-class post, service is deemed on the fourth business day following posting; or
- the notice is put into the internal mail system; and

- the time when you want the patient discharged.]

Signed ....   Date ....

Figure 3.1   Illustrative standard letter for nearest relatives to use to discharge patients

In other cases further inquiries would be needed such as contacting the patient's GP and, if at any stage a decision is made not to proceed with an application, the AMHP would need to write to the nearest relative. As the Code states at para. 14.102:

> *Such a letter should contain, as far as possible, sufficient details to enable the nearest relative to understand the decision while at the same time preserving the patient's right to confidentiality.*

The Code no longer indicates that authorities should issue AMHPs with guidance on what would constitute such a request from a nearest relative and whether they should include referrals routed via GPs or other professionals. This is an unfortunate omission and such guidance would certainly be helpful as referrals from nearest relatives will rarely make an explicit reference to section 13(4). Jones (2015, footnote to section 13(4)) submits the view that:

> *If a nearest relative indicates concern about the patient by saying, for example, that the patient 'ought to be in hospital' or that 'something ought to be done' about the patient, the nearest relative should be informed of the power under this subsection and asked whether he or she wishes to exercise it.*

Yeates (2005) has argued from a nearest relative perspective that she is very much in favour of the section 13(4) right and would use it in preference to seeking to be the applicant. In the lead-up to the law reform Yeates also argued for the retention of the nearest relative function rather than the proposed 'nominated person' as she was concerned about close blood relatives being excluded from Mental Health Act matters. The late change in the government's plans met her preference while giving the patient the right to seek to displace an NR if they can show that they are 'unsuitable'.

Information from hospital managers

Unless the patient objects, or the nearest relative requests otherwise, the hospital managers have a duty under section 132 to give information to the nearest relative of a detained patient. This will cover information on the relevant section, tribunal rights, consent to treatment information, etc. Section 132A requires similar information to be given regarding community patients.

Notice of discharge

Section 133 requires hospitals to give the nearest relative seven days' notice of the intended discharge of a patient from detention unless the patient or nearest relative has asked for this information not to be given, or unless it was the nearest relative who ordered the discharge. This duty would include information on those patients being discharged on to section 17A.

This requirement appears to be a much-ignored part of the Act which adds fuel to the fire of some relatives' arguments that they are not kept properly informed.

Patients on CTOs are also covered in that this section has been extended to include a duty on the responsible hospital to give seven days' notice where there is an intention to discharge a patient from the order.

Responsible clinicians in particular need to be made aware of this duty.

Quick route to the nearest relative

(Table 3.1 is for use with any complicated cases. This could be expanded or included within other documentation.)

Table 3.1   Quick route to the nearest relative

Relationship (where there is more than one person in a category underline the eldest)	Name and contact address or telephone number where this might be useful	One tick for each person in category	Tick if 18 or over. Insert age if under 18	Tick if living with or caring** for patient at point of assessment or at time of admission to hospital/ guardianship
Husband, wife or civil partner* Include anyone who has lived as if husband, wife or civil partner for last six months or more				
Son or daughter				
Father or mother				
Brother or sister				
Grandparent				
Grandchild				
Uncle or aunt				
Nephew or niece				
Five-year rule Anyone with whom patient has ordinarily resided for five years or more				

* Unless permanently separated by agreement or court order or where a partner has deserted the other.

** 'Caring for' is a matter of AMHP judgement but should usually be substantial and sustained.

1.   *Insert brief details* of any listed in the left column who are ordinarily resident in the UK, Channel Islands or Isle of Man (assuming the patient is ordinarily so resident; if not, the nearest relative may be someone who is, similarly, not so resident). *Ensure that anyone who qualifies for the list, and who is living with or caring for the patient, is included.*

In compiling the list, include half-blood relationships, treat illegitimate children as the legitimate children of their mothers, and do not include in-law relationships.

2.   If only one person is ticked in both of the final two columns they are the nearest relative.

3.   Rank in order of priority. If more than one person is ticked under (2) above, the nearest relative is the highest of those listed. If no one was so ticked, the ranking applies to everyone on the list. If there is more than one person in a category, whole-blood relatives are preferred to half-blood, and elder is preferred to younger.

Suggested documentation for Regulation 24

To use this form you need to be sure (a) that the first person named is indeed the nearest relative, and (b) that they are not incapable of acting as such through reasons of mental disorder or other illness. (See Appendix 11 for the form.)

ACTIVITY 3.1

Sample questions on relatives and carers

1a   *You are an AMHP and have determined the identity of a patient's nearest relative. You have decided an application under section 2 is appropriate. According to the Mental Health Act and the Code what should you do with regard to the nearest relative?*

1b   *From an early stage the patient makes it clear that they object to you speaking to the nearest relative and that, if detained, they will block the hospital from making contact with the nearest relative. Why is the Human Rights Act 1998 relevant here?*

2a   *Who can apply to the county court for the appointment of a nearest relative?*

2b   *What aspects of this area of law have been amended to be compliant with the European Convention on Human Rights?*

2c   *What arguments might be put for or against seeking a nearest relative for someone who does not seem to have one at the point of assessing for a section 3 admission?*

3a   *You are trying to determine who is a patient's nearest relative.*

Having made a list of relatives, what would be the significance of one or more of them living with the patient at the time of the admission to hospital?

3b   *Give two examples of when this issue might cause a problem and how the AMHP could possibly help to resolve this?*

Multiple choice questions

(Answers in Appendix 9)

1.   *Which of the following can make a written order to discharge a patient detained in hospital under Part 2 of the Act?*

   (a) The hospital managers ☐

   (b) The nearest relative ☐

    (c) Any relative ☐

    (d) An approved mental health professional ☐

    (e) The responsible clinician ☐

2. *Which of these may apply to the county court for the appointment of someone to act as nearest relative?*

    (a) Any relative of the patient ☐

    (b) The hospital managers ☐

    (c) Any other person with whom the patient is residing ☐

    (d) The patient ☐

    (e) An approved clinician ☐

    (f) An approved mental health professional ☐

    (g) The responsible clinician ☐

Chapter 4

The role of the approved mental health professional

AMHP functions under the MHA

The following list summarises the main functions of the AMHP as laid down in the Mental Health Act 1983. This chapter will look at some of these functions in detail:

- deciding whether to make an application for compulsory admission to hospital for assessment or for treatment under Part 2 of the Act (s13);

- deciding whether to make an application for guardianship under section 7 of the Act (s13);

- informing or consulting with the nearest relative (NR) about an application (s11);

- conveying a patient to hospital (or a place of residence) on the basis of an application as above (s6);

- responding to a referral from an NR for an MHA assessment, and, if an application is not made, giving the reasons for this in writing to the NR (s13(4));

- providing a social circumstance report for the hospital for any patient detained on the basis of an application made by the NR (s14);

- confirming that a CTO should be made and agreeing to any conditions (s17A);

- agreeing to the extension of a CTO (s20A);

- agreeing to the revocation of a CTO (s17F);

- applying to the county court for the displacement of an existing nearest relative and/or the appointment of an acting nearest relative (s29);

- having the right to enter and inspect premises where a mentally disordered patient is living (s115);

- applying for a warrant to enter premises under section 135 to search for and remove a patient to a place of safety (s135);

- having the power to take a patient into custody and take them to the place they ought to be when they have gone absent without leave (AWOL) (s138);

- interviewing a patient arrested by the police on section 136 (s136(2));

- making a decision on whether a patient subject to section 136 should be moved from one place of safety to another (s136(3)).

Guiding principles

Section 118 requires a number of principles to be covered in the Code of Practice and these should govern the practice of AMHPs. Note that the principles are set out with different emphases in the Welsh Code. The mental health strategy document *Adult Mental Health Services for Wales* (Welsh Assembly, 2001) established four underpinning principles to guide those involved in planning, commissioning, managing, working in, or using mental health services. They are: empowerment, equity, effectiveness and efficiency. The Welsh principles are grouped under these headings.

In the English Code the following headings are used to group the topics given in section 118 of the Act: least restrictive option, empowerment and involvement, respect and dignity, purpose and effectiveness, and finally efficiency and equity. The English Code then elaborates on these as follows:

Least restrictive option and maximising independence

Where it is possible to treat a patient safely and lawfully without detaining them under the Act, the patient should not be detained. Wherever possible a patient's independence should be encouraged and supported with a focus on promoting recovery wherever possible.

Empowerment and involvement

Patients should be fully involved in decisions about care, support and treatment. The views of families, carers and others, if appropriate, should be fully considered when taking decisions. Where decisions are taken which are contradictory to views expressed, professionals should explain the reasons for this.

Respect and dignity

Patients, their families and carers should be treated with respect and dignity and listened to by professionals.

Purpose and effectiveness

Decisions about care and treatment should be appropriate to the patient, with clear therapeutic aims, promote recovery and should be performed to current national guidelines and/or current, available best practice guidelines.

Efficiency and equity

Providers, commissioners and other relevant organisations should work together to ensure that the quality of commissioning and provision of mental healthcare services are of high quality and are given equal priority to physical health and social care services. All relevant services should work together to facilitate timely, safe and supportive discharge from detention.

These summaries are all developed further in Chapter 1 of the Code. In its advice on using the principles the Code states that all decisions should be lawful which would require compliance with the Human Rights Act 1998. This is of great importance. AMHPs could depart from the Code if they had cogent reasons for doing so (see later discussion on the *von Brandenburg* case below in this chapter and in Chapter 7 and the reference to the *Munjaz* case in Chapter 10). The European Convention on Human Rights would be of critical importance if this were to happen (see Appendix 2).

Assessment for possible compulsory admission or guardianship

The key professionals in assessing a person's need for possible compulsory admission to hospital, or for guardianship, are two doctors and an approved mental health professional. Although the nearest relative may apply for detention, the Code of Practice states at para. 14.30:

> *An AMHP is usually a more appropriate applicant than a patient's nearest relative, given their professional training and knowledge of the legislation and local resources. This also reduces the risk that an application by the nearest relative might have an adverse effect on their relationship with the patient.*

In practice, nearest relative applications are very rare.

The Mental Health Act 1983 sets out the criteria which must be satisfied before a person can be detained. These have already been considered in Chapter 2 of this guide. This chapter will consider the process of assessment and the guidance contained in the Code of Practice. Chapter 4 of the Code of Practice covers applications for detention. There are separate chapters on guardianship and community treatment orders.

Interpreters

There are a number of places where the Code refers to interpreters. Those occasions where this relates to the work of an AMHP are grouped together here for convenience. The first is a general statement from Chapter 4 of the Code (para. 4.6):

> *Where an interpreter is needed, every effort should be made to identify who is appropriate to the patient, given the patient's sex, religion or belief, dialect, cultural background and age. Interpreters need to be skilled and experienced in medical or health-related interpreting. Using the patient's relatives and friends as intermediaries or interpreters is not good practice, and should only exceptionally be used, including when the patient is a child or young person. Interpreters (both professional and non-professional) must respect the confidentiality of any personal information they learn about the patient through their involvement.*

A Mental Health Act assessment provides a thorough test of a worker's skills even in their first language. It would be wise for all AMHPs to be sure that they have developed skills for working with interpreters. Para. 14.42 states:

> *Given the importance of good communication, it is essential that those professionals who assess patients are able to communicate with the patient effectively and reliably to prevent potential misunderstandings. AMHPs should establish, as far as possible, whether patients have particular communication needs or difficulties and take steps to meet these, for example by arranging a signer or a professional interpreter. AMHPs should also be in a position, where appropriate, to supply appropriate equipment to make communication easier with patients who have impaired hearing, but who do not have their own hearing aid.*

In the paragraphs on working with people who are deaf the Code indicates that the AMHP would normally be expected to be the one to book the interpreters. At para. 14.116:

> *Unless different arrangements have been agreed locally, the AMHP involved in the assessment should be responsible for booking and using registered qualified interpreters with expertise in mental health interpreting, bearing in mind that the interpretation of thought-disordered language requires particular expertise. Relay interpreters (interpreters who relay British Sign Language (BSL) to hands-on BSL or visual frame signing or close signing) may be necessary, such as when the deaf person has a visual impairment, does not use BSL to sign or has minimal language skills or a learning disability.*

In para. 14.117 the point made in Chapter 4 of the Code is developed:

> *Reliance on unqualified interpreters or health professionals with only limited sign-ing skills should be avoided. Subject to the normal considerations about patient confidentiality family members may occasionally be able to assist a professional interpreter in understanding a patient's idiosyncratic use of language. Family members should not be relied upon in place of a professional interpreter, even if the patient is willing for them to be involved.*

One final piece of information which might be helpful for AMHPs to know is given in para. 12.40 of the Code, in the chapter on mental health tribunals:

> *It is important that patients and their representatives are able to understand and participate in the Tribunal hearing. This includes providing information in formats that they understand and, if required, providing interpretation services free of charge, including sign language. Hospital managers and LSSAs should inform the Tribunal well in advance if they think any such services might be necessary.*

Informing or consulting the nearest relative

The AMHP's responsibilities towards the nearest relative are dealt with in some detail in Chapter 3 of this book. Paras 14.58–60 of the Code summarise the main requirements:

> *When AMHPs make an application for admission under section 2, they must take such steps as are practicable to inform the nearest relative and, if different, carer, that the application is to be (or has been) made and of the nearest relative's power to discharge the patient.*

The reference to the carer is not based on the MHA itself but presumably reflects the emphasis on carers' rights to information contained in the Care Act, although, as with much of the Code, the authority for statements is not made explicit and it may be that the use of the word 'must' in this case is open to debate.

> *Before making an application for admission under section 3, AMHPs must consult the nearest relative, unless it is not reasonably practicable or would involve unreasonable delay.*

There is no reference here to the carer which seems rather inconsistent.

> *Circumstances in which the nearest relative need not be informed or consulted include those where:*
>
> - *it is not practicable for the AMHP to obtain sufficient information to establish the identity or location of the nearest relative, or where to do so would require an excessive amount of investigation involving unreasonable delay; and*
> - *consultation is not possible because of the nearest relative's own health or mental incapacity.*

The consultation with the nearest relative can take place before the two medical recommendations are obtained (*Re Whitbread,* 1997).

AMHPs should not assume that the person listed as nearest relative on a previous detention is still necessarily in that role. The Code of Practice has never covered this issue but the Reference Guide gives an opinion when it states at para. 2.18:

> *The identity of the nearest relative will change if the current nearest relative dies or if (for example) the nearest relative is a spouse or civil partner and the marriage or civil partnership ends.*

And then at para. 2.19:

> *It may also change for some other reason not directly involving the existing nearest relative, e.g. the patient marries, or another relative reaches the age of 18, or comes to live in the UK, and therefore becomes eligible to be the nearest relative.*

The appendices to this guide provide AMHPs with checklists for assessments under sections 2, 3, 4 and 7 to ensure that all necessary actions have been taken. These should be read in conjunction with any local procedures.

AMHP responsibility for actions and section 139

There are a number of myths concerning the AMHP's position in terms of responsibility for actions that they take under the Mental Health Act. For example, some people seem to consider that AMHPs are acting as free agents and that their approving or authorising authorities have no responsibility for their actions. While it would be true to say that the AMHP has a personal duty to make the decision on whether to apply for detention, the local authority still carries some responsibility and, of course, decides whether an AMHP is currently competent to perform as such.

Section 139 of the Mental Health Act is of importance when considering the liability of an AMHP for actions taken in relation to the Act. It states at section 139(1):

> *No person shall be liable, whether on the grounds of want of jurisdiction or any other ground, to any civil or criminal proceedings to which he would have been liable apart from this section in respect of any act purporting to be done in pursuance of this Act or any regulations or rules made under this Act unless the act was done in bad faith or without reasonable care.*

It then sets out the procedure which must be followed before proceedings can be taken. Section 139(2):

> *No civil proceedings shall be brought against any person in any court in respect of any such act without the leave of the High Court; and no criminal proceedings shall be brought against any person in any court in respect of any such act except by or with the consent of the Director of Public Prosecutions.*

This does not prevent the patient from applying to the High Court for a writ of habeas corpus so that the lawfulness of the detention can be tested.

Whether a person has acted in bad faith or without reasonable care is a question of fact with the burden of proof lying with the applicant. The relevance of the Code of Practice to any action against an AMHP can be seen in para. V of the Introduction, which states:

> The people listed above [which includes AMHPs] to whom the Code is addressed must have regard to the Code. It is important that these persons have training on the Code and ensure that they are familiar with its requirements. As departures from the Code could give rise to legal challenge, reasons for any departure should be recorded clearly. Courts will scrutinise such reasons to ensure that there is sufficiently convincing justification in the circumstances.

The ability of the AMHP to make an independent decision was seen as important by Parliament. Jones (2015, footnote to section 13(1A)) comments on this when he considers the AMHP's position when deciding whether or not to make an application as per section 13 of the Act:

> The responsibilities under this provision are placed on the Approved Mental Health Professional and not on the employing authority (Nottingham City Council v Unison [2004] EWHC 893, para 18). However, as an AMHP acts on behalf of the local authority (section 145 (1AC)), that authority will be vicariously liable for any lack of care or bad faith on behalf of the AMHP (TTM v London Borough of Hackney [2010] EWHC 1349 (Admin), para 35: affirmed by the Court of Appeal at [2011] EWCA Civ 4, even though the authority might not be the AMHP's employer (DD v Durham CC [2012] EWHC 1053 (QB), para 21)). The AMHP should exercise his or her own judgement, based upon social and medical evidence, and not act at the behest of his or her employer, medical practitioners or other persons who might be involved with the patient's care . . . The judgement to be exercised applies not only to the decision on whether an application should be made in respect of the patient; it also applies to the question of what section of this Act to invoke.

In terms of good practice which would be consistent with acting in good faith and reasonable care, it could be suggested that an AMHP needs to be 'angst-ridden but strangely decisive', i.e. concerned to respect a person's right to freedom, but prepared to intervene decisively where the level of mental disorder and risk requires it. They need to show an awareness of relevant law and procedures and, in particular, as public authorities, a good grasp of, and commitment to, the European Convention on Human Rights.

The importance of the AMHP role was emphasised by Lord Bingham in the House of Lords judgement on *R (von Brandenburg) v East London* when he said:

> I would, secondly, resist the lumping together of the ASW [approved social worker] and the recommending doctor or doctors as 'the mental health professionals'. It is the ASW who makes the application, not the doctors.

The question being raised was:

> When a mental health review tribunal has ordered the discharge of a patient, is it lawful to readmit him under section 2 or section 3 of the [Mental Health Act 1983] where it cannot be demonstrated that there has been a relevant change of circumstances?

The outcome was essentially that an AMHP must not fly in the face of a tribunal decision of which they are aware:

> An ASW may not lawfully apply for the admission of a patient whose discharge has been ordered by the decision of a mental health review tribunal of which the ASW is aware unless the ASW has formed the reasonable and bona fide opinion that he has information not known to the tribunal which puts a significantly different complexion on the case as compared with that which was before the tribunal.
>
> (R v East London and the City Mental Health NHS Trust and another (Respondents) ex parte von Brandenburg (2003))

Management and supervision of AMHPs

This part of the chapter gives details of some key issues involved in the management and supervision of AMHPs. It places the role of the approved mental health professional in context and clarifies which tasks can be performed only by an AMHP. It also lists tasks that they are likely to be involved in, but which can also be performed by other staff.

Statutory basis for employing AMHPs

Section 114 of the Mental Health Act 1983 states the following:

1. *A local social services authority may approve a person to act as an approved mental health professional for the purposes of this Act.*

2. *But a local social services authority may not approve a registered medical practitioner to act as an approved mental health professional.*

3. *Before approving a person under subsection (1) above, a local social service authority shall be satisfied that he has appropriate competence in dealing with persons who are suffering from mental disorder.*

AMHPs replace ASWs (approved social workers) who came into existence in 1984. The functions of the AMHP remain essentially unchanged from those of the ASW other than the new roles in relation to community treatment orders. ASWs were social workers who had undertaken additional training to equip them to perform specific tasks under the Act. In addition to social workers registered with the Health and

Care Professions Council or Care Council for Wales (CCfW) the following professional groups are able to train to become AMHPs:

- nurses (who need to be first-level mental health or learning disability nurses);
- registered occupational therapists; and
- chartered psychologists (who need to hold a relevant practising certificate issued by the British Psychological Society).

The vast majority of AMHPs are still social workers (as at December 2015). The author is not aware of any psychologists who have become AMHPs; there are a handful of occupational therapists and about 80 nurses, a quarter of whom come from just two authorities.

AMHPs need to be approved by an LSSA even if they are employed by an NHS Trust or other body. As we noted earlier the LSSA cannot direct the decisions of an AMHP, who must reach their own independent judgement.

An AMHP may be approved by only one local authority. That authority can support them in making an application outside of its area (e.g. where a local resident has turned up in another area of England or Wales). If an AMHP works part time in two local authorities, the second one could authorise the AMHP to act on its behalf when appropriate. NIMHE (2008) has provided helpful guidance on these issues.

Training courses for AMHPs are delivered by accredited universities (approved by the Health and Care Professions Council in England or by the Care Council for Wales). Successful candidates may then be approved by a local authority for a period of five years before they are required to go through a re-approval process.

ASWs automatically became AMHPs in November 2008. Most completed short courses to learn the implications of the changes brought about by the MHA 2007 but the key to eligibility now would be whether they were warranted to act as an ASW at midnight on 2 November 2008 when the transition from ASW to AMHP occurred. If a member of staff wanted to return to AMHP work after several years of not practising, authorities would be well advised to require staff to undertake some refresher training and to shadow colleagues before submitting evidence of their current competence. Although the basic AMHP courses are fairly standardised, arrangements for re-approval vary considerably between authorities.

If an AMHP exercises their power under section 115 to enter and inspect premises where a mentally disordered patient is living they are required to have some form of identification. Ideally, this should be a sealed ID card and include: photograph, name, approving local authority details and contact number, date of appointment as AMHP and/or expiry date, signature of relevant senior officer. Some authorities find it helpful to quote section 115 rights of access on the reverse.

Management, consultation and supervision

Apart from legal advice, which should be available from the approving local authority, AMHPs need management, consultation and supervision which is specific to their role.

As far as legal advice is concerned, the National Institute for Mental Health in England (NIMHE, 2008, p14) has suggested that local authorities:

> *review the legal advice service that is available to AMHPs (and other professionals) and how it can be organised across organisations. A clear pathway should be agreed locally, ensuring that the AMHP can access impartial advice in situations where there are conflicting views or opinions between different professionals and organisations.*

The issue of management, consultation and supervision which is specific to the role of the AMHP is dealt with in the same document (NIMHE, 2008, p13):

> *All organisations employing AMHPs (and the LSSAs on whose behalf they act, if different) will wish to consider the following issues in supporting them in their role – that the AMHP has access to:*
>
> * *professional supervision from an approved and experienced AMHP;*
>
> * *information about AMHP practice in general;*
>
> * *advice on any problems the AMHP might encounter (for example regarding access to beds, the police, or ambulance services); and*
>
> * *advice and support on how to work to resolve problems with partner organisations.*
>
> *Employers should also act in circumstances where an AMHP may require further training, mentoring or support, for example after an unusual or controversial situation.*

The importance of maintaining the AMHP's independence became clearer to the government in the latter stages of the mental health reform process leading up to the 2007 Amending Act. Guidance which has now been issued places considerable emphasis on this as, for example, in the passage below from NIMHE (2008, p14):

> *Even before the changes brought about by the Act, with the formation of partnership arrangements in mental health services, some LSSAs do not currently employ any senior managers with responsibility for, or experience and knowledge of, the ASW (now AMHP) role.*
>
> *To support the independence of the AMHP role, and to ensure that AMHPs are appropriately supported in undertaking their duties, LSSAs may wish to consider having at least one directly employed senior manager or lead officer who has direct knowledge and experience of the AMHP role or service. This would be one way of helping to ensure that AMHPs have:*
>
> * *access to advice and support independent of the hospital to which the patient may be admitted or from which they may receive treatment;*
>
> * *a senior level 'champion' to highlight any problems identified by the AMHP, and to protect the role's independence.*

The integration of health and social services in the mental health field led to the need for some guidance on joint working (NIMHE, 2008, p14):

> *LSSAs and NHS Trusts who co-operate to provide an AMHP service will need to consider and agree the following issues so that they are explicitly covered by their s75 and other agreements:*
>
> - *details of how the daytime service will be configured, for example central AMHP service versus team-based AMHP service;*
>
> - *details of supervision and support arrangements, including access to senior support from the LSSA where serious issues arise, such as those related to conflicts of interest;*
>
> - *agreement to release staff for initial and refresher AMHP training;*
>
> - *agreement on governance issues . . . including:*
>
>   - *the collection of statistics on AMHP activity (whose responsibility it is to collect each set of information, and when and how this data will be reported, used and reviewed)*
>
>   - *regular reporting to management, and how and in what circumstances to share feedback on issues of concern regarding services as a whole or on poor performance by an individual AMHP.*

AMHPs and their employers and supervisors should watch the Department of Health website for news of any further advice or guidance on this area.

Policy requirements from the Code of Practice

There are a number of points in the Code of Practice where local authorities are required to have a policy. Those managing AMHPs may find the following exercise helpful. Table 4.1 identifies the topic and paragraph number of references in the Code to the need for some sort of policy. *Tick if there is already a policy and note the date it was last amended (if available).*

Table 4.1   Policy requirements from the Code of Practice

Para.	Topic	Policy? tick/date	Comments on existing policy or key points if new policy required
14.47 & 14.48	Police assistance. For people undertaking MHA assessments.		
14.86	Delays in placing patients. Mechanism to report delays in finding beds.		
15.11	Monitoring use of s4 to ensure it is not misused and to look at availability of doctors.		
5.17	Displacement of nearest relatives. Advice to AMHPs on whether to make an application to county court.		

5.17	Displacement of nearest relatives. Advice to AMHPs on who to nominate when applying to court.		
16.9	Section 135 warrants. Guidance for AMHPs on how and when to apply.		
16.30	Local partnership arrangements to deal with people experiencing mental health crises.		
16.31	Sections 135 and 136. Agreed local policy needed covering all aspects.		
17.25–17.28	Conveyance of patients. Joint policy and procedure with ambulance and police.		
19.126	Duties of local authorities relating to children and young people in hospital.		
35.15	Receipt of guardianship applications. Checklist for responsible staff.		
28.13	Guardianship patients who go AWOL. Policy needed on action to take.		
30.16	Guardianship Policy needed on how the LA will discharge its responsibilities.		

Tasks for AMHPs involved in MHA assessments

The following tasks can form the basis of an exercise near the beginning of an AMHP course (Table 4.2). See Appendix 6 for the answers.

Table 4.2   Tasks for AMHPs involved in MHA assessments

No.	AMHP task – identify source of words within quotation marks	Source (Act, Code or Guide)
1	To interview the patient in a 'suitable manner'.	
2	To have 'regard to any wishes expressed by relatives'.	
3	Consider all the circumstances of the case including: 'the past history of the patient's mental disorder, the patient's present condition and the social, familial and personal factors bearing on it, as well as the other options available for supporting the patient, the wishes of the patient and the patient's relatives and carers, and the opinion of other professionals involved in caring for the patient'.	
4	'Because a proper assessment cannot be carried out without considering alternative means of providing care and treatment, AMHPs and doctors should, as far as possible in the circumstances, identify and liaise with services which may potentially be able to provide alternatives to admission to hospital. That could include crisis and home treatment teams.'	
5	Decide whether 'detention in a hospital is in all the circumstances of the case the most appropriate way of providing the care and medical treatment of which the patient stands in need'.	

(Continued)

Table 4.2 (Continued)

No.	AMHP task – identify source of words within quotation marks	Source (Act, Code or Guide)
6	Ensure that it is 'necessary or proper for the application to be made by' the AMHP.	
7	'Take such steps as are practicable' to inform the nearest relative that an application for section 2 has been, or is about to be, made and inform them of their powers of discharge under section 23.	
8	If considering section 3 consult NR to ensure that they do not object to the application being made unless 'such consultation is not reasonably practicable or would involve unreasonable delay'.	
9	'Take the patient and convey him to hospital' if an application is made by the AMHP.	
10	'If they do not consult or inform the nearest relative, AMHPs should record their reasons. Consultation must not be avoided purely because it is thought that the nearest relative might object to the application.'	
11	If the patient is admitted, the AMHP should make sure that any 'moveable property' of the patient is protected.	
12	If the nearest relative applies for section 2 or 3, an AMHP must 'interview the patient and provide the [hospital] managers with a report on his social circumstances'.	
13	If required to do so by the nearest relative, the SSD must direct an AMHP 'to consider the case with a view to making an application for his admission to hospital'. If AMHP does not apply he must give his reasons in writing to NR.	
14	'. . . provide an outline report for the hospital at the time the patient is first admitted or detained, giving reasons for the application and details of any practical matters about the patient's circumstances which the hospital should know.'	

Code of Practice guidance

It is no longer feasible to gather together in a short table the Code guidance that is addressed to AMHPs. Nearly every statutory duty of the AMHP is commented on in the Code. Wherever possible these have been referred to in the relevant parts of this book. For AMHPs in Wales significant training will be needed when the Welsh Code is published in 2016.

ACTIVITY 4.1

Sample questions on the role of the AMHP

1a What are the main aspects of law concerned with the appointment of AMHPs?

1b What legal protection does an AMHP have in carrying out duties under the Mental Health Act 1983?

1c Identify a couple of possible dilemmas for an AMHP working in a home treatment team.

2a What are the main responsibilities of an AMHP, in terms of interviewing and assessing a patient in their area with a view to a possible section 3 admission?

2b Take any one of these responsibilities and identify potential difficulties for an AMHP.

ACTIVITY 4.1 *continued*

Multiple choice questions

(Answers in Appendix 9)

1. Which of the following may apply to admit a patient to hospital in an emergency under section 4?

    (a) Any relative ☐
    (b) The nearest relative ☐
    (c) An approved mental health professional ☐

2. An applicant who conveys a patient to hospital has all the powers that police officers have when they take someone into custody.

    (a) True ☐
    (b) False ☐

Chapter 5
Patients concerned in criminal proceedings

Patients involved with the police and the courts

Introduction

Some patients are detained in hospital or received into guardianship as a result of a court order. Part 3 of the Mental Health Act 1983 covers these situations as well as those where the Secretary of State can direct people to be transferred from prisons into hospital. There were minimal amendments made by the 2007 Act reforms. This contrasted with the major changes which occurred under the 1983 Act which had contained significant changes from the position under the 1959 Act. Several of these gave effect to recommendations which were made in the Butler Report of 1975 (DHSS, 1975). One of the report's main conclusions was that too many mentally abnormal offenders were being inappropriately placed in prison. Sections 35, 36 and 38 of the 1983 Act were all new attempts to tackle this problem. There was a delay in their implementation until 1984 when it was believed resources would be in place to cope with these new patients but they are still little used today. In 2014–15 section 35 was only used 75 times in England and section 36 was used only 15 times. Section 38 is aggregated with section 44 (a remand to hospital from the magistrate's court while waiting for a Crown Court hearing) but still only amounted to 106 occasions. This can be compared with section 37 hospital orders of which there were 429 in the same period. This in itself is a small number compared with the use of Part 2 of the Act. In 2014–15 there were over 50,000 occasions when patients were made subject to section 2 or 3 while only 880 patients were detained under Part 3.

AMHPs are increasingly being asked to take on the function of social supervisor for conditionally discharged patients. As a result there is some new material in this chapter for social supervisors.

Table 5.1 provides a summary of the main sections noting their purpose, duration, whether there is access to mental health tribunals and whether consent to treatment provisions apply. Section 136 is included at the end of the chapter because it involves the police and is sometimes used with offenders. There is further legislation, apart from the Mental Health Act, which affects patients who offend. This is included here in a brief summary of relevant law. AMHPs are not directly involved with Part 3 of the Act so this chapter just provides a brief overview of the key sections.

Table 5.1   Part 3 patients: periods of detention and further information (consent to treatment, access to MH tribunals)

Section number and purpose	Maximum duration	Can patient apply to MHT?	Can nearest relative apply to MHT?	Will there be an automatic MHT hearing?	*Do consent to treatment rules apply?
35 Remand to hospital for psychiatric report	**28 days** May be renewed by court for further 28 days to max. 12 weeks	No	There is no nearest relative	No	No
36 Remand to hospital for psychiatric treatment	**28 days** May be renewed by court for further 28 days to max. 12 weeks	No	There is no nearest relative	No	Yes
37 Guardianship order by court	**6 months** May be renewed for six months and then yearly	Within first six months and then in each period	Within first year and then yearly	No	No
37 Hospital order by court	**6 months** May be renewed for six months and then yearly	In second six months and then in each period	In second six months and then in each period	If one has not been held, the hospital managers refer to MHT every three years	Yes
37/41 Restriction order by court	**Without limit of time**	In second six months and then yearly	There is no nearest relative	If one has not been held, Justice Secretary refers every three years	Yes
38 Interim hospital order by court	**12 weeks** May be renewed by 28 days at a time to max. one year	No	There is no nearest relative	No	Yes

(Continued)

Table 5.1 (Continued)

Section number and purpose	Maximum duration	Can patient apply to MHT?	Can nearest relative apply to MHT?	Will there be an automatic MHT hearing?	*Do consent to treatment rules apply?
42 Conditional discharge	Without limit of time	In second year and then every two years	There is no nearest relative	No	No
45A Hospital and limited directions	Variable	In second six months and then yearly	No	If one has not been held, the Justice Secretary refers to MHT every three years	Yes
47 Transfer to a hospital of a person serving prison sentence	6 months May be renewed for six months and then yearly	Within first six months and then in each period	Within first six months and then in each period	If one has not been held, the hospital managers refer to MHT every three years	Yes
47/49 Transfer from prison plus restrictions	Restriction order expires on earliest prison release date	In second six months period after transfer and then yearly	There is no nearest relative	If one has not been held, the Home Secretary refers to MHT every three years	Yes
48 Transfer to hospital of other prisoners	Variable	Within first six months and then in each period	Within first six months and then in each period	If one not has been held, the Justice Secretary refers to MHT every three years	Yes
48/49 Transfer from prison and restrictions	Restriction order expires on the earliest date of release from prison	In second six months period after transfer and then yearly	There is no nearest relative	If one has not been held, the Justice Secretary refers to MHT every three years	Yes
136 Police power in public places	72 hours Not renewable	No	No	No	No

* Where consent to treatment rules do not apply, a patient is in the same position as an informal patient and should not be treated without their consent except in an emergency under common law or where it is possible to rely on the Mental Capacity Act. Chapter 6 has fuller information on consent to treatment.
– under section 67 the Secretary of State for Health (or Welsh Minister) can refer section 37 patients to the MHT at any time;
– under section 71 the Justice Secretary can refer restricted patients to the MHT at any time;
Note also:
– conditionally discharged restricted patients may apply to the MHT after one year and then every two years but if the patient is recalled to hospital the Justice Secretary must refer to the MHT within one month.

There is a presumption in favour of remanding a person on bail rather than in custody. This could even include a condition of residence at a hospital while, for example, reports are prepared. In these circumstances, however, the patient would be informal and not subject to detention. Where a person might otherwise be remanded to prison, the Mental Health Act 1983 introduced two new powers (see next section).

Section 35: Remand to hospital for report on accused's mental condition

Subsection (3) allows an order to be made if:

(a) the court is satisfied, on the written or oral evidence of a registered medical practitioner, that there is reason to suspect that the accused person is suffering from mental disorder; and

(b) the court is of the opinion that it would be impracticable for a report on his mental condition to be made if he were remanded on bail . . .

There must also be evidence that a hospital bed would be available within seven days, beginning with the date of the remand. While waiting for a bed, the accused must be kept in a 'place of safety' which for the purposes of this section could be any police station, prison or remand centre, or any hospital willing to receive the patient.

The remand is for a maximum 28 days although the court may renew this for further periods of 28 days to a maximum of 12 weeks. Part 4 provisions on consent to treatment do not apply so the person should not be treated without their consent except in an emergency under common law or in situations where the MCA can be relied on. To overcome this, some psychiatrists have sought a section 2 or 3 detention to run alongside the section 35. Section 5 does not specifically rule this out and the Code of Practice at para. 22.41 states that it might be considered if there is a delay in getting to court. The use of section 36 might be more appropriate in most such cases.

Section 36: Remand of accused person to hospital for treatment

This may be used only by the Crown Court and is restricted to those cases where it would be an alternative to a remand in custody. It applies to people waiting for trial or sentence and requires the written or oral evidence of two doctors that the person is suffering from mental disorder of a nature or degree which makes it appropriate for him to be detained in a hospital for treatment. There also needs to be appropriate medical treatment available. The remand is for a maximum of 28 days although the court may renew this for further periods of 28 days to a maximum of 12 weeks. Part 4 provisions on consent to treatment apply. Again there must be evidence that a hospital bed would be available within seven days, beginning with the date of the remand. While waiting for a bed, the accused must be kept in a place of safety as defined above. It is possible that someone may have to wait for more than three months to appear in the Crown Court. In these circumstances, the general powers of the Secretary of State to transfer prisoners may apply.

Section 37: Hospital or guardianship order

Where an offender is convicted a hospital or guardianship order may be made by the Crown Court. A magistrates' court may also make an order, even if there has not been a conviction, if they are satisfied that the offender committed the act or made the omission in question. In either case the court needs to be satisfied on the evidence of two doctors that the patient is suffering from a mental disorder and that either:

(i) *the mental disorder from which the offender is suffering is of a nature or degree which makes it appropriate for him to be detained in a hospital for medical treatment and, appropriate medical treatment is available to him; or*

(ii) *in the case of an offender who has attained the age of 16 years, the mental disorder is of a nature or degree which warrants his reception into guardianship under this Act; and*

(iii) *the Court is of the opinion, having regard to all the circumstances including the nature of the offence and the character and antecedents of the offender, and to the other available methods of dealing with him, that the most suitable method of disposing of the case is by means of an order under this section.*

The order lasts for up to six months in the first instance. It may be renewed for a further six months and then for a year at a time. The effect of a hospital order is very similar to the person being subject to section 3. Part 4 applies for consent to treatment purposes. There must be evidence that a hospital bed would be available within 28 days, beginning with the date of the order. Guardianship orders are not made very often. Only 14 were made in 2014–15. An order can be made only if the proposed guardian agrees to it. If the patient absconds from the place where they are required to live, they may be recaptured and returned there.

Section 37/41: Hospital order with restrictions

To make a restricted hospital order the court needs the same evidence as is required for a hospital order and, in addition, one of the doctors must attend court to give evidence in person. Only the Crown Court can impose restrictions and they must now be without limit of time (it used to be possible to set a specific time limit). The grounds are that it appears to the court:

having regard to the nature of the offence, the antecedents of the offender and the risk of his committing further offences if set at large, that it is necessary for the protection of the public from serious harm.

This means that the patient can be discharged, given leave of absence or transferred to another hospital only with the approval of the Justice Secretary. The Secretary of State may discharge the patient absolutely or conditionally. If conditionally discharged the patient will be subject to compulsory after-care from a responsible clinician. In practice a social supervisor is appointed (often an AMHP). If an AMHP takes on this role they would be well advised to undertake a two-day course to prepare for the responsibility. It is a far more 'welfarist' function (see pp2–3) than that of an AMHP. There is detailed advice from the Ministry of Justice available in *Guidance for Social Supervisors* (2009).

The mental health tribunal can also discharge restricted patients but the hospital managers cannot discharge and there is no nearest relative in law.

Section 38: Interim hospital order

Where a court is trying to decide whether a full hospital order is needed they can check this by making an interim hospital order. The order can be made for up to 12 weeks in the first instance and can be renewed by the court for periods of up to 28 days at a time, to a maximum of one year. Two doctors must give written or oral evidence. The court will then receive reports on how the patient reacts to treatment. Part 4 of the MHA 1983 applies so treatment may be given as with section 37.

Section 45A: Hospital and limitation directions

This is a prison sentence combined with a requirement for hospital treatment with limitation directions. Until 2008 its use was limited to patients with psychopathic disorder. Now that classifications have been abolished by the 2007 Act (leaving us with just 'any disorder or disability of mind') the measure is open to people with any kind of mental disorder. However there were only nine occasions in 2014–15 when a section 45A was made. The order is available only to the Crown Court. The grounds set out in subsection (2) are:

(a) *that the offender is suffering from mental disorder; and*

(b) *that the mental disorder from which the offender is suffering is of a nature or degree which makes it appropriate for him to be detained in a hospital for medical treatment; and*

(c) *that appropriate medical treatment is available for him.*

The written or oral evidence from two doctors is required.

Section 47: Transfers of sentenced prisoners

It is still possible for a prisoner to be transferred to a psychiatric hospital even after sentencing. The Home Secretary can order their transfer under section 47 if satisfied by reports from at least two doctors:

(a) *that the said person is suffering from mental disorder;*

(b) *that the mental disorder from which that person is suffering is of a nature or degree which makes it appropriate for him to be detained in a hospital for medical treatment; and*

(c) *that appropriate medical treatment is available to him.*

The transfer direction has the same effect as a section 37 hospital order made without restrictions and the patient is subject to consent to treatment provisions. Commonly, a restriction direction is also made under section 49. This has the same effect as a restriction order under section 41 described above. If the offender was sentenced to a fixed term of imprisonment the restriction lifts on the expiry of the sentence (allowing for remission).

Table 5.2   Detentions under Part 3

Section no.	2007–08	2009–10	2011–12	2014–15
35 Remand for report	145	106	107	75
36 Remand for treatment	17	30	16	15
37/41 Restricted hospital orders	455	547	522	486
37 Unrestricted hospital orders	352	456	459	307
45A Hospital and limited directions	11	5	8	9
47/49 Transfers of sentenced prisoners with restrictions	361	458	427	429
47 Unrestricted transfers of sentenced prisoners	41	45	41	60
48/49 Transfers of unsentenced prisoners with restrictions	384	360	398	440
48 Unrestricted transfer of unsentenced prisoners	17	4	9	3
Other sections (38, 44, 46)	134	180	143	106
Total	1,917	2,191	2,130	1,930

Section 48: Removal to hospital of other prisoners

This section gives the Secretary of State for Justice powers to direct the transfer to hospital of a person who is waiting for trial or sentence and who has been remanded in custody. Two medical reports are needed stating that:

(a)   *the person is suffering from mental disorder of a nature or degree which makes it appropriate for him to be detained in hospital for medical treatment; and*

(b)   *he is in urgent need of such treatment; and*

(c)   *appropriate medical treatment is available for him.*

Part 4 provisions on consent to treatment apply to this group of patients.

Numbers of detentions under Part 3

These have remained fairly stable, as can be seen from Table 5.2. There was a slight increase in the first full year of the changes, then the figures levelled off and now they have fallen back to 2007–8 figures.

Other relevant law apart from the Mental Health Act

Unfit to plead (Criminal Procedure (Insanity and Unfitness to Plead) Act 1991)

If an accused person is found to be unfit to be tried, there is provision for a 'trial of the facts' to determine whether the jury is satisfied beyond reasonable doubt that the accused did the act or made the omission charged against him. The Ministry of Justice provides guidance on aspects of the trial of the facts and a circular summarises the disposal options for the court which include a guardianship order, a supervision and treatment order, a hospital admission order or absolute discharge.

The insanity defence

This applies to murder where the sentence is fixed by law and is phrased as the accused was 'labouring under such defect of reason from disease of the mind as to not know the nature and quality of the act he was doing, or, if he did know it, that he did not know it was wrong' (the M'Naghten Rules). If the defence is successful the judge must make the equivalent of a hospital order with restrictions on discharge. This measure is used infrequently.

Diminished responsibility

This is set out in section 2 of the Homicide Act 1957. The accused was suffering from such abnormality of mind as to substantially impair mental responsibility for the killing. If this argument is successful, the judge has discretion in sentencing. Any conviction will be for manslaughter rather than murder so there is no mandatory life sentence.

The Infanticide Act 1938

This can apply where the mind of a woman who kills a child under 1 'is disturbed by reason of not having fully recovered from the effect of giving birth to the child or by reason of the effect of lactation consequent on the birth'. The court may impose any appropriate sentence.

Community rehabilitation orders supervised by probation

These orders can be made in any court and for any offence other than one with a fixed penalty but they do require a conviction. The offender is then supervised by a probation officer for a specified period between six months and three years. The court must have evidence from a doctor approved under the Mental Health Act 1983. The doctor must state that the person's mental condition requires, and may be susceptible to, treatment but that the person does not need to be subject to a hospital order. The court may then specify where treatment should take place: this could be as an in-patient in a hospital or mental nursing home; as an out-patient at a specified hospital or place; by or under the direction of a named doctor. The court must explain all the requirements of the order to the offender and obtain their consent to the order. If, subsequently, the person refuses to co-operate with one of the conditions, the doctor can report this only to the supervising officer who may take proceedings for breach of probation.

Supervision Orders

There seems to have been an increase in the use of these orders, in domestic violence cases, among others, and AMHPs may find themselves asked to take on the role of supervisor. Appendix 10 reproduces the new Schedule which has been inserted into the Criminal Procedures (Insanity) Act 1964 and sets out further information on these orders.

Police powers under section 136

The wording of this section is straightforward:

(1) If a constable finds in a place to which the public have access a person who appears to him to be suffering from mental disorder and to be in immediate need of care or control, the constable may, if he thinks it necessary to do so in the interests of that person or for the protection of other persons, remove that person to a place of safety within the meaning of section 135 above.

(2) A person removed to a place of safety under this section may be detained there for a period not exceeding 72 hours for the purpose of enabling him to be examined by a registered medical practitioner and to be interviewed by an approved mental health professional and of making any necessary arrangements for his treatment or care.

(3) A constable, an approved mental health professional or a person authorised by either of them for the purposes of this subsection may, before the end of the period of 72 hours mentioned in subsection (2) above, take a person detained in a place of safety under that subsection to one or more other places of safety.

(4) A person taken to a place of a safety under subsection (3) above may be detained there for a purpose mentioned in subsection (2) above for a period ending no later than the end of the period of 72 hours mentioned in that subsection.

The officer does not have to suspect that any criminal offence has been committed.

For many years there have been concerns that this (and other controlling powers of the MHA) is used disproportionately with black and ethnic minority individuals. The Code of Practice (para. 16.63) states that its use with people from ethnic minorities should be monitored.

The Code has been strengthened in its advice that police stations should be used as places of safety in only a minority of cases. Para. 16.38 of the Code states:

A police station should not be used as a place of safety except in exceptional circumstances, for example it may be necessary to do so because the person's behaviour would pose an unmanageably high risk to other patients, staff or other users if the person were to be detained in a healthcare setting.

A police station should not be used as the automatic second choice if there is no health-based place of safety immediately available.

Para. 16.39 then states:

If, exceptionally, a police station is used, the locally agreed policy should set out the time within which the appropriate health and social care professionals will attend the police station to assess the person or to assist in arranging to transfer them to a more suitable place of safety.

Finally, para. 16.43 states:

> *In identifying the most appropriate place of safety for an individual, consideration should be given to the impact that the proposed place of safety (and the journey to it) may have on the person and on their examination and interview. It should always be borne in mind that the use of a police station can give the impression that the person detained is suspected of having committed a crime. This may cause distress and anxiety to the person concerned and may affect their co-operation with, and therefore the effectiveness of, the assessment process. In the event that a person is taken to a police station, it should be clearly explained to them that they are not suspected of any crime or other wrongdoing, and they are being kept there until they can be assessed to see if they need any care or treatment.*

Patients arrested under section 136 have the right to have another person of their choice informed of the arrest and of their whereabouts. If a police station is used as the place of safety, they have a right of access to legal advice. If a hospital is used, the Code (para. 16.69) recommends giving access to legal advice if it is requested.

Section 136(2) makes it clear that an assessment should be carried out by both an AMHP and a doctor. Para.16.47 states:

> *Assessment by the doctor and AMHP should begin as soon as possible after the arrival of the individual at the place of safety. In cases where there are no clinical grounds to delay assessment, it is good practice for the doctor and AMHP to attend within three hours; this is in accordance with best practice recommendations made by the Royal College of Psychiatrists. Where possible, the assessment should be undertaken jointly by the doctor and the AMHP.*

If the doctor arrives first and concludes admission to hospital is unnecessary or the person agrees to informal admission, the individual should still be seen by an AMHP. Only if the doctor concludes that the person is not mentally disordered at all should they be released before the arrival of the AMHP (Code, para. 16.50).

If it is discovered that a patient who has been arrested on section 136 is currently subject to a CTO or is on section 17 leave or absent without leave, the Code (para. 15.16) advises that the RC be contacted. Out of hours there will normally be a senior clinician on duty who will be designated by the responsible hospital as the patient's RC. In relation to CTO patients the Code then states at para. 10.55:

> *Where the person is known to be on a CTO and compulsory admission is indicated, the recall power should be used. An application for detention should not be made in respect of a person who is known to be on a CTO.*

Diversion, interrogation and prosecution

Apart from section 136 the police have a number of options to choose from when they are dealing with a possible offender who they think might be mentally disordered: check if the person is an absconding detained patient and then return them to the hospital under section 18 or section 138; persuade the person to co-operate while the police set up an informal or compulsory admission; use their statutory powers of arrest. Under the Police and Criminal Evidence Act 1984 (PACE) there is a Code of Practice which covers the detention, treatment and questioning of persons by police officers (Home Office, 2012). This will apply where the officer suspects, or is told in good faith, that a person may be mentally ill or have significant learning difficulties or be unable to understand the significance of questions or, indeed, the significance of their own answers. If the person is detained, an 'appropriate adult' (AA) must be informed and asked to come to the police station. A person who is trained or experienced in dealing with mentally disordered people may often be seen as more appropriate than an unqualified relative. The appropriate adult should be present when the individual is told of their rights or can have them read again. They can also require the presence of a lawyer. Unless delay would involve serious risk to person or property, a mentally disordered person should not be interviewed or asked to sign a statement until the appropriate adult is present. The appropriate adult is not just an observer. They have a role in advising the person being interviewed, observing the fairness of the interview and facilitating communication with the interviewee. If a decision is taken to prosecute, the case is passed to the Crown Prosecution Service. Among other factors, they will consider the likely effect of prosecution on people who are young, old, infirm or mentally ill. In the case of mental illness, the Crown Prosecutor will require independent evidence of the illness and the likely adverse effects of prosecution.

Other relevant police powers

Section 17 of the PACE Act 1984 allows a constable to enter and search any premises for the following purposes: to execute a warrant; to arrest a person for an offence; to recapture someone who is unlawfully at large whom is he pursuing; or, finally, to save life or limb or to prevent serious damage to property.

There are also limited circumstances in which a common-law power of arrest may be made. In *Bibby v Chief Constable of Essex Police* (Court of Appeal, 2000) these circumstances were summarised: a sufficiently real and present threat to the peace; the threat coming from the person to be arrested; conduct clearly interfering with the rights of others with its natural consequence being 'not wholly unreasonable violence' from a third party; and, finally, unreasonable conduct from the person to be arrested. However, in line with recent police guidance, the Code states at para.16.29:

> Police should generally use section 135 or 136, rather than their common law power of arrest for breach of the peace, when the person appears to be suffering from mental disorder which makes it necessary for them to be taken to a place of safety.

The role of the appropriate adult

This role does not sit very comfortably with that of the AMHP but the two functions often coincide and AMHPs need to be familiar with the work of the appropriate adult (AA). Some staff will perform this task on some occasions but rarely with the same patient that they have dealt with under the Mental Health Act. A brief outline of the function was given above, noting that the appropriate adult is not just an observer. They advise the person being interviewed, observe the fairness of the interview and facilitate communication with the interviewee. What follows is a selection of key elements of the recently revised PACE Codes of Practice (Code C as implemented from June 2014).

C1.7 The 'appropriate adult' means, in the case of a . . . (b) 'person who is mentally disordered or mentally vulnerable':

- *a relative, guardian or other person responsible for their care or custody;*
- *someone experienced in dealing with mentally disordered or mentally vulnerable people but who is not a police officer or employed by the police;*
- *failing these, some other responsible adult aged 18 or over who is not a police officer or employed by the police.*

Note 1D to this part of the Code states:

In the case of people who are mentally disordered or otherwise mentally vulnerable, it may be more satisfactory if the appropriate adult is someone experienced or trained in their care rather than a relative lacking such qualifications. But if the detainee prefers a relative to a better qualified stranger or objects to a particular person, their wishes should, if practicable, be respected.

Under Code C11.17 if an appropriate adult is present at an interview, they should be informed:

- *that they are not expected to act simply as an observer; and*
- *that the purpose of their presence is to:*
  - *advise the person being interviewed;*
  - *observe whether the interview is being conducted properly and fairly;*
  - *facilitate communication with the person being interviewed.*

C1.4 of the Code states:

If an Officer has any suspicion, or is told in good faith, that a person of any age may be mentally disordered or otherwise mentally vulnerable, in the absence of clear evidence to dispel that suspicion, the person shall be treated as such for the purposes of this Code.

'Mentally vulnerable' applies to any detainee who, because of their mental state or capacity, may not understand the significance of what is said, of questions, or of their replies. The Code links the term 'mental disorder' to section 1 of the Mental Health Act but also states that if the Custody Officer has any doubts about the mental state/capacity of a person an AA should be called.

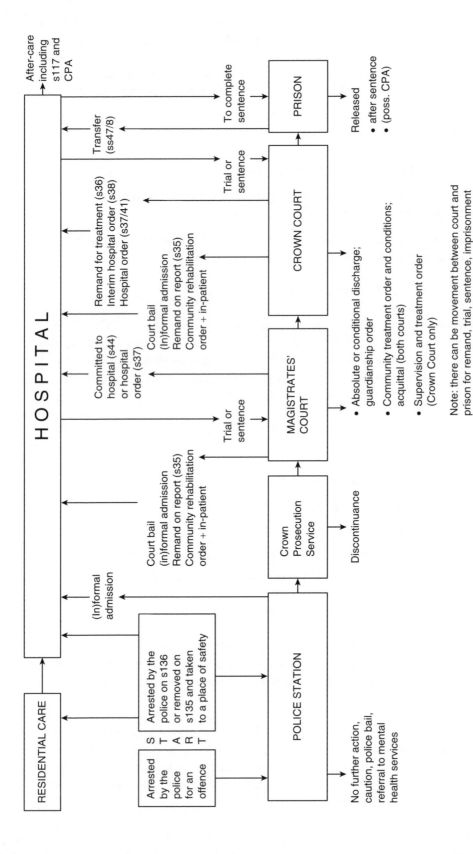

Figure 5.1   Flowchart on patients involved with the police and the courts

Source: Extracts from Puri et al., *Mental Health Law* (2012). © 2012 Basant K Puri, Robert A Brown, Heather J McKee and Ian H Treasaden. Reproduced by permission of Hodder & Stoughton.

A person should always be given an opportunity to consult a solicitor privately without the AA being present.

Summary of main provisions

The flowchart in Figure 5.1 summarises the main provisions covered in this chapter. It shows a number of options from the moment a person is arrested for an offence or under section 136 of the Mental Health Act onwards. The possible outcomes are traced by the arrows and the relevant section numbers should match up with information given earlier in the chapter.

ACTIVITY **5.1**

Sample questions on patients involved in criminal proceedings

1a *What grounds need to exist before a person can be placed on a section 37 hospital order under the Mental Health Act 1983?*
1b *In what circumstances might restrictions be put on such an order and what are the main likely effects of such restrictions?*
1c *What aspects of the Mental Health Act might lead an AMHP to become involved with such a patient?*
2a *A woman is arrested by the police and is brought to the police station. The police suspect that she may be suffering from a mental disorder. Give two reasons why an AMHP might be called to the station.*
2b *List some of the issues about using a police station to hold someone who might be mentally ill. How could an AMHP ameliorate any problems?*

Multiple choice questions

(Answers in Appendix 9)

1. *A patient remanded to a hospital on an interim hospital order under section 38 may be detained after renewals for a maximum of:*

   (a) *28 days*   ☐
   (b) *12 weeks*   ☐
   (c) *six months*   ☐
   (d) *a year*   ☐

2. *A patient who is subject to a hospital order made by the court under section 37 is first entitled to apply to the mental health review tribunal:*

   (a) *after six months*   ☐
   (b) *within six months*   ☐
   (c) *after one year*   ☐

Chapter 6
Consent to treatment and mental capacity

Consent to treatment under the MHA 1983

Introduction

The purpose of Parts 4 and 4A of the Act is to clarify the circumstances in which treatment for mental disorder may be given without the consent of a patient subject to compulsion. This was often a contentious issue under the 1959 Mental Health Act, which gave no specific guidance on treatment. Although the 1983 Act introduced a fairly clear set of rules to follow, these have, in turn, become somewhat contentious and there are a number of complications which have arisen from case law.

The main principle adopted by the Act is that there are some patients who are liable to be detained who may need to be given treatment without their consent. Furthermore, this may be seen as reasonable given the fact of their detention. Certain procedures, however, should be followed to offer safeguards. These essentially involve a second medical opinion from outside the hospital for more serious forms of treatment in those cases where valid consent cannot be obtained from the patient. This absence of consent could be the result either of the patient objecting to the treatment or of their being unable to give valid consent (e.g. because of mental incapacity). For the most serious treatments (such as psychosurgery), a second opinion *and* the consent of the patient are required. Because of the invasive nature of these treatments, the safeguards are also extended to informal patients. The community treatment orders have brought with them a new set of rules which are set out in Part 4A.

The Care Quality Commission has a general duty to oversee the operation of these parts of the Act.

Detained patients who are not covered by Part 4 of the Act are in the same position as any other patients in a general hospital and cannot be treated without their consent except where the Mental Capacity Act applies or where common law would allow it (e.g. in an emergency). It is particularly important to understand not just what the procedures are, but which patients are covered by them, as not all detained patients are included. Generally, those patients liable to detention for periods of more than 72 hours are covered, with the exception of people remanded for reports by the courts under section 35. Details of which sections are covered by the rules are included in full in the flowchart and checklist later in this chapter. The grids which can be found in this guide for patients detained under Parts 2 or 3 also provide a quick visual guide as to which patients are covered by the Part 4 or 4A rules and which are not.

A definition of medical treatment

Section 145 provides a definition of medical treatment as:

> *nursing, psychological intervention and specialist mental health habilitation, rehabilitation and care . . . the purpose of which is to alleviate, or prevent a worsening of, the disorder or one or more of its symptoms or manifestations.*

The second part of the definition was an amendment designed to stress the need for therapeutic intent but it is not a requirement that this is likely. In *MD v Nottinghamshire Health Care NHS Trust* (2010) it was stated:

> *it is sufficient if the treatment is for the purpose of preventing a worsening of the symptoms or manifestations. That envisages that the treatment required may not reduce risk. It is also sufficient if it will alleviate but one of the symptoms or manifestations, regardless of the impact on the risk posed by the patient.*

Part 4 – Consent to treatment for patients liable to be detained

Sections 57, 58 and 58A set out which types of medical treatment attract specific rules. Some treatments require the approval of a second opinion appointed doctor

(SOAD) who has been appointed by the Secretary of State or the Welsh Ministers for this purpose. The categories of treatment which are specified in the Act are:

- Section 57:
  - any surgical operation for destroying brain tissue or for destroying the functioning of brain tissue (generally known as neurosurgery);
  - surgical implantation of hormones to reduce male sex drive.
- Section 58:
  - medicine after three months of treatment while detained.
- Section 58A:
  - electro-convulsive therapy (ECT) and related medicine.

These sections are considered in more detail below. Other forms of treatment could be added to this list in future by regulations.

Approved clinicians

There are some situations when the person in charge of the treatment must be registered as an approved clinician (AC). For a detained patient this will be:

- where treatment is given without the patient's consent;
- where the patient has consented under section 58 or 58A and the certificate has been completed by an AC rather than a SOAD;
- where:
  - a CTO patient has been recalled or the CTO revoked, and
  - where the section 58 requirements have not yet been met, but
  - there is consent and the treatment is necessary to prevent serious suffering to the patient.

Where a CTO patient is in the community there needs to be an AC in charge of the treatment being given if the patient lacks capacity to consent. The exception to this rule would be where there is the consent of an attorney (from a lasting power of attorney), a deputy or the Court of Protection. The Code notes at para. 25.6 that:

> Hospital managers should keep a record of approved clinicians who are available to treat patients for whom they are responsible and should ensure that approved clinicians are in charge of treatment where the Act requires it.

Section 57

This deals with any surgical operation for destroying brain tissue or for destroying the functioning of brain tissue (generally known as neurosurgery), and the surgical implantation of hormones to reduce male sex drive. This section is unusual for Part 4 in that it covers informal as well as detained patients.

There are considerable safeguards under section 57. A SOAD and two other people who are appointed by the Care Quality Commission need to certify in writing that the patient is capable of understanding the nature, purpose and likely effects of the treatment in question and has consented to it. The SOAD then has to certify in writing that it is appropriate for the treatment to be given, having consulted two other persons who have been professionally concerned with the patient's medical treatment. One of these consultees needs to be a nurse and the other should be someone other than a nurse or a doctor. This could be an AMHP but neurosurgery under section 57 is very rare. There are usually only three or four cases per year in the whole of England and Wales.

Even less likely is a referral concerning the surgical implantation of hormones to reduce male sex drive as this has not been requested for more than 25 years.

Section 58

This section used to include ECT but this is now regulated by section 58A. Section 58 deals only with medication for mental disorder after three months of treatment under detention. This means it relates in practice to patients who are subject to section 3, section 37 or the equivalent. It does not cover medication if this is administered as part of ECT treatment as this is also covered by section 58A.

The safeguards provided by section 58 are that medication cannot be given unless:

- the patient has consented to the treatment and either the approved clinician in charge of it or a SOAD has certified in writing that the patient is capable of understanding its nature, purpose and likely effects and has consented to it; *or*

- a SOAD has certified in writing that the patient is not capable of understanding the nature, purpose and likely effects of that treatment, or is capable but has not consented to it, and that it is appropriate for the treatment to be given. The SOAD must have consulted two other persons who have been professionally concerned with the patient's medical treatment. One of these must be a nurse and the other shall be neither a nurse nor a registered medical practitioner; and neither can be the responsible clinician or the person in charge of the treatment in question.

If treatment is based on this procedure the Code recommends that there should be a record in the patient's notes of the relevant discussion where capacity was confirmed and full details of the specific treatment covered. The Code states at para. 25.18:

Certificates under this section must clearly set out the specific forms of treatment to which they apply. All the relevant drugs should be listed, including medication to be given 'as required' (prn), either by name or by the classes described in the British National Formulary (BNF). If drugs are specified by class, the certificate should state clearly the number of drugs authorised in each class, and whether any drugs within the class are excluded. The maximum dosage and route of administration should be clearly indicated for each drug or category of drugs proposed. This can exceed the dosages listed in the BNF, but particular care is required in these cases.

The *AMHP's Guide to Psychiatry and Medication* (Brown et al., 2009) provides some detail on treatments covered by this section.

Section 58A: ECT and related medication

This new section covers ECT and any medication administered as part of the ECT process. The rules apply to adult detained patients and to all patients under the age of 18, whether they are detained or not. No patient under 18 may be given ECT without the approval of a SOAD. There are some new safeguards and this is the first occasion where the Mental Health Act does not automatically take precedence over the Mental Capacity Act. For example, a competent refusal or a valid and applicable advance decision will prevent treatment from being given under section 58A.

ECT may not be given to an adult unless:

- the patient has consented to that treatment and either the approved clinician in charge of it or a SOAD has certified in writing that the patient is capable of understanding its nature, purpose and likely effects and has consented to it; *or*

- a SOAD has certified in writing that the patient is not capable of understanding the nature, purpose and likely effects of the treatment, and that it is appropriate for the treatment to be given, and that this will not conflict with a valid and applicable advance decision or a decision made by a donee or a deputy or the Court of Protection. The SOAD must have consulted two other persons who have been professionally concerned with the patient's medical treatment. One of these must be a nurse and the other shall be neither a nurse nor a registered medical practitioner; and neither can be the responsible clinician or the person in charge of the treatment in question.

If the patient is under 18 a certificate from a SOAD is needed whether they have capacity or not. However, the certificate by itself is not sufficient authority to treat. The relevant clinician must also have the patient's own valid consent or some other legal authority at the time of giving the treatment.

Section 62

This deals with urgent treatment. It covers sections 57, 58 and 58A but in practice it will not be used in relation to section 57. It provides for emergency situations (e.g. where a patient withdraws consent during a course of treatment) and even then it allows treatment only:

- (a) *which is immediately necessary to save the patient's life; or*
- (b) *which (not being irreversible) is immediately necessary to prevent a serious deterioration of his condition; or*

(c) which (not being irreversible or hazardous) is immediately necessary to alleviate serious suffering by the patient; or

(d) which (not being irreversible or hazardous) is immediately necessary and represents the minimum interference necessary to prevent the patient from behaving violently or being a danger to himself or to others.

With ECT only (a) and (b) apply so the risk level needs to be very high before the normal requirements can be dispensed with. The grounds set out in (c) and (d) are no longer acceptable for ECT and this may be a significant change for practitioners. These grounds are still applicable for emergency treatment with medication.

The definition of 'irreversible' is where it has 'unfavourable irreversible physical or psychological consequences' and hazardous means 'significant physical hazard'.

There is no prescribed form for use when treating under section 62.

Section 63

This section covers treatment which does not require the consent of the patient. This is the source of much concern to many patients. The implications are that, apart from ECT and the section 57 treatments, any treatment can be given in the first three months of a patient's detention without their valid consent. After three months the safeguard of the SOAD's involvement applies but only in relation to medication. Many other treatments can continue to be given without the SOAD safeguard.

The Code contains a number of pointers on treatment, such as encouraging staff to seek the patient's consent wherever practicable and to record this, or the refusal as the case may be, in the notes. Para. 24.43 states:

- compulsory administration of treatment which would otherwise require consent is invariably an infringement of Article 8 of the Convention (respect for family and private life). However, it may be justified where it is in accordance with law (in this case the procedures in the Mental Health Act) and where it is proportionate to a legitimate aim (in this case, the reduction of the risk posed by a person's mental disorder and the improvement of their health);

- compulsory treatment is capable of being inhuman treatment (or in extreme cases even torture) contrary to Article 3 of the Convention, if its effect on the person concerned reaches a sufficient level of severity. But the European Court of Human Rights has said that a measure which is convincingly shown to be of therapeutic necessity from the point of view of established principles of medicine cannot in principle be regarded as inhuman and degrading.

Para. 24.44 goes on to state:

Scrupulous adherence to the requirements of the legislation and good clinical practice should ensure that there is no such incompatibility. If clinicians have concerns about a potential breach of a person's human rights they should seek senior clinical and, if necessary, legal advice.

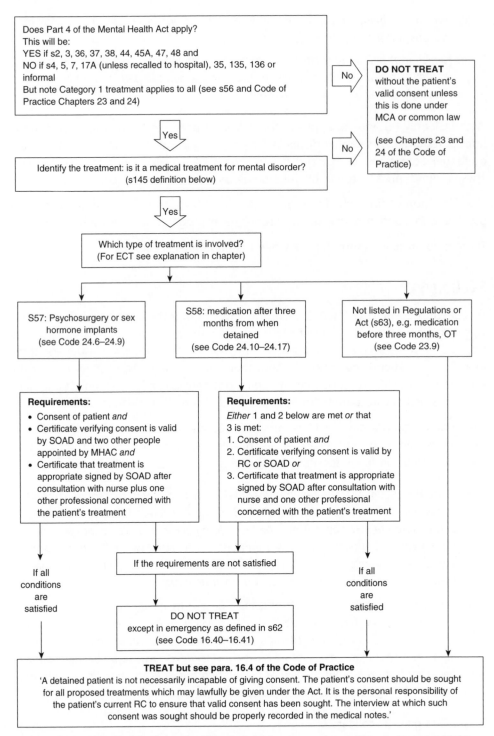

Figure 6.1   Consent to treatment flowchart for Part 4 (adapted from Puri et al. (2012))

It is quite possible that there will be legal challenges to the forcible administration of medication, especially to competent adults where they do not pose a risk to others.

Part 4A: Treatment of community patients not recalled to hospital

This sets out the law concerning treatment for patients who have been made subject to community treatment orders (CTOs). It is not always easy to follow and AMHPs may need to consider the implications for a few cases before it becomes easier to understand. This situation has arisen partly because the Bill was amended several times as it went through Parliament leaving the resulting Act a series of compromises between competing views.

A patient on section 17 leave in the community is covered by Part 4 of the Act but a community patient (one subject to a CTO) is covered by the different rules contained in Part 4A. For a community patient to be made subject to Part 4 they need to be recalled to hospital. In effect recalls may therefore take place to make it easier to give compulsory treatment to a mentally capable refusing patient.

If a patient is subject to a CTO (and has not been recalled) they cannot be given treatment for mental disorder unless the requirements of Part 4A are met. These are:

- the person giving the treatment must have the authority to do so; and

- (in most cases) there must be a certificate unless the patient has given valid consent.

Form CTO11 is needed for treatments which would require a certificate under section 58 or 58A if the patient were detained. In effect this means medication after the initial three-month period of detention and ECT and any related medication. However, a certificate is not required for medication during the first month following a patient's discharge from detention on to a CTO. This is the case even if the three-month period for section 58 has already expired or expires during this first month. If the patient gives valid consent the AC in charge of the treatment can complete a CTO 12 and no SOAD will be required. This change came into effect in June 2012.

When they are giving Part 4A certificates, SOADs are not asked to certify whether a patient has capacity to consent to the treatments in question. The question is whether the treatment is appropriate. The SOAD may make it a condition of their approval that particular treatments are given only in certain circumstances. They could specify that a certain treatment only is to be given if the patient consents.

Para. 25.32 of the Code, elaborating on this point, states:

> *[The SOAD] might specify that a medication may be given up to a certain dosage if the patient lacks capacity to consent, but that a higher dosage may be given with the patient's consent.*

SOADs can also decide which treatments to approve should the patient be recalled to hospital and whether to impose any conditions on that approval. Unless it states otherwise, a certificate will authorise medication even if the patient has capacity to refuse it.

Before issuing a certificate the SOAD must consult two people who have been pro-fessionally concerned with the patient's medical treatment. Only one of these may be a doctor and neither of them can be the patient's responsible clinician or the approved clinician in charge of any of the treatments that are to be specified on the certificate.

Where a patient has capacity to consent to treatment this provides the authority to treat. In other cases there may be a donee of an LPA, or a deputy who has been appointed by the Court of Protection, who is able to consent on the patient's behalf.

If a community patient lacks capacity to consent to the treatment, the clinician wish-ing to have authority to treat must:

- take reasonable steps to establish that the patient lacks capacity to consent to the treatment; then, when giving the treatment, he must reasonably believe that the patient lacks capacity to consent to it;

- have no reason to believe that the patient objects to being given the treatment; or, if he does have reason to believe that the patient objects, it is not necessary to use force against the patient in order to give the treatment;

- be the person in charge of the treatment and an approved clinician; or the treatment must be given under the direction of that clinician;

- ensure that giving the treatment will not conflict with an advance decision which he is satisfied is valid and applicable, or with a decision made by a donee or deputy or the Court of Protection.

Emergency treatment

In an emergency, if treatment is to be given without a certificate, the treatment must fall into one of the categories set out in section 64G(5):

(a) *it is immediately necessary to save the patient's life; or*

(b) *it is immediately necessary to prevent a serious deterioration of the patient's condition and is not irreversible; or*

(c) *it is immediately necessary to alleviate serious suffering by the patient and is not irreversible or hazardous; or*

(d) *it is immediately necessary, represents the minimum interference necessary to prevent the patient from behaving violently or being a danger to himself or others and is not irreversible or hazardous.*

If it is necessary to use force against the patient in order to give the treatment this can only be to prevent harm to the patient. The use of such force must be proportionate to the likelihood of the patient's suffering harm, and to the seriousness of that harm.

Recalled patients

When a patient is recalled by the RC they revert to being covered by Part 4 and can be treated accordingly, except as noted in the Code at para. 25.33:

- *a certificate under section 58 is not needed for medication if less than one month has passed since the patient was discharged from hospital and became a CTO patient;*

- *a certificate is not needed under either section 58 or 58A if a Part 4A certificate or Part 4A consent certificate has been issued;*

- *a certificate is not needed under either section 58 or 58A if the treatment in question is already explicitly authorised for administration on recall on the patient's Part 4A certificate; and*

- *treatment that was already being given on the basis of a Part 4A certificate may be continued, even though it is not authorised for administration on recall, if the approved clinician in charge of the treatment considers that discontinuing it would cause the patient serious suffering. But it may only be continued pending compliance with section 58 or 58A (as applicable) – in other words while steps are taken to obtain a new certificate.*

The Mental Capacity Act 2005

The bulk of the Mental Capacity Act (MCA) came into effect in October 2007. The Act is having a significant impact on mental health care. The MCA definition of incapacity would apply to decisions under the MHA. Also, where the Mental Health Act does not provide authority for treating patients who are subject to compulsion the MCA may be relevant. This would include treatments that are not for mental disorder. Where patients have capacity they would be entitled to refuse such treatments but clinicians might be able to rely on the MCA in situations where patients lack capacity.

The MCA provides a statutory framework for decision-making on behalf of people who lack the capacity to consent to their care or treatment. Before the Act came into effect incapacitated individuals were most commonly dealt with under the common law doctrine of necessity. This provided for the care or treatment of incapacitated adults in their best interests.

There is more detailed information on the MCA in *The Mental Capacity Act 2005: A Guide for Professionals* by Brown *et al.* (2015).

The five principles

Section 1 of the MCA sets out five principles that should be applied by anyone relying on the Act for any purpose. The principles are intended to protect people who lack capacity, and to help them participate in decision-making as fully as possible. Section 1 of the Act states:

(1) *A person must be assumed to have capacity unless it is established that he lacks capacity.*

(2) *A person is not to be treated as unable to make a decision unless all practicable steps to help him to do so have been taken without success.*

(3) *A person is not to be treated as unable to make a decision merely because he makes an unwise decision.*

(4) *An act done, or decision made, under this Act for or on behalf of a person who lacks capacity must be done, or made, in his best interests.*

(5) *Before the act is done, or the decision is made, regard must be had to whether the purpose for which it is needed can be as effectively achieved in a way that is less restrictive of the person's rights and freedom of action.*

Definition of incapacity

The first principle requires any decision-maker to assume capacity unless it can be established that the person in question lacks capacity. The test for incapacity is set out in sections 2 and 3 of the Act. Section 2 states:

> *for the purpose of this Act, a person lacks capacity in relation to a matter if at the material time he is unable to make a decision for himself in relation to the matter because of an impairment of, or a disturbance in the functioning of, the mind or brain.*

This requires two questions to be answered:

1. Is there a specific decision to be made now?

2. Is the person unable to make the decision because of an impairment of, or a disturbance in the functioning of the mind or brain, whether this be temporary or permanent?

This is sometimes referred to as 'the diagnostic test'.

If the potential decision-maker answers 'no' to either of these questions the MCA will not apply. However, if the answer is 'yes' to both questions the decision-maker must go on to establish whether the person is able to make their own decision. This must be done before the decision-maker is able to make decisions on behalf of the person. Section 3 of the MCA sets out the test for determining whether a person is incapable of making their own decisions ('the functional test'):

a person is unable to make decisions for himself if he is unable –

(a) *to understand the information relevant to the decision,*

(b) *to retain the information,*

(c) *to use or weigh that information as part of the process of making the decision, or*

(d) *to communicate his decision (whether by talking, using sign language or any other means).*

Any decision-maker must decide what information about the decision is relevant and give that information in a way that the person can understand. If a person shows that they are able to use that information to weigh up the benefits and/or risks of the proposed action, and understand the consequences of inaction, retain the information for long enough to weigh the information up, and finally communicate a decision then they would be regarded as having capacity. So if the potential decision-maker is satisfied that the person is able to meet all four of the above requirements (a)–(d) they must regard the person as having the capacity to make the decision in question and would have no authority to make that decision on the person's behalf. If, however, they believe (on the balance of probability) that the person is unable to demonstrate one or more of the four requirements then the person would be deemed to lack the capacity to make the decision in question. The decision-maker would then be able to make the decision on the person's behalf as long as they were acting in the person's best interests.

Best interests

There is no definition of 'best interests' in section 4 of the Act. Rather there is a checklist of factors that any decision-maker must consider. The aim of the checklist is to ensure that any decisions made, or actions taken, are in the best interests of the incapacitated person. The factors to consider are broad, enabling them to be applied to all decisions and actions.

Figure 6.2 provides a best interests checklist. It is based on the checklist from the statute as summarised at the beginning of Chapter 5 of the Code of Practice to the MCA.

There are no statutory forms for the best interests checklist, or for the capacity test. However, decision-makers are well advised to record their decision-making process as this will provide authority for their actions and help protect them from liability.

'Section 5 acts'

This is the expression used when referring to acts made in connection with the care or treatment of people where section 5 is relied on to provide protection from liability. In effect, section 5 of the MCA allows decision-makers to carry out acts in connection with the care or treatment of people provided that they have followed the requirements of the Act. There are limitations in that certain actions are not permitted as section 5 acts.

Encourage participation

- Do whatever is possible to permit and encourage the person to take part, or to improve their ability to take part, in making the decision.

Identify all relevant circumstances

- Try to identify all the things that the person who lacks capacity would take into account if they were making the decision or acting for themselves.

Find out the person's views

- Try to find out the views of the person who lacks capacity, including:

    - the person's past and present wishes and feelings – these may have been expressed verbally, in writing or through behaviour or habits;
    - any beliefs and values (e.g. religious, cultural, moral or political) that would be likely to influence the decision in question;
    - any other factors the person themselves would be likely to consider if they were making the decision or acting for themselves.

Avoid discrimination

- Do not make assumptions about someone's best interests simply on the basis of the person's age, appearance, condition or behaviour.

Assess whether the person might regain capacity

- Consider whether the person is likely to regain capacity (e.g. after receiving medical treatment). If so, can the decision wait until then?

If the decision concerns life-sustaining treatment

- Do not be motivated in any way by a desire to bring about the person's death. They should not make assumptions about the person's quality of life.

Consult others

- If it is practical and appropriate to do so, consult other people for their views about the person's best interests and to see if they have any information about the person's wishes and feelings, beliefs and values. In particular, try to consult:

    - anyone previously named by the person as someone to be consulted on either the decision in question or on similar issues;
    - anyone engaged in caring for the person;
    - close relatives, friends or others who take an interest in the person's welfare;
    - any attorney appointed under a lasting power of attorney or enduring power of attorney made by the person;
    - any deputy appointed by the Court of Protection to make decisions for the person.

- For decisions about major medical treatment or where the person should live and where there is no one who fits into any of the above categories, an independent mental capacity advocate (IMCA) must be consulted.
- When consulting, remember that the person who lacks capacity to make the decision or act for themselves still has a right to keep their affairs private – so it would not be right to share every piece of information with everyone.

Avoid restricting the person's rights

- See if there are other options that may be less restrictive of the person's rights.

Take all of this into account

- Weigh up all of these factors in order to work out what is in the person's best interests.

Figure 6.2   The best interests checklist

Section 5 acts must not conflict with a person's advance refusal of treatment, the authority of an attorney appointed by the person, or the authority of a deputy appointed by the Court of Protection.

As long as none of these situations exists then someone can make decisions and carry out actions for or on behalf of an incapacitated person provided that:

- before doing the act the decision-maker takes reasonable steps to establish that the person lacks capacity in relation to the matter;
- when doing the act they believe the person lacks capacity in relation to the matter; and
- the act will be in the person's best interests (determined in accordance with section 4).

If these criteria are met the decision-maker would be protected from liability, assuming that they do not exceed the limitations detailed below or act negligently. Section 6 sets out a number of conditions which must be met if section 5 acts are to be regarded as lawful. If decision-makers have followed the correct procedures and do not exceed the limitations detailed below, their acts of care or treatment will fall within the scope of section 5.

Restraint can be used provided that the following criteria are met:

- the decision-maker believes that the restraint is necessary to do the act in order to prevent harm to the person; and
- the act is a proportionate response to:
    - the likelihood of the person suffering harm; and
    - the seriousness of that harm.

Where the person is causing harm to others the MCA cannot be relied on. In these circumstances decision-makers need to consider whether the Mental Health Act or the common law would provide a way of intervening to protect others. Restraint must also fall short of deprivation of liberty if someone is relying on the MCA.

Lawful responses to deprivation of liberty

If a decision-maker decides that the care or treatment being proposed amounts to a deprivation of liberty, then the following provisions are available, assuming that the criteria are met:

- detention under an appropriate section of the MHA 1983;
- a personal welfare order of the Court of Protection, under section 16 of the MCA 2005;
- Deprivation of Liberty Safeguards (DoLS);
- life-sustaining treatment, or treatment to prevent a deterioration, while awaiting a decision by the Court of Protection.

Detention under the Mental Health Act is covered in some detail in this book.

A personal welfare order can be made by the Court of Protection where a person lacks capacity. The order can include decisions about where the person lives, what contact they should have with others, consent to treatment issues, and determining who is responsible for the person's health care. The court can also make orders in relation to a person's property and affairs.

The Deprivation of Liberty Safeguards (DoLS) are an amendment to the Mental Capacity Act introduced in April 2009. They are intended to provide a procedure for the lawful deprivation of liberty of individuals living in care homes or in hospital settings. They apply to people aged 18 or over, who lack capacity and who have a mental disorder (see Chapter 11 for a detailed description).

The MCA 2005 allows life-sustaining treatment or treatment to prevent a deterioration in someone's condition if an application is being made to the Court of Protection for determination of lack of capacity and best interests (section 4B).

Advance decisions

An advance decision can be made by a capacitated adult (18 or over). It need not be in writing unless it is for life-sustaining treatment. The advance decision would need to state what treatment cannot be given and under what circumstances. If the specific treatment is proposed and the person at that point lacks capacity in relation to the treatment decision then the advance decision may be valid and applicable. Advance decisions are limited to refusals of medical treatment (they cannot cover social care). They cannot be used to require a specific treatment to be given. With the exception of ECT an advance refusal of treatment for mental disorder can be overridden if a person is detained under a section of the Mental Health Act 1983 to which Part 4 applies. Additional safeguards for people who make advance refusals of ECT have been introduced, to ensure that their refusal is respected unless certain criteria are met.

Lasting powers of attorney

A lasting power of attorney (LPA) can be made by capacitated adults (aged 18 and over) to cover either personal welfare decisions or property and affairs. It must be witnessed and registered. The information required depends on whether it is a personal welfare matter LPA or a financial one. LPAs provide for the appointment of someone (the donee) to make decisions on behalf of the donor once they lose the capacity to make their own decisions. Other statutory interventions can sometimes override the donee's decision-making powers (e.g. if the patient is detained under the Mental Health Act).

If a person loses capacity before they have made an LPA the Court of Protection could intervene either by making a one-off decision or by appointing a deputy to make certain decisions on behalf of the person.

ACTIVITY 6.1

Sample questions on consent to treatment and mental capacity

1a What is an advance decision as defined in the Mental Capacity Act 2005 and how might this relate to psychiatric medication?

1b What issues may arise if someone makes an advance decision in relation to the use of a particular anti-psychotic drug and is later admitted to psychiatric hospital under section 3?

1c What difficulties might an AMHP face in these circumstances (before and after admission)?

2a A patient has been detained in hospital on section 3 for ten weeks and has consented to be on psychiatric medication for most of that period. The RC considers that a change in medication is now needed and is concerned that the patient may not agree. What are the legal options in terms of proceeding with the proposed treatment in this case?

2b Why might an AMHP who is working with the patient and their family become involved?

2c What dilemmas might an AMHP face in these circumstances?

Multiple choice questions

(Answers in Appendix 9)

1. Key principles of the Mental Capacity Act include:

    (a) A presumption of capacity exists for all those aged 16 or over. ☐

    (b) All practicable steps should be taken to help a person make a decision before they're considered incapable. ☐

    (c) An unwise decision implies a lack of capacity. ☐

    (d) Acts done on behalf of an incapacitated person must be in his/her best interests. ☐

    (e) All decisions made on behalf of and for an incapacitated person must be registered with the Court of Protection. ☐

    (f) Decisions should be the least expensive available in terms of cost to the person. ☐

    (g) Decisions should seek to be less restrictive in terms of the person's rights and freedom of action. ☐

2. A decision on a person's mental capacity needs to be made in relation to the particular matter at the time when the decision has to be made.

    (a) True ☐

    (b) False ☐

(Continued)

ACTIVITY **6.1** *continued*

3. *The test for capacity under the Mental Capacity Act is whether the person can:*

   (a) *understand the relevant information* ☐

   (b) *retain the relevant information* ☐

   (c) *believe the relevant information* ☐

   (d) *use or weigh the relevant information as part of the decision-making process* ☐

   (e) *communicate the decision* ☐

   (f) *read and sign a consent form* ☐

Chapter 7

Mental health tribunals and hospital managers' reviews

Summary of provisions concerning mental health tribunals

See Table 2.1 (p17) and Table 5.1 (pp87–8) for summaries of when patients and their nearest relatives can apply to the mental health tribunal and for information on when there will be an automatic hearing.

Introduction

Mental health review tribunals were established with the radical provisions of the 1959 Mental Health Act. The main function of a tribunal is to review the justification for continued detention, a community treatment order or guardianship at the time of a hearing. In an important judgement in 2001 influenced by the Human Rights Act, *R (on the application of H)* v *London North and East Region Mental Health Review Tribunal* (2001), the Court of Appeal ruled that a tribunal should express its decision in terms of a positive view (i.e. that the grounds for section 2 existed at the time of the hearing) rather than the traditional negative view (i.e. that the tribunal could not see that the grounds did not exist). Sections 72 and 73 were amended by a remedial order to reverse the burden of proof. It is no longer the case that the patient needs to show that the grounds for compulsion do not exist but rather that the detaining authority needs to show the tribunal that the grounds are still present. At a tribunal hearing, an AMHP is likely, therefore, to be asked if they would apply for or recommend detention if they were assessing on that day.

If a patient considers the original detention was unlawful, he can consider an application to the High Court for a writ of habeas corpus or an application for judicial review. This is increasingly used and may be linked to the limitations of legal aid in other areas at present. A number of actions have been taken on the basis of the inadequacy of the AMHP's assessment, and particularly on the failure to consult the nearest relative properly before applying for section 3 (see *GD* v *Edgware and Barnet* (2008) and *CX* v *LA* (2011)).

The main references to tribunals are to be found in Part 5 of the Mental Health Act 1983, in Schedule 2 to the Act and in the Tribunal Rules 2008 (SI 2699) as amended. These documents are all reprinted in Barber *et al.* (2012). The Practice Directions, which have been updated twice since that text was published, form Appendix 7 of this book. These are a useful reference as they contain the headings for the various reports that are required by the tribunal.

Key provisions

Section 65 provides for the establishment of the mental health review tribunal for Wales.

For the Welsh tribunals Schedule 2 of the MHA states at para.1:

Each of the Mental Health Review Tribunals shall consist of

(a) *a number of persons (referred to in this Schedule as 'the legal members') appointed by the Lord Chancellor and having such legal experience as the Lord Chancellor considers suitable;*

(b) *a number of persons (referred to in this Schedule as 'the medical members') being registered medical practitioners appointed by the Lord Chancellor; and*

(c) *a number of persons appointed by the Lord Chancellor and having such experience in administration, such knowledge of social services or such other qualifications or experience as the Lord Chancellor considers suitable.*

The First-tier Tribunal for England was set up by the Tribunals, Courts and Enforcement Act 2007. In both England and Wales each tribunal hearing will have at least one legal member (who will preside), one medical member and one 'lay' member (Wales) or mental health expert (England).

Section 66 sets out when a Part 2 patient (subject to civil detention, a CTO or guardianship) or their nearest relative may apply for a hearing (see Table 2.1, p17).

Section 67 allows the Secretary of State to refer any Part 2 patient to the MHT (e.g. if the Secretary of State thinks there should be a hearing before a patient would next be eligible to apply).

Sections 67, 68 and 76 allow access for any doctor or approved clinician who is acting for a patient in connection with the MHT to:

> *visit the patient and examine him in private and require the production of and inspect any records relating to the detention or treatment of the patient in any hospital or to any after-care services provided to the patient under section 117 below.*

Section 68 sets out when the hospital managers must refer the patient to the MHT.

Sections 69 and 70 state when Part 3 patients (those involved in court proceedings) and their nearest relatives have access to MHT hearings (see Table 5.1 on pp87–8).

Section 71 allows, and sometimes requires, the Secretary of State (on this occasion this would be the Justice Secretary) to refer restricted patients to the MHT.

Section 72 gives details of MHT powers. In some circumstances, they must direct the patient's discharge, e.g. if they are not satisfied that the grounds for detention exist.

The MHT has the following powers:

- to decide that a patient should continue to be subject to compulsion;
- to direct that a patient should be discharged immediately;
- to direct that a patient should be discharged on a specified future date.

If the tribunal has not exercised its power to discharge the patient, it may recommend:

- leave of absence;
- transfer to another hospital with a view to future discharge;
- transfer into guardianship;
- or (for section 3) it may recommend the RC to consider making a CTO.

If any such recommendation is not complied with, the MHT can reconsider that case and make a further decision.

Section 77 limits applications to one per eligible person per period of detention and states that applications should be submitted in writing.

Wales is covered by the Mental Health Review Tribunal Rules for Wales 2008. In England the procedure of MHTs is now regulated by the Tribunal Procedure (First-tier Tribunal) (Health Education and Social Care Chamber) Rules 2008. Both sets of rules introduce a new appeal process to the Upper Tribunal Administrative Appeals Chamber. The Rules are reprinted in *Mental Health Law in England and Wales* (Barber *et al.*, 2012) but reports for England are covered by the revised Practice Directions which are reprinted here at Appendix 7. In Wales the report headings are much shorter and contained within the Tribunal Rules.

Applying for the detention of a patient discharged by a tribunal

This issue was considered in *R (von Brandenburg)* v *East London and City* (2003). The question raised in this case was in what circumstances can a patient who has been discharged by a tribunal be further detained without breach of Article 5(4) of the ECHR? The decision of the Law Lords was that a patient may not be re-sectioned following tribunal discharge unless the ASW (now AMHP) in good faith believes he has information not known to the tribunal which would have placed a significantly different complexion on the matter.

The Law Lords stressed the different roles of the ASW who made the decision whether to admit and the doctors who provided the recommendations upon which the ASW had a discretion whether to act.

The case is often misquoted as saying there needs to be a 'change of circumstances' before a fresh application can be made. The actual test is whether there is information not previously known to the tribunal.

If the tribunal has apparently erred in law it might be possible for the detaining authority to apply for a stay and then challenge the tribunal decision by judicial review. The details of the *von Brandenburg* case will be of some interest to AMHPs.

On 15 March 2000 the patient was lawfully admitted to St Clement's Hospital for assessment after an emergency application made under section 4 of the 1983 Act. The application was made by an ASW and was supported by the required medical recommendation. A second medical recommendation was obtained, and on the same day the patient's admission was converted, again lawfully, into an admission for assessment for a period not exceeding 28 days under section 2 of the Act. On 22 March the patient applied for a tribunal hearing. This hearing took place on 31 March. The patient's application for discharge was resisted by the responsible medical officer (RMO), who gave oral evidence to the tribunal, by a staff grade medical practitioner working with the RMO, and by the hospital. The tribunal ordered that the patient should be discharged with effect from 7 April, deferring the discharge for seven days to allow accommodation in the community to be found and a care plan to be made, including possible medication. On 6 April 2000 the patient, who had not left the hospital, was again detained, this time under section 3 of the Act. The application was made by the same ASW. The necessary medical recommendations were made by the RMO and the second doctor who had supported the earlier admission under section 2.

Extracts from the Lords' judgement:

> *It is plainly of importance that the ASW is subject to a statutory duty to apply for the admission of a patient where he is satisfied that such an application ought to be made and is of the opinion specified . . . The problem at the heart of this case is to accommodate the statutory duty imposed on ASWs (by whom, in practice, most applications for admission are made) within the principles referred to . . . above. The correct solution is . . . that an ASW may not lawfully apply for the admission*

of a patient whose discharge has been ordered by the decision of a MHR tribunal of which the ASW is aware unless the ASW has formed the reasonable and bona fide opinion that he has information not known to the tribunal which puts a significantly different complexion on the case as compared with that which was before the tribunal. It is impossible and undesirable to attempt to describe in advance the information which might justify such an opinion.

Lord Bingham gave three hypothetical examples for illustration only. The essential elements were:

- new information on risk of self-harm;
- the patient tells the tribunal that he will take medication but then refuses to do so after discharge; or
- after the tribunal hearing the patient's mental condition significantly deteriorates.

Hospital managers' reviews

Section 23(2)(a) gives hospital managers the power to discharge some patients from compulsion. These are patients detained under Part 2 of the Act, unrestricted section 37 patients and patients who are subject to community treatment orders. This is not a function that can be exercised by employees or officers of the Trust. Those appointed to sit on panels are sometimes referred to as 'associate managers'. The managers' panel must consist of at least three authorised people. The Reference Guide has a useful table at 27.7 which sets out who can be authorised, depending on the type of hospital (see Table 7.1).

Table 7.1 Delegation of discharge decisions by hospital managers (Figure 77 in the Reference Guide)

If the managers are	the discharge function may be performed on their behalf by	who are
an NHS trust	three or more: • directors of the trust board (including the Chairman); or • members of an authorised committee or subcommittee of the trust	not employees of the trust.
an NHS foundation trust	three or more people authorised by the board of the trust	neither executive directors of the board of the trust, nor employees of the trust.
a special health authority or local health board	three or more: • authorised members of the body (including the Chairman); or • members of an authorised committee or subcommittee of the body	not officers of the body (within the meaning of the NHS Act 2006 or NHS (Wales) Act 2006).
another body of persons (e.g. company)	three or more: • authorised members of the body; or • members of an authorised committee or subcommittee of the body	

In this table 'authorised' means that the person, committee or subcommittee (as the case may be) has been authorised by the managers (i.e. the body in question) specifically for this purpose.

The Reference Guide goes on to state at para. 27.9:

> *Patients can only be discharged when all three people acting on behalf of the managers agree that they should be discharged. A two to one majority decision is not sufficient (R. [on the application of Tagoe-Thompson] v the hospital managers of the Park Royal Centre [2003] EWCA Civ 330). If the decision is taken by more than three people, as well as a majority being in favour, the majority must consist of at least three people in favour of discharge before a decision to discharge can be made.*

Hospital managers have discretion to undertake a review at any time but they must review a patient's detention if the RC submits a report under section 20 renewing detention. They must consider holding a review if they receive a request from a patient and also if the RC makes a report under section 25 opposing a nearest relative's application for a patient's discharge. The Code of Practice advises at para. 38.13 that, in deciding whether to conduct a review where they have a discretion, the managers are entitled to take into account whether there has been a recent tribunal hearing or whether one is due in the near future.

In exercising the power to discharge the managers must consider whether the criteria for detention under the relevant section continue to be met. In addition (if the review follows the RC's use of the barring order under section 25 to prevent discharge by the NR) they should consider whether the patient, if discharged, would be likely to act in a manner dangerous to other people or to themselves. Dangerousness, which is a more stringent test than the basic risk criteria which refer to health, safety or protection of others, might include psychological as well as physical harm.

The managers should be provided with CPA documentation and written reports from the RC and other appropriate professionals, and the patient should normally be given copies. There is no prescribed procedure for the conduct of managers' hearings but the Code of Practice states at para. 38.34:

- *the patient should be given a full opportunity, and any necessary help, e.g. from an IMHA to explain why they should be no longer be detained or on a CTO;*

- *the patient should be allowed to be accompanied by a representative of their own choosing to help in putting their point of view to the panel. If the patient lacks capacity to put their point of view, their deputy, attorney or other representative of their choosing should be allowed to represent them;*

- *the patient should also be allowed to have a relative, friend, carer, deputy, attorney or advocate attend to support them; and*

- *the responsible clinician and other professionals should be asked to give their views on whether the patient's continued detention or a CTO is justified and to explain the grounds on which those views are based.*

Where there are disagreements between those giving evidence the Code gives the following guidance at para. 38.37:

> Members of managers' panels will not normally be qualified to form clinical assessments of their own. They should give full weight to all the evidence in relation to the patient's care. If there is a divergence of views among the professionals about whether the patient meets the clinical grounds for continued detention or CTO, managers' panels should reach an independent judgement based on the evidence that they hear. Regard should be had to the least restrictive option and maximising independence principle . . . In some cases it might be necessary to consider adjourning to seek further medical or other professional advice.

AMHP reports for managers' hearings will usually follow the same headings that are used for tribunals.

Social circumstances reports

Introduction

The preparation of social circumstances reports is a familiar task for many mental health workers but the purpose of these, and the required content, vary considerably. Equally, expectations of social reports have changed significantly over the last thirty years. No longer do social workers, for example, expect to produce reports with a history of an individual's early childhood and a comprehensive list of psychological and social factors which may, or may not, have a crucial bearing on the matters currently under consideration. Instead, they expect reports to have a clear focus. On the other hand, the expectations of reports for computer-based systems often seem to lack the key elements required for AMHP reports. There have also been major changes in conventions on what is acceptable and appropriate to include. Increased rights of access to information have probably hastened these changes, as well as reinforcing the need to base conclusions and recommendations on a proper assessment of available facts, observed behaviour and expressed needs.

The question of making recommendations in tribunal reports has been a difficult one, and again practice has varied over time. For the last few years most mental health workers have made recommendations in tribunal reports whereas 20 years ago they were often advised not to do this. The new guidelines in the Practice Directions for tribunals in England do include a heading for recommendations in social circumstances reports.

AMHPs may find that they are expected to contribute reports in the following areas:

- assessments for possible admission to hospital;
- cases where the nearest relative has made the application for detention (s14);
- general review reports on a patient's progress;
- assessments for possible reception into guardianship;

- assessments for access to resources;

- mental health tribunals;

- hospital managers' reviews;

- assessments for after-care arrangements under section 117;

- where an application for a community treatment order is considered;

- social supervisor reports for conditionally discharged patients.

Each of these is considered, in varying detail, on the following pages.

Assessments for possible admission to hospital

Apart from the requirement in the Code of Practice (which will be considered below) there are various reasons for completing a report at the time of making an assessment for a possible admission to hospital and many local authorities have an in-house form for such occasions. Information in such reports can be useful for a number of purposes, including:

- providing a record of the circumstances leading up to any decision reached and documenting the assessment of risk factors;

- for hospital staff in the case of an admission occurring (whether formal or informal);

- subsequent review of the person's needs;

- a mental health tribunal (especially for section 2) or hospital managers' review;

- in the case of a compulsory admission, to provide a much fuller account of the reasons for admission than would be apparent from the application form and recommendations.

The process of completing a social report form can have its own value, especially if this is done at the time of assessment. For example, the form might contain reminders of certain key issues: Is an interpreter needed? Has the nearest relative been contacted and informed of their rights under section 23?

A typical form might cover the following:

- *Personal information* – name, address, date of birth, gender, ethnic origin, religion, relatives, GP;

- *Language* – and whether an interpreter is needed;

- *Origin of referral* – particularly note if it came from the nearest relative (s13(4));

- *Information at referral* – any particular concerns or risks;

- *Previous involvement with mental health services* – including any admissions to, discharge from and recall to hospital;

- *Interview with patient* – their wishes and views;

- *The patient's capacity to make key decisions on admission or treatment;*

- *Any known past wishes of the patient;*

- *Details of relatives and their views* – especially nearest relative's attitude;

- *Details of significant others;*

- *Medical opinions;*

- *Social, family and personal factors* (including visits by children – see below);

- *Alternatives to compulsory admission* (informal admission, guardianship, day care, GP, community psychiatric nurse (CPN), out-patient care, friends, relatives, etc.);

- *If deprivation of liberty is needed but the patient is compliant would the MCA be more appropriate and less restrictive?;*

- *Outcome of assessment and the reasons for this* – summary of mental health and risk issues;

- **Accommodation* – and what is available on discharge;

- **Employment/occupation/education;*

- **Financial position* (including benefits entitlements);

- **Family history and relationships;*

- **Community support available on discharge* – if being admitted to hospital + patient's previous response to community support;

- *Summary and recommendations for future action.*

(*Starred items may be more or less relevant at the time of assessment but may be worth noting in case of a subsequent mental health tribunal as they mirror headings for tribunal social circumstances reports.)

There are similarities between this list and the factors identified in the Code of Practice as key points to be taken into account when making an assessment (paras 14.6–14.13).

These reports, completed at the time of admission, are required by the Code of Practice and, together with the section papers, they must show justification for the decision taken. Para. 14.93 of the Code states that:

> The AMHP should provide an outline report for the hospital at the time the patient is first admitted or detained, giving reasons for the application and details of any practical matters about the patient's circumstances which the hospital should know. Where possible, the report should include the name and telephone number of the AMHP or a care co-ordinator who can give further information. Local authorities should use a standard form on which AMHPs can make this outline report.

The Code, in an earlier passage, at para. 14.88, states that before making an application:

> *AMHPs should ensure that appropriate arrangements are in place for the immediate care of any dependent children the patient may have and any adults who rely on the patient for care. Their needs should already have been considered as part of the assessment. Where relevant, AMHPs should also ensure that practical arrangements are made for the care of any pets and for the local authority to carry out its other duties under the Care Act 2014 to secure the patient's home and protect their property.*

In light of recent cases it is crucial that AMHPs set out how they identified the nearest relative and that there is some detail on information given and on any consultation for section 3 or section 7. Local authorities could assist by providing a checklist of key factors so AMHPs could just tick them and add brief comments where needed. This would be in line with current practice in hospitals where nurses are given checklists of section 132 rights for patients.

Cases where the nearest relative has made the application for detention

Section 14 of the Mental Health Act 1983 requires the hospital managers to notify the local social services authority as soon as a patient is admitted on an application from the nearest relative on either a section 2 or 3. The local authority then, as soon as practicable, must arrange for an AMHP to interview the patient and provide the managers with a report on his social circumstances. It would be good practice for such a report to be provided in cases where the application was for a section 4, but this is not formally required.

Jones (2015, footnote to section 14) considers that the social circumstances report:

> *could include an account of the patient's family and social relationships (including the attitude of carers), history of mental disorder, previous contact with the local authority, access to community resources, his employment record, financial situation and accommodation. The report should also contain an account of the circumstances of the admission. If the nearest relative's application was made after an AMHP had refused to make one, it is suggested that the AMHP's report should include an account of the reasons for her decision.*

It would be helpful for such a report to follow similar headings to those used in reports on assessments for admission. The reasons for the nearest relative being the applicant should be clearly stated. If the AMHP has doubts about the appropriateness of detention, these should be clearly stated.

General review reports on a patient's progress

These may be designed to be shared with members of a multi-disciplinary team and sometimes with the patient and their family. They may contain a summary of aims, facilities and services needed and a review of progress so far. See under after-care arrangements below for typical headings when used with patients who are covered by section 117, and the section on access to resources for some current views on reports.

Assessments for possible reception into guardianship

Sometimes, the same format might be used as for assessments for possible admission to hospital and, indeed, one could argue that every such assessment for hospital should include a view on the possibility of using guardianship. In many cases, however, where guardianship is being actively considered, there is time to produce a comprehensive care plan as recommended by the Code of Practice at paras 30.20– 30.21. It suggests that the plan should identify the services which are needed by the patient and who will provide them. The plan should also indicate which of the guardianship powers are necessary to achieve the plan. At para. 30.22 it states that key elements of the plan are likely to be:

- *suitable accommodation to help meet the patient's needs;*
- *access to day care, education and training facilities, as appropriate;*
- *effective co-operation and communication between all persons concerned in implementing the care plan; and*
- *(if there is to be a private guardian) support from the local authority for the guardian.*

Assessments for access to resources

There is often a specific in-house format for requests for resources administered by the local authority. These have frequently been revised over the last few years as assessment procedures have changed. The Care Act (2014) has led to wholesale changes in this area in England.

Mental health tribunals (and hospital managers' reviews)

There are various advisory policy documents on social reports for tribunals but the simplest advice for AMHPs is to follow the headings which can be found in the Practice Directions (First-tier Tribunal). These are reprinted at Appendix 7. The Welsh Tribunal Rules set out what is expected in reports (other than for conditionally discharged patients) in Wales:

a. *the patient's home and family circumstances including the views of the patient's nearest relative or the person so acting;*

b. *the opportunities for employment or occupation and the housing facilities which would be available to the patient if discharged;*

c. *the availability of community support and relevant medical facilities;*

d. *the financial circumstances of the patient.*

It is worth comparing the report headings in England and Wales as they take completely different approaches to the issues.

Although it is the health authority which should ensure the provision of reports, it often falls to local authority mental health social workers (including AMHPs) to write them, although this is changing in some community teams who give the task to the care co-ordinator. The legal basis for the range of facilities which should be considered can be found in Chapter 9. Note that in the judicial review of *R v MHRT for West Midlands and North West ex parte H* (2000), it was held that restricted patients do not have a nearest relative and therefore one should not be named in any reports.

The Code of Practice asks hospital managers to ensure that they have relevant reports before they undertake a review. Social reports for reviews should probably be similar to those for tribunals.

After-care arrangements under section 117

A definition of after-care services was inserted into section 117 by the Care Act 2014. What amounts to 'after-care services' is now defined as:

> *services which have both of the following purposes:*
>
> (a) *meeting a need arising from or related to the person's mental disorder; and*
>
> (b) *reducing the risk of a deterioration of the person's mental condition (and, accordingly, reducing the risk of the person requiring admission to a hospital again for treatment of mental disorder).*

AMHPs are sometimes asked to contribute reports and assessments as to whether section 117 services are still needed and this can have significant financial implications for individuals and for health and social services authorities. The Code of Practice provides clear and helpful guidance on the issue of when section 117 services can be ended. Para. 33.20 states:

> *The duty to provide after-care services exists until both the CCG and the local authority are satisfied that the patient no longer requires them. The circumstances in which it is appropriate to end section 117 after-care will vary from person to person and according to the nature of the services being provided. The most clear-cut circumstance in which after-care would end is where the person's mental health improved to a point where they no longer needed services to meet needs arising from or related to their mental disorder. If these services included, for example, care in a specialist residential setting, the arrangements for their move to more appropriate accommodation would need to be in place before support under section 117 is finally withdrawn. Fully involving the patient and (if indicated) their carer and/or advocate in the decision-making process will play an important part in the successful ending of after-care.*

Para 33.21 goes on to say that section 117 services should not be withdrawn solely on the grounds that:

- the patient has been discharged from the care of specialist mental health services
- an arbitrary period has passed since the care was first provided
- the patient is deprived of their liberty under the MCA
- the patient has returned to hospital informally or under section 2, or
- the patient is no longer on a CTO or section 17 leave.

Even if the provision of after-care has been successful in that the patient is now doing well in the community, it may be necessary to continue to provide after-care services, e.g. to prevent a relapse or further deterioration in the patient's condition.

ACTIVITY 7.1

Sample questions on mental health tribunals

1a When a patient is appealing against a section 3 detention, the mental health tribunal has a number of powers at its disposal, as well as recommendations which it can make. These are conferred by section 72. What are the powers?

1b Identify any one of the recommendations which the MHT could make under section 72. In what circumstances might it be wise for the members of the tribunal to make this recommendation rather than use one of the powers at their disposal?

2a What powers does a mental health tribunal have in terms of making decisions about a patient who is detained on section 2?

2b Why might a tribunal ask an AMHP attending a tribunal hearing whether they would be likely to apply for the patient's detention had that person been an informal patient and the AMHP were assessing them on the day of the tribunal?

2c Identify one dilemma an AMHP might face in these circumstances and how they might deal with this.

Multiple choice questions

(Answers in Appendix 9)

1. A mental health tribunal can vary the conditions attached to a CTO.

   (a) True ☐
   (b) False ☐

2. A patient who is subject to a section 3 detention is first entitled to apply to the tribunal:

   (a) after six months ☐
   (b) within six months ☐
   (c) after one year ☐

Chapter 8

The Care Quality Commission for England and the Healthcare Inspectorate Wales

BECOMING AN APPROVED MENTAL HEALTH PROFESSIONAL

This chapter should help candidates to achieve the following competences:

Application of knowledge: the legal and policy framework

Applied knowledge of:

2(1)(a)(i)   *mental health legislation, related codes of practice, national and local policy guidance;*

2(1)(a)(ii)   *relevant parts of other legislation, codes of practice, national and local policy and guidance, in particular the Children Acts 1989 and 2004, the Human Rights Act and the Mental Capacity Act.*

Historical background

As statutory mental health law has developed in England and Wales so there have been a number of independent bodies seeking to protect the rights of detained patients. In 1815–16 there was a Parliamentary Inquiry into Madhouses which was followed by the Lunacy Commission and then the Board of Control. Both of these bodies reported to Parliament. The Mental Health Act Commission (MHAC) was established as a Special Health Authority in 1983 and had a specific focus on detained patients.

In 2009 the MHAC was subsumed within the Care Quality Commission (CQC) in England (a much larger body covering health and social services generally) and was replaced by the Healthcare Inspectorate in Wales. These changes were effected by the Health and Social Care Act 2008.

Overall functions of the Care Quality Commission

The CQC is an independent regulator of health and social care services in England. It has a broad remit in health and social care including:

- registering providers of healthcare and social care to ensure that they are meeting the essential standards of quality and safety;

- monitoring how providers comply with the standards – the CQC gathers information and visits providers if it thinks this is needed;

- using enforcement powers – this might include fines or public warnings if services drop below essential standards. The CQC has the power to close a service down if necessary;

- acting to protect patients whose rights are restricted under the Mental Health Act;

- promoting improvement in services by conducting regular reviews of how well those who arrange and provide services locally are performing;

- carrying out special reviews of particular types of services and pathways of care, or undertaking investigations on areas where there are concerns about quality;

- seeking the views of people who use services by involving them in the work of the CQC and publishing a statement on how this is done;

- telling people about the quality of their local care services to help providers and commissioners of services to learn from each other about what works best and where improvement is needed, and to help to shape national policy.

Some concerns have been expressed that these functions are so broad that the focused attention that the MHAC could bring to bear has been lost.

Mental Health Act functions of CQC and Healthcare Inspectorate Wales (HIW)

Section 120 requires:

(1) *The regulatory authority must keep under review and, where appropriate, investigate the exercise of the powers and the discharge of the duties conferred or imposed by this Act so far as relating to the detention of patients or their reception into guardianship or to relevant patients.*

(2) *Relevant patients are –*

   (a) *patients liable to be detained under this Act,*

   (b) *community patients, and*

   (c) *patients subject to guardianship.*

(3) *The regulatory authority must make arrangements for persons authorised by it to visit and interview relevant patients in private –*

   (a) *in the case of relevant patients detained under this Act, in the place where they are detained, and*

   (b) *in the case of other relevant patients, in hospitals and regulated establishments and, if access is granted, other places.*

(4) *The regulatory authority must also make arrangements for persons authorised by it to investigate any complaint as to the exercise of the powers or the discharge of the duties conferred or imposed by this Act in respect of a patient who is or has been detained under this Act or who is or has been a relevant patient.*

(5) *The arrangements made under subsection (4) –*

    (a) *may exclude matters from investigation in specified circumstances, and*

    (b) *do not require any person exercising functions under the arrangements to undertake or continue with any investigation where the person does not consider it appropriate to do so.*

In England the Mental Health Act Commissioners who visit patients have been replaced by Mental Health Act Reviewers. In Wales this function is now performed by Reviewers appointed by the Healthcare Inspectorate.

Contact details

CQC (Mental Health Act)

Citygate

Gallowgate Newcastle

NE1 4PA

Tel: 03000 616161

Healthcare Inspectorate Wales

Bevan House

Caerphilly Business Park, Van Road

Caerphilly

CF83 3ED

Tel: 029 2092 8850

Reviewing treatment

The CQC and the HIW appoint second opinion appointed doctors (SOADs) to provide second opinions when required by sections 57, 58 or 58A of the MHA. SOADs are required to give their own independent judgement on whether treatment proposed by the AC should go ahead. In *R (on the application of Wooder)* v *Fegetter and the Mental Health Act Commission* (2002) it was considered that the SOAD owes a duty to give reasons for his opinion in writing to the AC together with any opinion he may have on the desirability of withholding them from the patient on 'serious harm' grounds. Unless the AC agrees these exist he will give the information to the patient.

The Code of Practice describes the role of the SOAD as follows:

> *25.60 The SOAD's role is to provide an additional safeguard to protect the patient's rights, primarily by deciding whether certain treatments are appropriate and issuing certificates accordingly. Although appointed by the Commission, SOADs act as independent professionals and must reach their own judgement about whether the proposed treatment is appropriate.*

> *25.61 When deciding whether it is appropriate for treatment to be given to a patient, SOADs are required to consider both the clinical appropriateness of the treatment to the patient's mental disorder and its appropriateness in the light of all the other circumstances of the patient's case.*

> *25.62 SOADs should, in particular:*

> - *seek to understand the patient's views on the proposed treatment, and the reasons for them. This includes involving an advocate, carers or making any reasonable adjustments, as appropriate;*

> - *give due weight to the patient's views, including any objection to the proposed treatment and any preference for an alternative;*

> - *consider the appropriateness of alternative forms of treatment, not just that proposed;*

> - *balance the potential therapeutic efficacy of the proposed treatment against the side effects and any other potential disadvantages to the patient;*

> - *take into account any previous experience of comparable treatment for a similar episode of disorder; and*

> - *give due weight to the opinions, knowledge, experience and skills of those consulted.*

If AMHPs are consulted by SOADs they should record any views they have expressed.

Visiting compulsory patients

Both the CQC and HIW arrange for visits to detained patients and feedback to the relevant hospital. In 2014–15 Mental Health Act Reviewers met with 5,937 patients. The regulatory bodies' annual reports contain their overall findings. The major concerns that emerged from these visits in 2014–15 were: treatment and medication; choice and access, including food options and ward activities; S17 leave; patient information and rights; and personal needs such as care planning. In recent years, the CQC has not really engaged effectively with AMHPs whereas a few years ago there was more emphasis on looking at the quality of their work and related issues such as police and ambulance involvement. There were supposedly some moves to approach this in a new way and it had been hoped that the CQC would address a number of issues that concern AMHPs: the impact of bed shortages; the problems associated with the numbers of CTOs; lack of support from police and ambulance services in some areas; and problems with places of safety for section 135 and section 136 patients etc. However the 2014–15 Annual Report only mentions AMHPs on four pages and one of these is a definition! It would also be helpful if the CQC could fulfil its duty towards guardianship patients. Again there is no significant mention of guardianship in the 2014–15 report. The Health Inspectorate for Wales has even less material on AMHPs and on guardianship in its latest reports. Given AMHPs' central role in the compulsory processes, and the pressures that they face, this is very disappointing.

Investigating complaints

The CQC and HIW have duties to investigate complaints concerning detained patients, community patients and those subject to guardianship. The CQC has highlighted a number of factors that emerged from complaints in 2014–15.

- *Issues with medication, including allegations of inappropriately prescribed medication and/or poor side effects of drugs.*

- *Concerns with the care and services provided by doctors and nurses. These related to the detention process, medical professionals not explaining rights, or not providing documents to make an appeal.*

- *Challenges with taking leave from hospital, including leave not being granted on clinical grounds, or escorted leave being agreed but the patient not being able to take it because there were not enough staff.*

- *Safeguarding concerns, including issues or allegations of offences against the person, and allegations of physical or verbal abuse by staff or other patients.*

(CQC, 2016, p21)

ACTIVITY **8.1**

Sample questions on the CQC and Healthcare Inspectorate Wales

1a *Identify three of the main functions of the regulatory bodies which might relate to consent to treatment issues.*

   (i)
   (ii)
   (iii)

1b *In relation to any one of these, what would you see as the likely main strengths and weaknesses of the CQC/HIW from a detained patient's point of view?*

ACTIVITY 8.1 *continued*

(Function)

(Strengths and weaknesses)

2a Identify three of the main functions of the regulatory bodies (other than those which relate to consent to treatment).

(i)

(ii)

(iii)

2b In relation to any one of these, what would you see as the likely main strengths and weaknesses of the CQC/HIW from a detained patient's point of view?

(Function)

(Strengths and weaknesses)

Multiple choice questions

(Answers in Appendix 9)

1. Which of the following functions might be performed by the Care Quality Commission/ Health Inspectorate Wales?

   (a) investigating complaints by detained patients ☐
   (b) discharging patients from detention ☐
   (c) appointing second opinion doctors for consent to treatment provisions ☐
   (d) visiting and interviewing detained patients in private ☐
   (e) recommending leave of absence with a view to discharge ☐

2. The CQC/HIW does not have a remit to see patients subject to community treatment orders.

   (a) True ☐
   (b) False ☐

Chapter 9

Other relevant legislation

AMHPs are bound by various duties under the Human Rights Act 1998, the Mental Capacity Act 2005, the Equality Act 2010 and the Health and Safety at Work Act 1974. This is because their role makes them individuals with functions of a public nature. AMHPs also need to have an awareness of children's legislation and the Care Act 2014 (and Welsh equivalent when enacted). This chapter looks at the broader legal framework within which AMHPs undertake their duties.

The Human Rights Act is looked at in detail in Chapter 10. What follows here is a summary of law which may be relevant to mentally disordered people living in England and Wales. Welfare benefits law is not covered here: information about this may be accessed at **www.disabilityrightsuk.org**.

Summary of legislation

Local Authority Social Services Act 1970

This Act, which resulted from the Seebohm Report, brought together separate departments and identified legislation which would be the responsibility of the new social services departments. Local social services authorities are responsible for approving AMHPs, receiving patients into guardianship and for making after-care arrangements under section 117.

The Health and Safety at Work Act 1974

This Act stresses shared responsibility for safety. Everyone is to accept responsibility for the results of their actions and omissions. The Act sets out the following duties:

- *The employer: It shall be the duty of every employer, so far as it is reasonably practicable, to take care of the health, safety and welfare at work of all [their] employees. They must provide such information, instruction, training and supervision as is necessary to ensure, so far as it is reasonably practicable, the safety at work of . . . employees.*

- *The employee: It shall be the duty of every employee while at work (a) to take reasonable care for the health and safety of . . . self and of other persons who may be affected by . . . acts or omissions at work, and (b) to co-operate with the employer so far as is necessary to enable the employer to perform or comply with any statutory duty. AMHPs are advised to seek out local policies on prevention and management of violence.*

Mental Health Act 1983

See separate chapters covering most provisions of this Act.

Section 117   After-care services for those detained on long-term sections.

Public Health (Control of Disease) Act 1984

Sections 35–38   The magistrates' court can order the medical examination of a person thought to have or to be carrying a notifiable disease, and order their removal to hospital and their detention there. Section 67 provides a right of appeal to the Crown Court.

Section 46   Places a duty on local authorities to bury or cremate the body of a person if no other arrangements are being made and gives power to SSD to bury or cremate the body of a person who was accommodated in a Part III of the National Assistance Act home. A charge may be made for this.

Police and Criminal Evidence Act 1984

This sets out the rights of mentally disordered persons who are arrested and/or charged by the police. The most recent edition of the Codes of Practice which govern procedures under this Act was published in 2015. It includes details of the appropriate adult role.

Children Act 1989

(See also Chapter 19 in Code of Practice with regard to which legislation to use.)

Section 25   Secure accommodation order applies to children not detained under MH Act where risk exists of self-harm or of absconding followed by harm. No more than 72 hours detained per 28-day period without the authority of the court.

Section 31   Supervision order: LA may specify where child lives, have psychiatric examination, etc. Care order: LA becomes 'nearest relative' (MHA, section 27).

Section 38	Interim care order or supervision order: maximum initial eight weeks with renewals of four weeks. Interim care order also makes LA nearest relative.
Section 43	Child assessment order: maximum seven days. May include psychiatric examination.
Section 44	Emergency protection order: maximum initial eight days with extension of seven days. May be removed to accommodation or kept in hospital.
Section 46	Police protection: maximum 72 hours where police believe risk of significant harm; may be removed to accommodation or kept in hospital.
Section 47	Local authority enquiries – to safeguard or promote child's welfare.

Environmental Protection Act 1990

Section 80	If premises are a 'statutory nuisance' (defined in section 79) or prejudicial to health, council can serve notice setting time limit for repair – failure is a criminal offence leading to a fine of £5,000.

Human Rights Act 1998

(See Chapter 10 and Appendix 2 for further information.)

Commencement date 2 October 2000. Embodies European Convention on Human Rights within the British legal system. Individuals are able to pursue rights through British courts.

Housing Act 2004

Council has duty to inspect private premises for hazards. These are scored by following Housing Health and Safety Rating System (HHSRS). If category 1 hazard, council could serve improvement notice, ban use of premises and even make a demolition order.

Equality Act 2010

This replaces previous legislation such as the Race Relations Act 1976 and the Disability Discrimination Act 1995. The public sector 'Equality Duty' (PSED) came into effect in September 2011. Public bodies are required to publish information demonstrating their compliance with duties under the Act. In exercising public functions, AMHPs will need to have due regard to the need:

- to eliminate unlawful discrimination, harassment, victimisation and other conduct prohibited by the Act;
- to advance equality of opportunity between people who share a protected characteristic and those who do not;
- to foster good relations between people who share a protected characteristic and those who do not.

The Mental Health Act Code of Practice now gives much greater recognition to the importance of this legislation. Para. 3.9 notes that complying with the PSED may involve treating persons with mental health problems more favourably than others to achieve equality of access to services and outcomes. Para. 3.13 gives some helpful examples of reasonable adjustments for mentally disordered persons:

- *Assessment for detention is undertaken by professionals with the appropriate specialist skills to assess the person based on their individual needs, e.g. adjustments if the person has a learning disability, an autism spectrum disorder or is deaf.*

- *Ensuring the care environment is as accessible as possible, e.g. through appropriate signage and lighting.*

- *Ensuring information for patients is in a format accessible to the person, e.g. using pictures and big print, or providing translations into the person's first language.*

- *Ensuring there are adequate numbers of staff with the right skills and experience to communicate effectively with patients, e.g. staff who can use sign language or communicate in the person's first language.*

- *Providing specific or additional training for staff who work with people with learning disabilities or autism spectrum disorders.*

- *Ensuring meetings are accessible to people, e.g. providing materials in an appropriate format and holding the meeting in an accessible venue. The provision of an independent mental health advocate (IMHA) can support a patient to participate in decisions about their care and treatment.*

Compulsory removal under section 47 of the National Assistance Act 1948

This controversial power was repealed by the Care Act 2014.

The Care Act 2014

This is now in force in England. Welsh AMHPs will need to check for the latest information on the equivalent law in Wales. Although section 47 of the National Assistance Act has been repealed, one section that is the source of many AMHP stories (section 48 and the requirement to protect moveable property) has survived as section 47 of the Care Act 2014.

47 Protecting property of adults being cared for away from home

(1) This section applies where –

    (a) *an adult is having needs for care and support met under section 18 or 19 in a way that involves the provision of accommodation, or is admitted to hospital (or both), and*

(b) it appears to a local authority that there is a danger of loss or damage to movable property of the adult's in the authority's area because –

    (i) the adult is unable (whether permanently or temporarily) to protect or deal with the property, and

    (ii) no suitable arrangements have been or are being made.

(2) The local authority must take reasonable steps to prevent or mitigate the loss or damage.

(3) For the purpose of performing that duty, the local authority –

    (a) may at all reasonable times and on reasonable notice enter any premises which the adult was living in immediately before being provided with accommodation or admitted to hospital, and

    (b) may deal with any of the adult's movable property in any way which is reasonably necessary for preventing or mitigating loss or damage.

(4) A local authority may not exercise the power under subsection (3)(a) unless –

    (a) it has obtained the consent of the adult concerned or, where the adult lacks capacity to give consent, the consent of a person authorised under the Mental Capacity Act 2005 to give it on the adult's behalf, or

    (b) where the adult lacks capacity to give consent and there is no person so authorised, the local authority is satisfied that exercising the power would be in the adult's best interests.

(5) Where a local authority is proposing to exercise the power under subsection (3)(a), the officer it authorises to do so must, if required, produce valid documentation setting out the authorisation to do so.

(6) A person who, without reasonable excuse, obstructs the exercise of the power under subsection (3)(a) –

    (a) commits an offence, and

    (b) is liable on summary conviction to a fine not exceeding level 4 on the standard scale.

(7) A local authority may recover from an adult whatever reasonable expenses the authority incurs under this section in the adult's case.

For England the Care Act 2014 has repealed most of the main adult social care statutes with which most AMHPs will have become familiar. In terms of service provision the Act is light on detail, with much of the most important material tucked away in the regulations. A good place to look for the up-to-date position on the implementation of the Act is **www.lukeclements.com**.

ACTIVITY 9.1

Sample questions on other relevant legislation

1a   When does a local authority have a duty to protect a person's moveable property under section 47 of the Care Act 2014?

1b   Why might this aspect of law involve an AMHP who applies for someone's detention under section 2 of the Mental Health Act 1983?

1c   What difficulties can arise with the operation of this piece of legislation?

Multiple choice questions

(Answers in Appendix 9)

1.   Where a care order is made the local authority becomes the child's nearest relative.

   (a)   True   ☐
   (b)   False   ☐

2.   With the increasing problem of bed shortages, an AMHP would need to consider the Health and Safety at Work Act when deciding the timing of a visit to a patient as part of a Mental Health Act assessment.

   (a)   True   ☐
   (b)   False   ☐

3.   Meeting the requirements of section 47 of the Care Act 2014 specifically requires an AMHP to perform the functions.

   (a)   True   ☐
   (b)   False   ☐

Chapter 10
The Human Rights
Act 1998

BECOMING AN APPROVED MENTAL HEALTH PROFESSIONAL

This chapter should help candidates to achieve the following competences:

Application of knowledge: the legal and policy framework

Applied knowledge of:

2(1)(a)(i)   *mental health legislation, related codes of practice, national and local policy guidance;*

2(1)(a)(ii)   *relevant parts of other legislation, codes of practice, national and local policy and guidance, in particular the Children Acts 1989 and 2004, the Human Rights Act and the Mental Capacity Act.*

European Convention on Human Rights

The Act became operational on 2 October 2000. It does not incorporate the whole of the European Convention on Human Rights (ECHR) but it does include the following articles:

Article 2   *Right to life*
Everyone's right to life shall be protected by law.

Article 3   *Prohibition of torture*
No one to be subject to torture or inhuman or degrading treatment or punishment.

Article 5   *Right to liberty and security of person*

    5.1 No one shall be deprived of their liberty except for specific cases and in accordance with procedure prescribed by law e.g. after conviction, lawful arrest on suspicion of having committed an offence, lawful detention of person of unsound mind, to prevent spread of infectious diseases.

    5.4 Everyone deprived of liberty by arrest or detention shall be entitled to take proceedings by which the lawfulness of the detention shall be decided speedily by a court and release ordered if the detention is not lawful.

Note: In the *Bournewood* case (*HL* v *UK*, 2004) the European Court ruled there had been breaches of Articles 5.1 and 5.4. For a detailed description of this case and its long-term implications, see Chapter 2.

Article 6   *Right to a fair trial*
Everyone is entitled to a fair and public hearing within a reasonable time by an independent and impartial tribunal.

Article 8   *Right to respect for private and family life*
Everyone has the right to respect for his private and family life, his home and his correspondence.

Article 9   *Freedom of thought, conscience and religion*

Article 11   *Freedom of assembly and association*

Article 12   *Right to marry*
Men and women of marriageable age have the right to marry and to found a family.

Article 14   *Prohibition of discrimination*

Enjoyment of the rights and freedoms set forth in this Convention shall be secured without discrimination on any ground such as sex, race, colour, language, religion, political or other opinion, national or social origin, association with a national minority, property, birth or other status.

The full text of the relevant articles of the European Convention on Human Rights is set out in Appendix 2.

Advice on implications of the Act

Section 3 of the Act states:

So far as it is possible to do so, primary legislation and subordinate legislation must be read and given effect in a way which is compatible with the Convention rights.

This does not, however, affect the validity, continuing operation or enforcement of any incompatible primary legislation.

However, moving away from statute, where following the Mental Health Act Code of Practice would appear to be leading to a breach of a person's human rights this might provide cogent reasons for departing from the Code.

Public authorities

Public authorities are required to act in a way which is compatible with ECHR rights unless they are prevented from doing so by statute. Courts, tribunals, the NHS, local authorities, the CQC, the HIW, AMHPs, approved clinicians, SOADs and section 12 doctors would all be classed as public authorities.

Key terms

Absolute rights	These cannot be limited or qualified (e.g. Article 2).
Declarations of incompatibility	May be made by higher courts with the expectation that legislation will then be amended to make it compatible with the ECHR.
Limited rights	Specify limitations (e.g. the right to liberty allows for the detention of 'persons of unsound mind').
Living instrument	The European Court will interpret the ECHR in light of present-day conditions.
Margin of appreciation	Describes the measure of discretion given to the state in deciding on action under scrutiny (e.g. national security).
Positive obligations	Many articles expect positive action as well as non-interference with rights.
Proportionality	Interference with rights must be no more than necessary to achieve the intended objective.
Qualified rights	Set out when interference with such rights is permissible (where in accordance with the law, necessary in a democratic society, related to the tone of the aims in the relevant article).

Some examples of the impact of the Human Rights Act

The case of *Winterwerp* v *Netherlands* (1979) is important in that it established that a person must be reliably shown to be suffering from a true mental disorder based on objective medical expertise (except for emergencies). The mental disorder must be of a kind or degree justifying compulsory confinement and continued detention must be justified on the basis of the persistence of the disorder. There needs to be a true mental disorder and not just behaviour deviating from society's norms. This case may create dilemmas for AMHPs in at least two situations:

- if they are assessing someone with a paraphilia (such as paedophilia) and there is discussion as to whether the individual is presenting with a true mental disorder or just behaviour which deviates from society's norms;

- if they are put forward to train as an approved clinician, a role which is supposed to involve the ability to demonstrate objective medical expertise.

Another case of direct relevance to AMHPs was the case of *R (E)* v *Bristol City Council* (2005). In this case the judge decided that to interpret the words 'reasonably practicable' in relation to the obligation of the ASW under section 11(4) of the Act to consult with the nearest relative as meaning 'appropriate' rather than that the nearest relative was 'available' would avoid a potential infringement of the patient's rights under Article 8. This was in a situation where the patient did not wish that the nearest relative should be consulted. As we have seen, courts are required to interpret legislation if possible in a way which is compatible with Convention rights. This is what the judge did in the *Bristol* case and it has left the AMHP, in effect, with a decision to make as to when to consult the nearest relative in cases where this would cause a degree of distress to the patient.

However, as we saw in Chapter 3, this position was modified by the case of *TW* v *Enfield Borough Council* (2014). In terms of protecting the patient's Article 5 rights this case emphasised the role of the nearest relative. AMHPs are now required to show an awareness of this protective role and, if they still decide not to consult the nearest relative, they would usually be expected to apply to the county court for someone else to take on this function.

The status of the Code of Practice was considered in *R (Munjaz)* v *Mersey Care NHS Trust* (2005). The key questions in this case were the legal status and effect of the Code of Practice and whether Ashworth Hospital's use of seclusion was lawful. This had departed from the guidance then contained in the Code of Practice.

The Law Lords decided that the Code does not have statutory force but that it is guidance which should be considered with great care. It is more than advice which a person under an obligation to have regard to it is free to follow or not. The decision was that the Code should be departed from only for 'cogent reasons'.

The Appeal Court had earlier decided that seclusion could constitute medical treatment for mental disorder under section 63 and the Lords did not depart from this view. Where a patient is subject to the compulsory powers of the MHA it is not seclusion which constitutes a deprivation of liberty but the fact that he has been detained under a relevant section. The importance of the ECHR was emphasised and it was noted that appropriate local policies and procedures in relation to seclusion could prevent a breach of the patient's rights under Articles 3 and 8, even if they allow for a departure from the Code's guidance.

For further information and examples of how the Human Rights Act impacts on the Mental Health Act see Chapter 17 of Barber *et al.* (2012).

ACTIVITY **10.1**

Sample questions on the Human Rights Act

1a What were the key human rights issues in the HL v UK case decided in the European Court (the case formerly known as Bournewood)? (That is, identify the key articles which were relevant to the case and why.)

1b Which article(s) if any did the European Court decide had been breached and why?

1c What dilemmas does this judgement now pose for AMHPs in practice and how should they approach dealing with these dilemmas?

2a Who can apply to the county court for the appointment of a nearest relative?

2b What aspects of this area of law have been amended to be compliant with the European Convention on Human Rights?

2c What arguments might be put for or against seeking a nearest relative for someone who does not seem to have one at the point of assessing for a section 3 admission?

(Continued)

ACTIVITY *10.1* *continued*

Multiple choice questions

(Answers in Appendix 9)

1. Which rights are specifically enshrined in English law as a result of the Human Rights Act?

    (a) Freedom of thought, conscience and religion ☐
    (b) Freedom of expression ☐
    (c) Freedom to bear arms ☐
    (d) Freedom to give advance agreement to medical treatment ☐
    (e) The right to marry and found a family ☐
    (f) Freedom to travel without personal identification within Europe ☐
    (g) Prohibition of discrimination ☐

2. Under Article 3 (prohibition of torture) no one shall be subjected to:

    (a) inhuman or degrading treatment or punishment ☐
    (b) unwanted psychiatric treatment if detained but mentally capable ☐
    (c) seclusion for more than eight hours ☐
    (d) torture ☐

3. Everyone who is deprived of his liberty by arrest or detention shall be entitled to take proceedings by which the lawfulness of his detention shall be decided speedily by a court.

    (a) True ☐
    (b) False ☐

Chapter 11

The Deprivation of Liberty Safeguards

BECOMING AN APPROVED MENTAL HEALTH PROFESSIONAL

This chapter should help candidates to achieve the following competences:

Application of knowledge: the legal and policy framework

Applied knowledge of:

2(1)(a)(ii)   *relevant parts of other legislation, codes of practice, national and local policy and guidance, in particular the Children Acts 1989 and 2004, the Human Rights Act and the Mental Capacity Act.*

DoLS – BIA (Best Interests Assessor) competences:

6(a)   *an applied knowledge of the Mental Capacity Act 2005 and related Code of Practice;*

6(b)   *the ability to keep appropriate records and to provide clear and reasoned reports in accordance with legal requirements and good practice;*

6(c)   *the skills necessary to obtain, evaluate and analyse complex evidence and differing views and to weigh them appropriately in decision-making.*

Introduction

The Mental Health Act 2007 made amendments to the Mental Capacity Act which are covered in summary in this chapter.

There has been severe criticism of DoLS but it should be noted that many people who have effectively been deprived of their liberty (especially in community settings) have never been properly assessed or given any safeguards whatsoever. At least the process of assessment should provide some consideration of the need for safeguards during the assessment process itself. In some cases this may lead to the use of detention or guardianship under the Mental Health Act. For those who argue that a court hearing provides a greater safeguard it is also the case that many DoLS assessments lead to an eventual hearing at the Court of Protection.

The complexity of the statute has been eased by an excellent Code of Practice which explains the provisions in a far more accessible way than the statute. This chapter will draw heavily on the Code as a way of conveying information on the new procedures. For a detailed analysis of the new Deprivation of Liberty Safeguards (DoLS) procedures and for access to the statute itself see Brown *et al*. (2015).

The full title of the Code, which covers England and Wales, is *The Deprivation of Liberty Safeguards (Code to supplement the main Mental Capacity Act 2005 Code of Practice)* and will be referred to as the DoLS Code for the rest of this chapter. The DoLS Code needs to be read alongside the *Cheshire West* case that we considered in Chapter 2.

The essential characteristics of a deprivation of liberty are:

- the objective component of confinement in a particular restricted place for a not negligible length of time; and

- the subjective component of a lack of valid consent; and

- the attribution of responsibility to the state.

So where a person is under continuous supervision and control and not free to leave, then, unless they are able to give valid consent to the restrictions, they are likely to be seen as deprived of their liberty. Nevertheless the Code provides a summary of factors which are relevant in deciding what amounts to a deprivation of liberty when it states at para. 2.5:

> *The ECtHR and UK courts have determined a number of cases about deprivation of liberty. Their judgments indicate that the following factors can be relevant to identifying whether steps taken involve more than restraint and amount to a deprivation of liberty. It is important to remember that this list is not exclusive; other factors may arise in future in particular cases.*
>
> - *Restraint is used, including sedation, to admit a person to an institution where that person is resisting admission.*
>
> - *Staff exercise complete and effective control over the care and movement of a person for a significant period.*
>
> - *Staff exercise control over assessments, treatment, contacts and residence.*
>
> - *A decision has been taken by the institution that the person will not be released into the care of others, or permitted to live elsewhere, unless the staff in the institution consider it appropriate.*
>
> - *A request by carers for a person to be discharged to their care is refused.*
>
> - *The person is unable to maintain social contacts because of restrictions placed on their access to other people.*
>
> - *The person loses autonomy because they are under continuous supervision and control.*

It continues by stating at para. 2.6:

> *In determining whether deprivation of liberty has occurred, or is likely to occur, decision-makers need to consider all the facts in a particular case. There is unlikely*

to be any simple definition that can be applied in every case, and it is probable that no single factor will, in itself, determine whether the overall set of steps being taken in relation to the relevant person amount to a deprivation of liberty. In general, the decision-maker should always consider the following:

- *All the circumstances of each and every case*

- *What measures are being taken in relation to the individual? When are they required? For what period do they endure? What are the effects of any restraints or restrictions on the individual? Why are they necessary? What aim do they seek to meet?*

- *What are the views of the relevant person, their family or carers? Do any of them object to the measures?*

- *How are any restraints or restrictions implemented? Do any of the constraints on the individual's personal freedom go beyond 'restraint' or 'restriction' to the extent that they constitute a deprivation of liberty?*

- *Are there any less restrictive options for delivering care or treatment that avoid deprivation of liberty altogether?*

- *Does the cumulative effect of all the restrictions imposed on the person amount to a deprivation of liberty, even if individually they would not?*

In situations where an incapacitated adult is deprived of their liberty, or at risk of being deprived of their liberty, in a care home or hospital setting, the DoLS procedure should be set in motion. The managing authority has the responsibility of applying for an authorisation of deprivation of liberty. The managing authority is whoever is responsible for running the hospital or care home. They apply to the supervisory body which will, in England, be the local authority.

The supervisory body then sets in motion six assessments which must be carried out by two or more qualified people. In practice the assessors will usually be a doctor and a best interests assessor (referred to after this as a BIA). The assessments are: age, no refusals, mental capacity, mental health, eligibility and best interests. Each of these will be described below but before we consider the six assessments it is worth looking at the dramatic effect of the *Cheshire West* case on the number of referrals for DoLS.

DoLS referrals

In 2013–14 there were 13,714 recorded referrals for DoLS assessments in England. This increased dramatically to 129,688 in the following year. There were similar increases in Wales. The impact on practice has been enormous. As with guardianship there are significant variations between local authorities, as Table 11.1 shows. Dorset, for example, had 770 referrals per 100,000 population. The figure for Cumbria was just 87. The numbers of DoLS granted also vary as can be seen in Table 11.2.

Table 11.1   DoLS referrals for 14 English local authorities, 2013–14 and 2014–15

Local authority	Population	2013–14	per 100,000	2014–15	per 100,000	more referrals
Dorset	414,900	228	55	3195	770	14x
Bournemouth	186,744	148	79	1264	677	9x
Poole	148,615	88	59	978	658	11x
Cornwall*	537,914	158	29	2331	433	15x
Hampshire	1,344,610	361	27	5447	405	15x
Portsmouth	206,836	67	32	807	390	12x
Isle of Wight	140,500	29	21	534	380	18x
Southampton*	239,428	112	47	810	338	7x
Surrey	1,132,390	112	10	3013	266	27x
Somerset	530,100	95	18	1248	235	13x
Birmingham	1,085,417	192	18	2249	207	12x
Lambeth	318,200	47	15	384	121	8x
Lewisham	291,900	34	12	294	101	9x
Cumbria	499,900	98	20	434	87	4x
Total England	**54,316,600**	**13,714**	**25**	**129,688**	**239**	**9x**

* Some estimation because of incomplete returns.

Sources: Office for National Statistics and Health and Social Care Information Service.

Table 11.2   DoLS granted in 2014–15 for 14 English local authorities

Local authority	Population	DoLS granted	Per 100,000
Sunderland	275,500	1195	433
Bedford Borough	163,900	655	399
Portsmouth	206,836	700	338
Poole	148,615	415	279
Tower Hamlets	284,000	450	158
Bournemouth	186,744	255	137
Dorset	414,900	510	123
Southampton*	239,428	195	81
Hampshire	1,344,610	1080	80
Isle of Wight	140,500	70	50
Cumbria	499,900	235	47
Cornwall*	537,914	170	32
Surrey	1,132,390	275	24
Croydon	342,000	70	20
Total England	**54,316,600**	**54,775**	**101**

* Some estimation because of incomplete returns.

Sources: Office for National Statistics and Health and Social Care Information Service.

Table 11.3 DoLS not signed off in 2014–15 for 13 English local authorities

Local authority	Population	Applications for DoLS	Not signed off yet	% referrals outstanding
Cumbria	499,900	480	0	0
Sunderland	275,500	1350	0	0
Portsmouth	206,836	785	0	0
Poole	148,615	975	325	33
Bournemouth	186,744	1270	605	48
Dorset	414,900	3200	1750	55
Hampshire	1,344,610	5440	3380	62
Devon	744,282	2695	1755	65
Southampton	239,428	730	485	66
Isle of Wight	140,500	535	365	68
Cornwall	537,914	2415	1825	76
Surrey	1,132,390	3050	2475	81
Torbay	131,492	680	600	88
Total England	**54,316,600**	**137,875**	**56,820**	**41**

Sources: Office for National Statistics and Health and Social Care Information Service.

Finally, as a rather dramatic indication of the increase in workloads for BIAs (including many AMHPs) in 2014–15, over 40 per cent of the referrals were outstanding at the end of the year. Again, Table 11.3 shows some of the local authority variations.

The six assessments

In contrast with detention or guardianship under the Mental Health Act, there are no forms prescribed by the Regulations for these assessments. However, standard forms are available and the use of these is strongly advised. There are different forms for England and Wales. The forms take people through the complex procedures in a way that asks all the relevant questions and leaves them to concentrate on their own professional judgement.

Age

(This will be carried out by a BIA in England.)

The person must be, or believed to be, 18 years of age or older. If there is no documentary evidence of age the assessor has to use their own judgement.

No refusals

(This will be carried out by a BIA.)

The assessor needs to establish if a deprivation of liberty would conflict with any advance or substituted decision. This could be an advance decision made by the person refusing all or part of the proposed care and treatment, or it could be a refusal by either a donee/appointee (under an LPA), or it could be the objection of a deputy who has been appointed by the Court of Protection. If there is a conflict the DoLS procedures cannot be used.

Mental capacity

(This can be carried out by a BIA or by a doctor approved as a mental health assessor.)

The individual's capacity needs to be assessed in relation to the decision about residence in a residential care home or in a hospital for the purpose of providing care and treatment. The test for capacity is the one contained in the Mental Capacity Act. If the person has capacity then, again, the DoLS procedure cannot be used.

Mental health

(This needs to be carried out by a doctor approved under section 12 of the MHA, or a doctor with a minimum of three years' post-registration experience in the diagnosis or treatment of mental disorder. Both need to complete a DoLS course provided by the RCP. Separate requirements in Wales.)

The doctor must establish if the relevant person has a mental disorder as defined by the Mental Health Act 1983, i.e. 'any disorder or disability of the mind'. This will exclude those solely with dependence upon alcohol or drugs, but will include those with a learning disability whether or not they exhibit 'abnormally aggressive or seriously irresponsible conduct'. Therefore the DoLS procedure may be used for people with a learning disability who would not be eligible for guardianship (s7) or detention for treatment (s3) of the MHA. The requirement to meet the definition of mental disorder could also, in rare cases, exclude someone who lacks capacity because of an impairment in the functioning of the brain which has not affected their mind.

Eligibility

(This needs to be carried out by a doctor approved as a mental health assessor or a BIA who is also an AMHP.)

This involves establishing if there are requirements placed upon the relevant person that would mean that they are not eligible for DoLS. A patient subject to most forms of detention under the MHA would not be eligible for DoLS. Similarly a deprivation of liberty could not be granted if it would be inconsistent with an obligation placed upon a patient subject to section 17 leave of absence or a patient who is subject to guardianship, a community treatment order or to conditional discharge. A patient who could be detained under the MHA would not be eligible for DoLS.

Best interests

(This needs to be carried out by an AMHP, social worker, nurse, occupational therapist or psychologist who is two years post-qualification and has completed approved BIA training.)

Best interests assessors must satisfy themselves that: the person is, or is going to be, a detained resident in a care home or hospital. This requires them to establish if the person's care and treatment is, or will amount to, a deprivation of liberty. In some cases the supervisory body may want this part of the assessment to be carried out at an early stage. If the BIA were to find that there was no deprivation of liberty the whole process could be called to a halt (which could save considerable work and expense).

If there is a deprivation of liberty the BIA needs to assess if it would be in the person's best interests to be a detained resident or patient; if it is necessary for the person to be a detained resident or patient to prevent harm to himself, and if a deprivation of liberty is a proportionate response to the likelihood of the person suffering harm and the seriousness of that harm.

During this process the BIA will also:

- identify a representative for the person;

- consider any conditions to be attached to the deprivation of liberty; and

- suggest the length of time for which a deprivation of liberty should be granted.

As part of the assessment the BIA needs to see if there are appropriate persons such as friends or family members who can be consulted as part of the process of deciding on the person's best interests. If they decide that there is no such person then an independent mental capacity advocate (IMCA) must be appointed.

The best interests checklist from section 4 of the MCA applies to BIA assessments. In addition they must consider the additional factors outlined at para. 4.61 of the DoLS Code:

- whether any harm to the person could arise if the deprivation of liberty does not take place;

- what that harm would be;

- how likely that harm is to arise (i.e. is the level of risk sufficient to justify a step as serious as depriving a person of liberty?);

- what other care options there are which could avoid deprivation of liberty; and

- if deprivation of liberty is currently unavoidable, what action could be taken to avoid it in the future.

If they are satisfied from the written evidence that all of the assessments are met, the supervisory body will give a standard authorisation. This could last for up to a year. If any of the six assessments results in a negative answer, then a standard authorisation cannot be given.

Discussion

Many AMHPs are not best interests assessors despite the government's original expectations that all BIAs would be AMHPs. This is partly because many AMHPs were unhappy with the failure of pay and conditions to keep pace with the increased demands of their role under the Mental Health Act. An awareness of the complexity of the BIA role, together with professional experience, has led the author to form the opinion that it is a great pity that the potential importance of the BIA role was underestimated by the government. The training for the role is far shorter and less demanding than that of the AMHP.

Cases such as *London Borough of Hillingdon* v *Neary* (2011) suggest that the role might have been better performed by AMHPs. However, the sheer volume of work may lead to changes and learning from experience. It may also be the case that more AMHPs will now train to fulfil the function.

Where there is a deprivation of liberty there are questions about the value of the safeguards with DoLS. Hale (2010) points out that if the MHA is used, the time limits are shorter and there is speedy access to a tribunal rather than to the court. She compares the length and complexity of the proceedings in two Court of Protection (CoP) cases with tribunal proceedings, and notes that a patient can represent themselves before a tribunal whereas the CoP requires the person to be represented by a litigation friend. The MHA has detailed rules on consent to treatment whereas the MCA leaves this to the general principles. Having considered guardianship Hale states:

> One is left wondering whether the elaborate DoLS machinery would have been needed at all, if guardianship had been adapted to include a power to detain the patient in the place where the guardian required him to live. The MHA would have had to be used more often for compliant patients both in and out of hospital, but would that have been such a bad thing?

(2010, p308)

These issues are pursued in more depth in Chapter 2 in the conclusion to the material on guardianship.

DoLS vs detention under the Mental Health Act

Where AMHPs, BIAs and other decision-makers are faced with the compliant, mentally disordered person in hospital (or in need of admission) who is in effect deprived of their liberty, unless they decide that the person does not need detention, they are faced with a difficult decision as to which Act to rely on. Chapter 2 explored the legal reasons for that dilemma. Here, to assist in the decision-making process, is a summary of the key differences between the two pieces of legislation, with particular emphasis on the relevant safeguards. When making a decision an AMHP would need to record the key elements in their decision.

As we saw in Chapter 2 the Code states in para 13.59 that:

> *the nature of the safeguards provided under the two regimes are different and decision-makers will wish to exercise their professional judgement in determining which safeguards are more likely to best protect the interests of the patient in the particular circumstances of each individual case.*

This view is supported by Table 11.4 and the AMHP should consider the circumstances case by case.

Table 11.4   A comparison between the MHA and MCA when depriving someone of their liberty

Feature or safeguard	Mental Health Act	Mental Capacity Act
Urgent detention without full assessment involving AMHP/ BIA	Up to 72 hours	Up to 7 days, renewable for further 7 days
Who assesses	AMHP + medical practitioner(s)	BIA + medical practitioner
Who agrees to the DOL	Hospital managers	Supervisory body (LA)
Grounds	Mental disorder (of nature or degree), for health or safety of self or protection of others	Mental incapacity, mental disorder, 18+, no refusals, best interests, eligibility
Maximum time limits on DOL	Fixed e.g. 28 days, 6 months	Flexible up to a year
Who can discharge	Responsible clinician First-tier Tribunal Hospital managers Nearest relative	Supervisory body Court of Protection
Court appeal against detention	Tribunal + sometimes an automatic hearing	Court of Protection
Family or friend	Nearest relative	Relevant person's representative
Advocate	IMHA	IMCA
Inspection or review	CQC	CQC
Returning person who absconds	S18	Nothing specific
Treatment without consent	Part 4 of MHA + Code	S5 MCA
After-care	Eligibility for s117 after-care if detained on s3	No equivalent

---

ACTIVITY 11.1

Multiple choice questions

(Answers in Appendix 9)

1. Which of the following assessments form part of the Deprivation of Liberty Safeguards procedures?

    (a) Best interests ☐
    (b) No refusals (e.g. objection from LPA donee) ☐
    (c) Age ☐
    (d) Financial ☐
    (e) Eligibility ☐
    (f) Whether receiving MHA section 117 after-care ☐
    (g) Mental capacity ☐
    (h) Abnormally aggressive or seriously irresponsible conduct ☐
    (i) Mental disorder ☐

2. Under the DoLS procedure one professional could carry out all of the required assessments.

    (a) True ☐
    (b) False ☐

3. Under the DoLS procedure a representative will be appointed for the individual after deprivation of liberty has been authorised.

    (a) True ☐
    (b) False ☐

Appendix 1
Checklists for applications and forms

Applications for compulsory hospital admission or guardianship

YOU SHOULD BE ABLE TO ANSWER 'YES' TO ALL THE NUMBERED QUESTIONS OR BE ABLE TO FOLLOW THE INSTRUCTIONS. YOU MAY ALSO FIND HELPFUL THE GENERAL POINTS WHICH ARE PRINTED AT THE END OF SECTION 4 ADMISSIONS.

Important: All the forms were amended in 2008. Ensure you use current versions of the forms. Welsh forms are identified in Appendix 5.

SECTION 2 – Admission for assessment (lasting for up to 28 days)

(1) Are you of the opinion 'having regard to any wishes expressed by relatives of the patient or any other relevant circumstances' that your making an application would be necessary or proper?

(2) Have you interviewed the patient 'in a suitable manner'?

(3) Are you satisfied that 'detention in a hospital is in all the circumstances of the case the most appropriate way of providing the care and medical treatment of which the patient stands in need'? Have you considered and decided against: informal admission, out-patient treatment, community psychiatric nursing support, crisis intervention centres, primary health care support, local authority social services or private provision, support from friends, relatives or voluntary organisations?

(4) Have you got two medical recommendations, which state that the patient is suffering from mental disorder 'of a nature or degree which warrants detention in hospital for assessment' and that he ought to be detained 'in the interests of his own health or safety or with a view to the protection of other persons'?

(5) Has one of the doctors had previous acquaintance with the patient? If not, every effort should be made to find one who has. If unsuccessful, you must give your reasons at the bottom of your application.

(6) Has one doctor been approved as having special experience in psychiatry? See your local list of section 12 approved doctors if you have any doubts.

(7) Have you seen the patient within the last 14 days?

(8) Have the doctors personally examined the patient together or within five days of each other? (This means five clear days so one on the first and the other on the seventh of the month is acceptable.)

(9) Can you confirm that there is no conflict of interests (see Appendix 8) unless this is an emergency?

(10) Have you checked the validity of the medical recommendations (e.g. that they have been signed and are from doctors entitled to make recommendations)? If not, and a serious mistake has been made, you could be notified and have to make a new application. Less important mistakes (e.g. spelling of names) can be corrected within 14 days of the admission. (See section 15 for more information if needed.)

(11) Have you informed the nearest relative that the application is to be made and of their rights of discharge under section 23(2)(a)? If not, you must do so after the admission if this is practicable. Inform the hospital when you have done this.

(12) Are the dates of the signatures of both medical recommendations on or before the date of your application?

(13) After signing an application you have 14 days to get the patient admitted into hospital beginning with the date when the patient was last examined for the purpose of making one of the medical recommendations. You have the authority to remove compulsorily the patient to hospital and/or to authorise anyone else to do this but should have the recommendations and application to hand to demonstrate this.

Forms required

Application on Form A2 (nearest relative would use Form A1 and an AMHP would subsequently prepare a report).

Recommendation on Form A3 (joint) or Form A4.

Note: If the request for an application to be considered came from the nearest relative and you have decided against it, you must give them your reasons in writing.

SECTION 3 – Admission for treatment (lasting up to six months and renewable)

(1) Are you of the opinion 'having regard to any wishes expressed by relatives of the patient or any other relevant circumstances' that your making an application would be necessary or proper?

(2) Have you interviewed the patient 'in a suitable manner'?

(3) Are you satisfied that 'detention in a hospital is in all the circumstances of the case the most appropriate way of providing the care and medical treatment of which the patient stands in need'? Have you decided against: informal admission, out-patient treatment, CPN support, crisis intervention centres, LA social services or private provision, support from primary health care, friends, relatives or voluntary organisations?

(4) Have you got two medical recommendations, on one form or two, which state that the patient is suffering from a mental disorder 'of a nature or degree which makes it appropriate for him to receive medical treatment in a hospital' and 'it is necessary for the health or safety of the patient or for the protection of other persons that he should receive such treatment and it cannot be provided unless he is detained under section 3 of the Act'? and that 'appropriate medical treatment' is available at a specified hospital?

(5) If the clinical description of the mental disorder indicates that the patient has a learning disability, do the recommendations make it clear that there is also abnormally aggressive or seriously irresponsible conduct?

(6) Have the doctors identified a hospital where appropriate treatment can be delivered? If a treatment plan is not clearly apparent from their forms you may need to ask them for more detail.

(7) Has one doctor had previous acquaintance with the patient? If not, every effort should be made to find one who has. If unsuccessful you must give reasons on Form A6.

(8) Has one doctor been approved as having special experience in psychiatry? See your local list of section 12 approved doctors if you have any doubts.

(9) Have you seen the patient within the last 14 days?

(10) Have the doctors personally examined the patient together or within five days of each other? (This means five clear days so one on the first and the other on the seventh is acceptable.)

(11) Can you confirm that there is no conflict of interests (see Appendix 8) unless this is an emergency (which would be very unusual circumstances for a section 3)?

(12) Have you checked the validity of the medical recommendations (e.g. they are signed and are from doctors entitled to make them)? If not, and a serious mistake is made, you could be notified and have to make a new application. Less serious errors (e.g. spelling of names) can be corrected within 14 days of admission. (See section 15 for more information.)

(13) Have you consulted the nearest relative and checked that they have no objection to an application? If you have not, would you say this was not reasonably practicable or would have involved unreasonable delay? (If unable to consult the nearest relative you should try to see them as soon as possible to let them know their rights of discharge. Inform the hospital when you have done this.)

(14) Are the dates by both doctors' signatures on or before the date of your application?

159

(15) After signing an application you have 14 days to get the patient admitted into hospital beginning with the date when the patient was last examined for the purpose of making one of the medical recommendations. You have the authority to remove compulsorily the patient to hospital and/or to authorise anyone else to do this but should have the recommendations and application to hand to demonstrate this.

Forms required

Application on Form A6 (nearest relative would use Form A5 and an AMHP would subsequently prepare a report).

Recommendation on Form A7 (joint) or Form A8.

Note: If the request for an application to be considered came from the nearest relative and you have decided against it, you must give them your reasons in writing.

SECTION 4 – Admission for assessment in cases of emergency (lasts up to 72 hours)

(1) Are you of the opinion 'having regard to any wishes expressed by relatives of the patient or another relevant circumstances' that your making an application would be necessary or proper?

(2) Have you interviewed the patient 'in a suitable manner'?

(3) Are you satisfied that 'detention in hospital is in all the circumstances of the case the most appropriate way of providing the care and medical treatment of which the patient stands in need'? Have you considered: informal admission, out-patient treatment, community nursing support, crisis intervention centres, primary health care support, local authority social services or private provision, support from friends, relatives or voluntary organisations?

(4) Is it of urgent necessity the patient be admitted and detained in hospital for assessment?

(5) Would obtaining a second recommendation to meet the needs of section 2 involve undesirable delay?

(6) Have you got a medical recommendation which states 'that this patient is suffering from mental disorder of a nature or degree which warrants the patient's detention in a hospital for assessment' and 'ought to be so detained' in the interests of the patient's own health or safety or with a view to the protection of other persons?

(7) Has the doctor had previous acquaintance with the patient? If not, is it genuinely not practicable to find such a doctor? If unsuccessful you must give your reasons at the bottom of Form 6.

(8) Do the details on the medical recommendation correspond with those on your application?

(9) Have you and the doctor both seen the patient in the last 24 hours?

(10) After signing an application, you have 24 hours to get the patient admitted into hospital beginning with the time when the patient was examined for the purpose of making the medical recommendation or from when the application was made, whichever was the earlier. You have the authority to compulsorily remove the patient to hospital and/or to authorise anyone else to do this but should have the recommendation and application to hand to demonstrate this.

Forms required

Application on Form A10 (nearest relative would use Form A9 and if there were a conversion to section 2, through the provision of an additional medical recommendation, an AMHP would probably prepare a report).

Recommendation on Form A11.

Notes:

1. If the request for an application to be considered came from the nearest relative and you have decided against it, you must give them your reasons in writing.

2. The doctor providing the recommendation does not need to be section 12 approved and may not have previous acquaintance with the patient. This significantly reduces the safeguards for the patient and should be avoided if possible. It is important to remind the hospital to let the AMHP know if the section is converted to a section 2 so that the AMHP can inform the nearest relative as required by section 11(3).

General points for admissions to hospital from the community

If you have reached the point where you have signed an application form, the following points are worth checking:

- Has a doctor organised a bed in the hospital and is the hospital expecting you?

- Have you arranged transport? It is your job to make sure that the patient gets to the hospital. The ambulance service should assist if needed. Check any local agreements. If you are authorising someone else to transport the patient you should give them a written authority for this purpose.

- Have you made arrangements to protect any moveable property? Is there anyone to help with cancelling milk, etc.?

- You should leave a report at the hospital. This should include the patient's social circumstances and events leading up to the admission, including a note on alternatives that were not considered to be appropriate, plus any telephone numbers etc. Include details on how you identified the nearest relative and information given to them.

- Have you fully explained to the patient what is happening?

SECTION 7 – Application for guardianship (lasting up to six months and renewable)

(1) Are you of the opinion 'having regard to any wishes expressed by relatives of the patient or any other relevant circumstances' that your making an application would be necessary or proper?

(2) Is the patient at least 16 years old?

(3) If the clinical description of the mental disorder indicates that the patient has a learning disability, do the recommendations make it clear that there is also abnormally aggressive or seriously irresponsible conduct?

(4) Have you got two medical recommendations which specify the mental disorder as above and state that this is 'of a nature or degree which warrants his reception into guardianship' and this is 'necessary in the interests of the welfare of the patient or for the protection of other persons'?

(5) Has one of the doctors had previous acquaintance with the patient? If not, every effort should be made to find one who has. If unsuccessful you must give your reasons near the bottom of Form G2.

(6) Has one doctor been approved as having special experience in psychiatry? See your local list of section 12 approved doctors.

(7) Have you seen the patient within the last 14 days and have the doctors personally examined the patient together or within five days of each other? (This means five clear days, i.e. one on the first and the other on the seventh is acceptable.)

(8) Have you consulted the nearest relative and checked that they have no objections to an application? If you have not, would you say that this was not reasonably practicable or would have involved unreasonable delay?

(9) Have you checked the validity of the medical recommendations (e.g. that they have been signed and that the disorder described is appropriate for this section)? If not, and a mistake has been made, you could be notified and have to make a new application.

(10) Has the person you are naming as guardian (if not the local authority) given you a statement in writing that she/he is willing to act as guardian? Use Part 2 of Form G2.

(11) Are the dates of the signatures of both medical recommendations on or before the date of your application?

(12) You must now seek the approval of the social services department for the guardianship. You have 14 days from the date when the patient was last examined for one of the recommendations to forward the application to the responsible person in the social services department. There is no formal time limit on when the social services department then has to make a decision but any significant delay could lead to a complaint. You will almost certainly be asked to provide a detailed report on

the patient and, where necessary, on the proposed guardian to help whoever has to make these decisions. Note that the person approving the guardian and agreeing to the guardianship would not have to be an approved mental health professional.

Forms required

Application on Form G2 (nearest relative would use Form G1). The social services department would then make its assessment of the appropriateness of guardianship, usually involving an approved mental health professional in this process.

Recommendations on Form G3 (joint) or Form G4.

Note: It is also possible for someone to be transferred into guardianship from detention in hospital using Form G6. Transfers from guardianship to detention under section 3 are also possible but require two medical recommendations and a fresh application from an AMHP.

Form A2 *Regulation 4(1)(a)(ii)* Mental Health Act 1983

Section 2 – Application by an approved mental health professional for admission for assessment

To the managers of (*name and address of hospital*)

```
┌─────────────────────────────────────────────────────┐
│                                                       │
│                                                       │
│                                                       │
└─────────────────────────────────────────────────────┘
```

I (*PRINT your full name and address*)

```
┌─────────────────────────────────────────────────────┐
│                                                       │
│                                                       │
│                                                       │
└─────────────────────────────────────────────────────┘
```

apply for the admission of (*PRINT full name and address of patient*)

```
┌─────────────────────────────────────────────────────┐
│                                                       │
│                                                       │
│                                                       │
└─────────────────────────────────────────────────────┘
```

for assessment in accordance with Part 2 of the Mental Health Act 1983.

I am acting on behalf of (*PRINT name of local social services authority*)

```
┌─────────────────────────────────────────────────────┐
│                                                       │
│                                                       │
│                                                       │
└─────────────────────────────────────────────────────┘
```

and am approved to act as an approved mental health professional for the purposes of the Act by (*delete as appropriate*)

that authority

(*name of local social services authority that approved you, if different*)

```
┌─────────────────────────────────────────────────────┐
│                                                       │
│                                                       │
│                                                       │
└─────────────────────────────────────────────────────┘
```

Complete the following if you know who the nearest relative is.

Complete (a) or (b) as applicable and delete the other.

(a) To the best of my knowledge and belief (*PRINT full name and address*)

```
┌─────────────────────────────────────────────────────────────┐
│                                                               │
│                                                               │
│                                                               │
│                                                               │
└─────────────────────────────────────────────────────────────┘
```

is the patient's nearest relative within the meaning of the Act.

(b) I understand that (*PRINT full name and address*)

```
┌─────────────────────────────────────────────────────────────┐
│                                                               │
│                                                               │
│                                                               │
│                                                               │
└─────────────────────────────────────────────────────────────┘
```

has been authorised by a county court/the patient's nearest relative* to exercise the functions under the Act of the patient's nearest relative. (*Delete the phrase which does not apply*)

I have/have not yet* informed that person that this application is to be made and of the nearest relative's power to order the discharge of the patient. (*Delete the phrase which does not apply*)

Complete the following if you do not know who the nearest relative is. Delete (a) or (b).

(a) I have been unable to ascertain who is the patient's nearest relative within the meaning of the Act.

(b) To the best of my knowledge and belief this patient has no nearest relative within the meaning of the Act.

The remainder of the form must be completed in all cases.

I last saw the patient on

```
┌──────────────────┐
│   /      /       │
└──────────────────┘  [date],
```

which was within the period of 14 days ending on the day this application is completed.

I have interviewed the patient and I am satisfied that detention in a hospital is in all the circumstances of the case the most appropriate way of providing the care and medical treatment of which the patient stands in need.

This application is founded on two medical recommendations in the prescribed form.

If neither of the medical practitioners had previous acquaintance with the patient before making their recommendations, please explain why you could not get a recommendation from a medical practitioner who did have previous acquaintance with the patient –

(If you need to continue on a separate sheet please indicate here ( ) and attach that sheet to this form)

Signed   Date

/   /

Form A4 *Regulation 4(1)(b)(ii)* Mental Health Act 1983

Section 2 – Medical recommendation for admission for assessment

I (*PRINT full name and address of practitioner*)

```

```

a registered medical practitioner, recommend that

(*PRINT full name and address of patient*)

```

```

be admitted to a hospital for assessment in accordance with Part 2 of the Mental Health Act 1983.

I last examined this patient on

```
  /   /
```
[date],

* I had previous acquaintance with the patient before I conducted that examination.

* I am approved under section 12 of the Act as having special experience in the diagnosis or treatment of mental disorder.

(* *Delete if not applicable*)

In my opinion,

(a) this patient is suffering from mental disorder of a nature or degree which warrants the detention of the patient in hospital for assessment (or for assessment followed by medical treatment) for at least a limited period,

AND

(b) ought to be so detained
    (i) in the interests of the patient's own health
    (ii) in the interests of the patient's own safety
    (iii) with a view to the protection of other persons.
    (*Delete the indents not applicable*)

My reasons for these opinions are:

(Your reasons should cover both (a) and (b) above. As part of them: describe the patient's symptoms and behaviour and explain how those symptoms and behaviour lead you to your opinion; explain why the patient ought to be admitted to hospital and why informal admission is not appropriate.)

(If you need to continue on a separate sheet please indicate here ( ) and attach that sheet to this form)

Signed   Date

/   /

Form A6 *Regulation 4(1)(c)(ii)* Mental Health Act 1983

Section 3 – Application by an approved mental health professional for admission for treatment

To the managers of (*name and address of hospital*)

```
┌─────────────────────────────────────────────────────────────┐
│                                                               │
│                                                               │
│                                                               │
│                                                               │
└─────────────────────────────────────────────────────────────┘
```

I (*PRINT your full name and address*)

```
┌─────────────────────────────────────────────────────────────┐
│                                                               │
│                                                               │
│                                                               │
│                                                               │
└─────────────────────────────────────────────────────────────┘
```

apply for the admission of (*PRINT full name and address of patient*)

```
┌─────────────────────────────────────────────────────────────┐
│                                                               │
│                                                               │
│                                                               │
│                                                               │
└─────────────────────────────────────────────────────────────┘
```

for treatment in accordance with Part 2 of the Mental Health Act 1983.

I am acting on behalf of (*name of local social services authority*)

```
┌─────────────────────────────────────────────────────────────┐
│                                                               │
│                                                               │
│                                                               │
│                                                               │
└─────────────────────────────────────────────────────────────┘
```

and am approved to act as an approved mental health professional for the purposes of the Act by (*delete as appropriate*)

    that authority

    (*name of local social services authority that approved you, if different*)

```
┌─────────────────────────────────────────────────────────────┐
│                                                               │
│                                                               │
│                                                               │
└─────────────────────────────────────────────────────────────┘
```

Complete the following where consultation with the nearest relative has taken place.

Complete (a) or (b) and delete the other

(a) I have consulted (*PRINT full name and address*)

    who to the best of my knowledge and belief is the patient's nearest relative within the meaning of the Act.

169

(b) I have consulted (*PRINT full name and address*)

```
┌─────────────────────────────────────────────────────┐
│                                                       │
│                                                       │
│                                                       │
│                                                       │
└─────────────────────────────────────────────────────┘
```

who I understand has been authorised by a county court/the patient's nearest relative* to exercise the functions under the Act of the patient's nearest relative. (**Delete the phrase which does not apply*)

That person has not notified me or the local social services authority on whose behalf I am acting that he or she objects to this application being made.

Complete the following where the nearest relative has not been consulted.

Delete whichever two of (a), (b) and (c) do not apply.

(a) I have been unable to ascertain who is this patient's nearest relative within the meaning of the Act.

(b) To the best of my knowledge and belief this patient has no nearest relative within the meaning of the Act.

(c) I understand that (*PRINT full name and address*)

```
┌─────────────────────────────────────────────────────┐
│                                                       │
│                                                       │
│                                                       │
│                                                       │
└─────────────────────────────────────────────────────┘
```

is

(i)   this patient's nearest relative within the meaning of the Act,

(ii)   authorised to exercise the functions of this patient's nearest relative under the Act,

(*Delete either (i) or (ii)*)

but in my opinion it is not reasonably practicable/would involve unreasonable delay (delete as appropriate) to consult that person before making this application, because –

```
┌─────────────────────────────────────────────────────┐
│                                                       │
│                                                       │
│                                                       │
│                                                       │
│                                                       │
│                                                       │
│                                                       │
│                                                       │
│ (If you need to continue on a separate sheet please  │
│ indicate here ( ) and attach that sheet to this form)│
└─────────────────────────────────────────────────────┘
```

The remainder of this form must be completed in all cases

I saw the patient on

Signed   Date

	/	/

which was within the period of 14 days ending on the day this application is completed.

I have interviewed the patient and I am satisfied that detention in a hospital is in all the circumstances of the case the most appropriate way of providing the care and medical treatment of which the patient stands in need.

This application is founded on two medical recommendations in the prescribed form.

If neither of the medical practitioners had previous acquaintance with the patient before making their recommendations, please explain why you could not get a recommendation from a medical practitioner who did have previous acquaintance with the patient –

(If you need to continue on a separate sheet please indicate here ( ) and attach that sheet to this form)

Signed   Date

	/	/

Form A8 *Regulation 4(1)(d)(ii)* Mental Health Act 1983

Section 3 – Medical recommendation for admission for treatment

I (PRINT full name and address of practitioner)

	/ /

a registered medical practitioner, recommend that

(PRINT full name and address of patient)

	/ /

be admitted to a hospital for treatment in accordance with Part 2 of the Mental Health Act 1983.

I last examined this patient on

/   /

[date],

* I had previous acquaintance with the patient before I conducted that examination.

* I am approved under section 12 of the Act as having special experience in the diagnosis or treatment of mental disorder.

(* Delete if not applicable)

In my opinion,

(a) this patient is suffering from mental disorder of a nature or degree which makes it appropriate for the patient to receive medical treatment in a hospital,

AND

(b) it is necessary

  (i) for the patient's own health
  (ii) for the patient's own safety
  (iii) for the protection of other persons

  (Delete the indents not applicable)

  that this patient should receive treatment in hospital,

AND

(c) such treatment cannot be provided unless the patient is detained under section 3 of the Act,

because –

(Your reasons should cover (a), (b) and (c) above. As part of them: describe the patient's symptoms and behaviour and explain how those symptoms and behaviour lead you to your opinion; say whether other methods of treatment or care (e.g. out-patient treatment or social services) are available and, if so, why they are not appropriate; indicate why informal admission is not appropriate.)

(If you need to continue on a separate sheet please indicate here ( ) and attach that sheet to this form)

I am also of the opinion that, taking into account the nature and degree of the mental disorder from which the patient is suffering and all the other circumstances of the case, appropriate medical treatment is available to the patient at the following hospital (or one of the following hospitals) –

(Enter name of hospital(s). If appropriate treatment is available only in a particular part of the hospital, say which part.)

Signed   Date

/   /

Appendix 2
The Human Rights Act 1998

Some key sections of the Human Rights Act given below are followed by the Articles of the European Convention of Human Rights that are enshrined in English law and relevant to mental health law.

Section 1 identifies which of the Convention rights are covered by the Human Rights Act. These are:

(a) Articles 2 to 12 and 14 of the Convention

(b) Articles 1 to 3 of the First Protocol, and

(c) Articles 1 and 2 of the Sixth Protocol

as read with Articles 16 to 18 of the Convention.

Section 2 requires courts or tribunals determining questions which have arisen in connection with a Convention right to take into account the decisions of Strasbourg (the European Court and Commission of Human Rights and the Committee of Ministers) so far as is relevant.

Section 3 requires legislation to be interpreted as far as possible in a way which is compatible with the Convention rights.

Section 4 gives the higher courts a power to make a 'declaration of incompatibility' where they find that primary legislation is incompatible with a Convention right. This does not strike down the existing legislation but relies on the government making a remedial order or introducing new law.

Section 6 makes it unlawful for a public authority to act in a way which is incompatible with a Convention right unless it is required to do so by primary legislation. A public authority would include a court or tribunal or any person certain of whose functions are of a public nature.

Section 7 states that victims may rely on the Convention rights in legal proceedings in UK courts and tribunals or may institute separate proceedings. Separate proceedings must usually be brought within one year of the date on which the act complained of took place.

Section 10 allows the relevant minister to amend infringing legislation by order following a declaration of incompatibility or a finding of the European Court of Human Rights if he is satisfied that there is a compelling reason to do so.

Section 11 states that the Act does not restrict any existing rights that an individual might have under UK law or his right to bring proceedings under existing law.

Section 13 obliges courts to have particular regard to the importance of the right to freedom of thought, conscience and religion.

Section 19 requires that when legislation is introduced into either House for a second reading, the minister responsible must make a written statement that he considers the Bill is compatible with the Convention rights or that he is unable to make such a statement but wishes Parliament to proceed with the Bill anyway.

The text of the European Convention of Human Rights

(This includes those articles which are enshrined in English law as a result of the Human Rights Act.)

Article 2: Right to life

1. Everyone's right to life shall be protected by law. No one shall be deprived of his life intentionally save in the execution of a sentence of a court following his conviction of a crime for which this penalty is provided by law.

2. Deprivation of life shall not be regarded as inflicted in contravention of this Article when it results from the use of force which is no more than absolutely necessary:

    (a) in defence of any person from unlawful violence;

    (b) in order to effect a lawful arrest or to prevent the escape of a person lawfully detained;

    (c) in action lawfully taken for the purpose of quelling a riot or insurrection.

Article 3: Prohibition of torture

No one shall be subjected to torture or to inhuman or degrading treatment or punishment.

Article 4: Prohibition of slavery and forced labour

1. No one shall be held in slavery or servitude.

2. No one shall be required to perform forced or compulsory labour.

3. For the purpose of this Article the term 'forced or compulsory labour' shall not include:

    (a) any work required to be done in the ordinary course of detention imposed according to the provisions of Article 5 of this Convention or during conditional release from such detention;

    (b) any service of a military character or, in case of conscientious objectors in countries where they are recognised, service exacted instead of compulsory military service;

    (c) any service exacted in case of an emergency or calamity threatening the life or well-being of the community;

    (d) any work or service which forms part of normal civic obligations.

Article 5: Right to liberty and security

1. Everyone has the right to liberty and security of person. No one shall be deprived of his liberty save in the following cases and in accordance with a procedure prescribed by law:

    (a) the lawful detention of a person after conviction by a competent court;

    (b) the lawful arrest or detention of a person for non-compliance with the lawful order of a court or in order to secure the fulfilment of any obligation prescribed by law;

    (c) the lawful arrest or detention of a person effected for the purpose of bringing him before the competent legal authority on reasonable suspicion of having committed an offence or when it is reasonably considered necessary to prevent his committing an offence or fleeing after having done so;

    (d) the detention of a minor by lawful order for the purpose of educational supervision or his lawful detention for the purpose of bringing him before the competent legal authority;

    (e) the lawful detention of persons for the prevention of the spreading of infectious diseases, of persons of unsound mind, alcoholics or drug addicts or vagrants;

    (f) the lawful arrest or detention of a person to prevent his effecting an unauthorised entry into the country or of a person against whom action is being taken with a view to deportation or extradition.

2. Everyone who is arrested shall be informed promptly, in a language which he understands, of the reasons for his arrest and of any charge against him.

3. Everyone arrested or detained in accordance with the provisions of paragraph 1(c) of this Article shall be brought promptly before a judge or other officer authorised by law to exercise judicial power and shall be entitled to trial within a reasonable time or to release pending trial. Release may be conditioned by guarantees to appear for trial.

4. Everyone who is deprived of his liberty by arrest or detention shall be entitled to take proceedings by which the lawfulness of his detention shall be decided speedily by a court and his release ordered if the detention is not lawful.

5. Everyone who has been the victim of arrest or detention in contravention of the provisions of this Article shall have an enforceable right to compensation.

Article 6: Right to a fair trial

1. In the determination of his civil rights and obligations or of any criminal charge against him, everyone is entitled to a fair and public hearing within a reasonable time by an independent and impartial tribunal established by law. Judgement shall be pronounced publicly but the press and public may be excluded from all or part of the trial in the interest of morals, public order or national security in a democratic society, where the interest of juveniles or the protection of the private life of the parties so require, or to the extent strictly necessary in the opinion of the court in special circumstances where publicity would prejudice the interests of justice.

2. Everyone charged with a criminal offence shall be presumed innocent until proved guilty according to law.

3. Everyone charged with a criminal offence has the following minimum rights:

   (a) to be informed promptly, in a language which he understands and in detail, of the nature and cause of the accusation against him;

   (b) to have adequate time and facilities for the preparation of his defence;

   (c) to defend himself in person or through legal assistance of his own choosing or, if he has not sufficient means to pay for legal assistance, to be given it free when the interests of justice so require;

   (d) to examine or have examined witnesses against him and to obtain the attendance and examination of witnesses on his behalf under the same conditions as witnesses against him;

   (e) to have the free assistance of an interpreter if he cannot understand or speak the language used in court.

Article 7: No punishment without law

1. No one shall be held guilty of any criminal offence on account of any act or omission which did not constitute a criminal offence under national or international law at the time when it was committed. Nor shall a heavier penalty be imposed than the one that was applicable at the time the criminal offence was committed.

2. This Article shall not prejudice the trial and punishment of any person for any act or omission which, at the time when it was committed, was criminal according to the general principles of law recognised by civilised nations.

Article 8: Right to respect for private and family life

1. Everyone has the right to respect for his private and family life, his home and his correspondence.

2. There shall be no interference by a public authority with the exercise of this right except such as is in accordance with the law and is necessary in a democratic society in the interests of national security, public safety or the economic wellbeing of the country, for the prevention of disorder or crime, for the protection of health or morals, or for the protection of the rights and freedoms of others.

Article 9: Freedom of thought, conscience and religion

1. Everyone has the right to freedom of thought, conscience and religion; this right includes freedom to change his religion or belief and freedom, either alone or in community with others and in public or private, to manifest his religion or belief, in worship, teaching, practice and observance.

2. Freedom to manifest one's religion or beliefs shall be subject only to such limitations as are prescribed by law and are necessary in a democratic society in the interests of public safety, for the protection of public order, health or morals, or for the protection of the rights and freedoms of others.

Article 10: Freedom of expression

1. Everyone has the right to freedom of expression. This right shall include freedom to hold opinions and to receive and impart information and ideas without interference by public authority and regardless of frontiers. This Article shall not prevent States from requiring the licensing of broadcasting, television or cinema enterprises.

2. The exercise of these freedoms, since it carries with it duties and responsibilities, may be subject to such formalities, conditions, restrictions or penalties as are prescribed by law and are necessary in a democratic society, in the interests of national security, territorial integrity or public safety, for the prevention of disorder or crime, for the protection of health or morals, for the protection of the reputation or rights of others, for preventing the disclosure of information received in confidence, or for maintaining the authority and impartiality of the judiciary.

Article 11: Freedom of assembly and association

1. Everyone has the right to freedom of peaceful assembly and to freedom of association with others, including the right to form and to join trade unions for the protection of his interests.

2. No restrictions shall be placed on the exercise of these rights other than such as are prescribed by law and are necessary in a democratic society in the interests of national security or public safety, for the prevention of disorder or crime, for the protection of health or morals or for the protection of the rights and freedoms of others. This Article

shall not prevent the imposition of lawful restrictions on the exercise of these rights by members of the armed forces, of the police or of the administration of the State.

Article 12: Right to marry

Men and women of marriageable age have the right to marry and to found a family, according to the national laws governing the exercise of this right.

Article 14: Prohibition of discrimination

The enjoyment of the rights and freedoms set forth in this Convention shall be secured without discrimination on any ground such as sex, race, colour, language, religion, political or other opinion, national or social origin, association with a national minority, property, birth or other status.

Article 16: Restrictions on political activity of aliens

Nothing in Articles 10, 11 and 14 shall be regarded as preventing the High Contracting Parties from imposing restrictions on the political activity of aliens.

Article 17: Prohibition of abuse of rights

Nothing in this Convention may be interpreted as implying for any State, group or person any right to engage in any activity or perform any act aimed at the destruction of any of the rights and freedoms set forth herein or at their limitation to a greater extent than is provided for in the Convention.

Article 18: Limitation on use of restrictions on rights

The restrictions permitted under this Convention to the said rights and freedoms shall not be applied for any purpose other than those for which they have been prescribed.

Part 2: The First Protocol

Article 1: Protection of property

Every natural or legal person is entitled to the peaceful enjoyment of his possessions. No one shall be deprived of his possessions except in the public interest and subject to the conditions provided for by law and by the general principles of international law.

The preceding provisions shall not, however, in any way impair the right of a State to enforce such laws as it deems necessary to control the use of property in accordance with the general interest or to secure the payment of taxes or other contributions or penalties.

Article 2: Right to education

No person shall be denied the right to education. In the exercise of any functions which it assumes in relation to education and to teaching, the State shall respect the right of parents to ensure such education and teaching in conformity with their own religious and philosophical convictions.

Article 3: Right to free elections

The High Contracting Parties undertake to hold free elections at reasonable intervals by secret ballot, under conditions which will ensure the free expression of the opinion of the people in the choice of the legislature.

Part 3: The Sixth Protocol

Article 1: Abolition of the death penalty

The death penalty shall be abolished. No one shall be condemned to such penalty or executed.

Article 2: Death penalty in time of war

A State may make provision in its law for the death penalty in respect of acts committed in time of war or of imminent threat of war; such penalty shall be applied only in the instances laid down in the law and in accordance with its provisions. The State shall communicate to the Secretary General of the Council of Europe the relevant provisions of that law.

Appendix 3

The Mental Health Act 1983: sections relevant to AMHPs

Part Title and examples of sections that may involve AMHPs directly or indirectly

1. **Application of Act**
   s1   definition of mental disorder

2. **Compulsory admission to hospital and guardianship**
   s2   admission for assessment
   s3   admission for treatment
   s4   admission for assessment in cases of emergency
   s5   patient already in hospital
   s7   application for guardianship
   s11   general provisions as to applications
   s12   general provisions as to medical recommendations
   s13   duties of Approved Mental Health Professionals
   s17   leave of absence from hospital
   s17A   Community Treatment Orders
   s23   discharge of patients
   s25   restriction on discharge by nearest relative
   s26   definitions of 'relative' and 'nearest relative'
   s29   appointment by county court of acting nearest relative

3. **Patients concerned in criminal proceedings or under sentence**
   s35   remand to hospital for report on accused's mental condition
   s36   remand of accused person to hospital for treatment
   s37   powers of courts to order hospital admission or guardianship
   s38   interim hospital orders
   s47   removal to hospital of persons serving sentences of imprisonment etc.
   s48   removal to hospital of other prisoners

4. **Consent to treatment**
   s56   patients to whom Part 4 applies
   s57   treatment requiring consent and a second opinion
   s58   treatment requiring consent or a second opinion
   s62   urgent treatment
   s63   treatment not requiring consent

5. **Mental Health Review Tribunals**
   s65   Mental Health Review Tribunals
   s72   powers of tribunals

6. **Removal and return of patients within UK etc.**

7. **(Repealed – used to be Court of Protection)**

8. **Miscellaneous functions of local authorities and Secretary of State**
   s114   appointment of Approved Mental Health Professionals
   s115   powers of entry and inspection
   s117   after-care

9. **Offences**
   s129   obstruction
   s130   prosecutions by local authorities

10. **Miscellaneous and supplementary**
    s131   informal admission of patients
    s135   warrant to search for and remove patients
    s136   mentally disordered persons found in public places
    s137   provisions as to custody, conveyance and detention
    s139   protection for acts done in pursuance of this Act
    s145   interpretation (includes definition of AMHP)

Note: See also various regulations, rules, circulars and the Code of Practice.

Appendix 4A
The AMHP Regulations for England

The Mental Health (Approved Mental Health Professionals) (Approval) (England) Regulations 2008 (Statutory Instrument 2008 No. 1206 (England))

The Secretary of State, in exercise of the powers conferred by section 114 of the Mental Health Act 1983,[1] makes the following Regulations:

Citation, commencement and application

1. (1) These Regulations may be cited as the Mental Health (Approved Mental Health Professionals) (Approval) (England) Regulations 2008 and shall come into force on 3rd November 2008.

   (2) These Regulations apply to England only.

Interpretation

2. In these Regulations –

   'the Act' means the Mental Health Act 1983;

   'AMHP' means an approved mental health professional;

   'approve' and 'approval' include 're-approve' and 're-approval';

   'approving LSSA' means the local social services authority in England that has approved the person to act as an AMHP;

   'Care Council for Wales' has the meaning given by section 54(1) of the Care Standards Act 2000;[2]

   'General Social Care Council' has the meaning given by section 54(1) of the Care Standards Act 2000;

'LSSA' means a local social services authority in England;

'professional requirements' means the requirements set out in Schedule 1.

Granting approval

3. (1) An LSSA may only approve a person to act as an AMHP if it is satisfied that the person has appropriate competence in dealing with persons who are suffering from mental disorder.

   (2) In determining whether it is satisfied a person has appropriate competence, the LSSA must take into account the following factors –

   (a) that the person fulfils at least one of the professional requirements, and

   (b) the matters set out in Schedule 2.

   (3) Before an LSSA may approve a person to act as an AMHP who has not been approved, or been treated as approved, before in England and Wales, the person must have completed within the last five years a course approved by the General Social Care Council or the Care Council for Wales.

Period of approval

4. An LSSA may approve a person to act as an AMHP for a period of five years.

Conditions

5. When any approval is granted under these Regulations, it shall be subject to the following conditions –

   (a) in each year that the AMHP is approved, the AMHP shall complete at least 18 hours of training agreed with the approving LSSA as being relevant to their role as an AMHP;

   (b) the AMHP shall undertake to notify the approving LSSA in writing as soon as reasonably practicable if they agree to act as an AMHP on behalf of another LSSA, and when such agreement ends;

   (c) the AMHP shall undertake to cease to act as an AMHP and to notify the approving LSSA immediately if they are suspended from any of the registers or listings referred to in the professional competencies, or if any such suspension ends; and

   (d) the AMHP shall undertake to cease to act as an AMHP and to notify the approving LSSA immediately if they no longer meet at least one of the professional requirements.

Suspension of approval

6. (1) If at any time after being approved, the registration or listing required by the professional requirements of a person approved to act as an AMHP is suspended, the approving LSSA shall suspend that AMHP's approval for as long as the AMHP's registration or listing is suspended.

(2) Where an AMHP's approval is suspended, that person may not act as an AMHP unless and until the suspension of approval is ended by the approving LSSA in accordance with subsection (3).

(3) Where the approving LSSA is notified that the suspension of the AMHP's registration or listing has ended, the approving LSSA shall, unless it is not satisfied the AMHP has appropriate competence in dealing with persons suffering from mental disorder, end the suspension of approval.

(4) Where the suspension of approval has ended, the approval shall continue to run for any unexpired period of approval, unless the approving LSSA ends it earlier in accordance with regulation 7.

End of approval

7. (1) Except where paragraph (2) applies, a person shall cease to be approved to act as an AMHP at the end of the day on which their period of approval expires.

(2) Except where regulation 6 applies, the approving LSSA shall end the approval of a person it has approved to act as an AMHP before their period of approval expires –

(a) in accordance with a request in writing to do so from that AMHP;

(b) if it is no longer satisfied that the AMHP has appropriate competence taking into account the matters set out in Schedule 2;

(c) immediately upon becoming aware that the AMHP –

(i) is no longer a person who meets at least one of the professional requirements;

(ii) is in breach of any of the conditions set out in regulation 5; or

(iii) has been approved to act as an AMHP by another LSSA.

(3) When an approval ends, the approving LSSA shall notify the AMHP immediately that the approval has ended and give reasons for ending the approval.

(4) When an approval ends, the approving LSSA shall notify that fact to any other LSSA for whom it knows the AMHP has agreed to act as an AMHP.

(5) If an LSSA approves a person as an AMHP knowing that that AMHP is already approved by another LSSA, it shall notify the previous approving LSSA.

Records

8. (1) The approving LSSA shall keep a record of each AMHP it approves which shall include –

(a) the name of the AMHP;

(b) the AMHP's profession;

(c) the AMHP's date of approval;

(d) details of any period of suspension under regulation 6;

(e) details of the completion of training to comply with regulation 5(a);

(f) details of any previous approvals as an AMHP within the previous five years;

(g) the names of other LSSAs for whom the AMHP has agreed to act as an AMHP; and

(h) the date of and reason for the end of approval, if applicable.

(2) The record referred to in paragraph (1) shall be retained by the approving LSSA for a period of five years commencing with the day on which the AMHP's approval ended.

Signed by authority of the Secretary of State for Health.

Ivan Lewis

Parliamentary Under-Secretary of State, Department of Health, 28 April 2008

SCHEDULE 1   Regulation 2

PROFESSIONAL REQUIREMENTS

The professional requirements are as follows –

(a) a social worker registered with the General Social Care Council;

(b) a first level nurse, registered in Sub-Part 1 of the Nurses' Part of the Register maintained under article 5 of the Nursing and Midwifery Order 2001,[3] with the inclusion of an entry indicating their field of practice is mental health or learning disabilities nursing;

(c) an occupational therapist registered in Part 6 of the Register maintained under article 5 of the Health Professions Order 2001;[4] or

(d) a chartered psychologist who is listed in the British Psychological Society's Register of Chartered Psychologists and who holds a relevant practising certificate issued by that Society.[5]

SCHEDULE 2   Regulation 3(2)

MATTERS TO BE TAKEN INTO ACCOUNT TO DETERMINE COMPETENCE

1. Key Competence Area 1 : Application of Values to the AMHP Role

Whether the applicant has –

(a) the ability to identify, challenge and, where possible, redress discrimination and inequality in all its forms in relation to AMHP practice;

(b) an understanding of and respect for individuals' qualities, abilities and diverse backgrounds, and is able to identify and counter any decision which may be based on unlawful discrimination;

(c) the ability to promote the rights, dignity and self-determination of patients consistent with their own needs and wishes, to enable them to contribute to the decisions made affecting their quality of life and liberty; and

(d) a sensitivity to individuals' needs for personal respect, confidentiality, choice, dignity and privacy while exercising the AMHP role.

2. Key Competence Area 2: Application of Knowledge: The Legal and Policy Framework

(1) Whether the applicant has –

   (a) appropriate knowledge of and ability to apply in practice –

   (i) mental health legislation, related codes of practice and national and local policy guidance, and

   (ii) relevant parts of other legislation, codes of practice, national and local policy guidance, in particular the Children Act 1989,[6] the Children Act 2004,[7] the Human Rights Act 1998[8] and the Mental Capacity Act 2005;[9]

   (b) a knowledge and understanding of the particular needs of children and young people and their families, and an ability to apply AMHP practice in the context of those particular needs;

   (c) an understanding of, and sensitivity to, race and culture in the application of knowledge of mental health legislation;

   (d) an explicit awareness of the legal position and accountability of AMHPs in relation to the Act, any employing organisation and the authority on whose behalf they are acting;

   (e) the ability to –

   (i) evaluate critically local and national policy to inform AMHP practice, and

   (ii) base AMHP practice on a critical evaluation of a range of research relevant to evidence-based practice, including that on the impact on persons who experience discrimination because of mental health.

(2) In paragraph (1), 'relevant' means relevant to the decisions that an AMHP is likely to take when acting as an AMHP.

3. Key Competence Area 3: Application of Knowledge: Mental Disorder

Whether the applicant has a critical understanding of, and is able to apply in practice –

(a) a range of models of mental disorder, including the contribution of social, physical and development factors;

(b) the social perspective on mental disorder and mental health needs, in working with patients, their relatives, carers and other professionals;

(c) the implications of mental disorder for patients, their relatives and carers; and

(d) the implications of a range of treatments and interventions for patients, their relatives and carers.

4. Key Competence Area 4: Application of Skills: Working in Partnership

Whether the applicant has the ability to –

(a) articulate, and demonstrate in practice, the social perspective on mental disorder and mental health needs;

(b) communicate appropriately with and establish effective relationships with patients, relatives and carers in undertaking the AMHP role;

(c) articulate the role of the AMHP in the course of contributing to effective interagency and inter-professional working;

(d) use networks and community groups to influence collaborative working with a range of individuals, agencies and advocates;

(e) consider the feasibility of and contribute effectively to planning and implementing options for care such as alternatives to compulsory admission, discharge and aftercare;

(f) recognise, assess and manage risk effectively in the context of the AMHP role;

(g) effectively manage difficult situations of anxiety, risk and conflict, and an understanding of how this affects the AMHP and other people concerned with the patient's care;

(h) discharge the AMHP role in such a way as to empower the patient as much as practicable;

(i) plan, negotiate and manage compulsory admission to hospital or arrangements for supervised community treatment;

(j) manage and co-ordinate effectively the relevant legal and practical processes including the involvement of other professionals as well as patients, relatives and carers; and

(k) balance and manage the competing requirements of confidentiality and effective information-sharing to the benefit of the patient and other persons concerned with the patient's care.

5. Key Competence Area 5: Application of Skills: Making and Communicating Informed Decisions

Whether the applicant has the ability to –

(a) assert a social perspective and to make properly informed independent decisions;

(b) obtain, analyse and share appropriate information having due regard to confidentiality in order to manage the decision-making process including decisions about supervised community treatment;

(c) compile and complete statutory documentation, including an application for admission;

(d) provide reasoned and clear verbal and written reports to promote effective, account-able and independent AMHP decision-making;

(e) present a case at a legal hearing;

(f) exercise the appropriate use of independence, authority and autonomy and use it to inform their future practice as an AMHP, together with consultation and supervision;

(g) evaluate the outcomes of interventions with patients, carers and others, including the identification of where a need has not been met;

(h) make and communicate decisions that are sensitive to the needs of the individual patient; and

(i) keep appropriate records with an awareness of legal requirements with respect to record keeping and the use and transfer of information.

Notes

1. 1983 c.20. Section 114 was substituted by section 18 of the Mental Health Act 2007 (c.12). The Welsh Ministers are making separate Regulations in relation to Wales.

2. 2000 c.14.

3. SI 2002/253. The Register is divided into parts in accordance with the Nurses and Midwives (Parts of and Entries in the Register) Order of Council 2004 (SI 2004/1765).

4. SI 2002/254.

5. The British Psychological Society is a Royal Charter body, registered as a charity in England and Wales No. 229642 and is at St Andrews House, 48 Princess Road East, Leicester, LE1 7DR.

6. 1989 c.41.

7. 2004 c.31.

8. 1998 c.42.

9. 2005 c.9.

Appendix 4B
The AMHP Regulations for Wales

The Mental Health (Approval of Persons to be Approved Mental Health Professionals) (Wales) Regulations 2008 (Statutory Instrument 2008 No. 2436 (W.209) (Wales)

The Welsh Ministers, in exercise of the powers conferred upon them by section 114 of the Mental Health Act 1983,[1] hereby make the following Regulations:

Title, commencement and application

1. (1) The title of these Regulations is the Mental Health (Approval of Persons to be Approved Mental Health Professionals) (Wales) Regulations 2008 and they come into force on 3 November 2008.

   (2) These Regulations apply in relation to Wales.

Interpretation

2. In these Regulations –

   'the Act' ('*y Ddeddf*') means the Mental Health Act 1983;
   'AMHP' ('*GPIMC*') means an approved mental health professional;
   except in the context of regulation 3, 'approve' ('*cymeradwyo*') and 'approval' ('*cymeradwyaeth*') include 're-approve' ('*ail gymeradwyo*') and 're-approval' ('*ail gymeradwyaeth*');
   'approving LSSA' ('*AGCLI sy'n cymeradwyo*') means the LSSA that has approved the person to be an AMHP;
   'Care Council for Wales' ('*Cyngor Gofal Cymru*') has the meaning given by section 54(1) of the Care Standards Act 2000;[2]
   'LSSA' ('*AGCLI*') means a local social services authority in Wales;

'professional requirements' ('*gofynion proffesiynol*') means the requirements set out in Schedule 1;

'relevant competencies' ('*cymwyseddau perthnasol*') means the skills set out in Schedule 2.

Granting approval

3. (1) Subject to paragraph (2), an LSSA may only grant approval to a person to be an AMHP, where that person is not already approved as an AMHP under these Regulations, or has not been so approved within the previous five years, if that person –

    (a) fulfils the professional requirements;

    (b) is able to demonstrate that he or she possesses the relevant competencies; and

    (c) has completed within the last two years a course for the initial training of AMHPs approved by the Care Council for Wales.

    (2) An LSSA may only approve a person to be an AMHP, where the person is not already approved as an AMHP under these Regulations, but is approved to act in relation to England, or has been so approved within the previous five years if that person –

    (a) fulfils the professional requirements; and

    (b) is able to demonstrate that he or she possesses the relevant competencies such as will enable that person to act within Wales, or if not, completes such course as the approving LSSA deems necessary to enable him or her to do so.

    (3) In determining whether a person seeking approval as an AMHP possesses the relevant competencies as required under paragraphs (1)(b) or (2)(b) above, the LSSA must have regard to the references of that person.

Period of approval

4. Subject to regulation 5, an LSSA may approve a person to be an AMHP for a period of up to five years.

End of approval

5. (1) Subject to paragraph (2) below, the approval of an AMHP will cease as soon as the period of the approval has expired.

    (2) The approval of a person as an AMHP will cease before the period of approval has expired in the following circumstances –

    (a) if that person ceases to carry out functions as an AMHP on behalf of the approving LSSA;

    (b) if that person fails to meet any of the conditions attached to his or her approval in accordance with regulation 7;

    (c) if, in the opinion of the approving LSSA, that person no longer possesses the relevant competencies;

    (d) if that person no longer fulfils the professional requirements;

    (e) if that person becomes approved as an AMHP by another LSSA;

    (f) if that person makes a written request for cessation of approval.

(3) Following the end of an approval, the approving LSSA must notify that fact to any other LSSA for whom it knows that person has agreed to act as an AMHP.

(4) If the approval of a person as an AMHP ends in the circumstance provided in paragraph (2)(e) above, the new approving LSSA must notify that fact to the previous approving LSSA.

(5) Where an approving LSSA ends the approval of an AMHP under paragraph (2), that LSSA must immediately notify that person in writing of the date of the ending of and the reasons for ending that approval.

Suspension of or conditions attaching to registration

6. (1) If at any time after being approved, an AMHP's registration or listing in accordance with fulfilment of the professional requirements as required under regulation 3(1) is suspended, the approving LSSA must suspend that person's approval for the duration of the suspension of his or her registration or listing.

    (2) In the event of conditions being attached to an AMHP's registration or listing, as the case may be, the LSSA may attach such conditions to the approval as it may deem necessary, or it may suspend the approval.

    (3) Where the suspension of approval has ended, the approval will continue to run for any unexpired period of approval, unless the approving LSSA ends it earlier in accordance with regulation 5.

Conditions of approval

7. Any approval is subject to the following conditions –

    (a) the AMHP must complete whilst he or she remains approved such training as required by the approving LSSA, at such intervals as determined by the LSSA as being necessary;

    (b) the AMHP must provide evidence to the reasonable satisfaction of the approving LSSA, at no less than annual intervals of the date of his or her approval, that he or she continues to have appropriate competence to carry out functions as an AMHP;

    (c) the AMHP must notify the approving LSSA in writing as soon as reasonably practicable if he or she agrees to carry out duties as an AMHP on behalf of another LSSA, and when such agreement ends;

    (d) the AMHP must notify the approving LSSA, in writing as soon as reasonably practicable, if the AMHP is approved by a different LSSA;

    (e) the AMHP must notify the approving LSSA immediately if he or she no longer meets any of the requirements set out in regulation 3 or regulation 8 as the case may be;

    (f) the AMHP must notify the approving LSSA immediately in the event of him or her being suspended from registration or listing, as the case may be, or having conditions attached to the same.

Reapproval

8. (1) An LSSA may grant approval of a person who has previously been approved within Wales, such approval having been in force within the previous five years prior to the proposed date of reapproval, in accordance with these Regulations where that person –

    (a) fulfils the professional requirements; and

    (b) is able to demonstrate that he or she possesses the relevant competencies.

   (2) In determining whether the person seeking approval as an AMHP possesses the relevant competencies as required under paragraph (1)(b) above, the LSSA must have regard to the references of that person.

Monitoring and records

9. (1) The approving LSSA must keep a record of all persons that it approves as AMHPs, including –

    (a) their names;

    (b) their professions;

    (c) the dates of approval;

    (d) the periods for which approval is given;

    (e) details of completion of any training referred to in regulation 7(a);

    (f) evidence provided to it by the AMHPs under regulation 7(b);

    (g) names of other LSSAs for whom such persons act as an AMHPs;

    (h) any details of the ending or suspension of approval, or conditions attached to the same.

   (2) The approving LSSA must keep the records referred to in paragraph 1 above relating to persons approved by it as AMHPs for three years following the ending of such persons' approval.

Edwina Hart, Minister for Health and Social Services, one of the Welsh Ministers, 15 September 2008

SCHEDULE 1   Regulations 2 and 3

PROFESSIONAL REQUIREMENTS

1. In order to fulfil the professional requirements, a person must be one of the following –

    (a) a social worker registered with the Care Council for Wales;

    (b) a first level nurse, registered in Sub-Part 1 of the Register maintained under article 5 of the Nurses and Midwifery Order 2001,[3] with the inclusion of an entry indicating that his or her field of practice is mental health or learning disabilities nursing;

(c) an occupational therapist registered in Part 6 of the Register maintained under article 5 of the Health Professions Order 2001;[4]

(d) a chartered psychologist listed in the British Psychological Society's Register of Chartered Psychologists and who holds a relevant practising certificate issued by that Society.[5]

SCHEDULE 2   Regulation 3(4) and (5)

FACTORS TO BE TAKEN INTO ACCOUNT TO DETERMINE COMPETENCE

Key Competence Area 1: Values-based Practice

1.1 The ability to identify what constitutes least restrictive health and social care for those dealt with or who may be dealt with under the Act;

1.2 The ability to identify, challenge and, where practicable, redress discrimination and inequality in all its forms in relation to AMHP practice;

1.3 Understanding and respect for diversity and the ability to identify and counter any decision which may be based upon oppressive practice;

1.4 Understanding and respect for individuals' qualities, abilities and diverse backgrounds;

1.5 Race and culturally-sensitive understanding in the application of knowledge of mental health legislation;

1.6 Consideration of the needs of individuals for whom Welsh is their language of choice;

1.7 The ability to promote the rights, dignity and self-determination of patients consistent with their own needs and wishes, to enable them to contribute to the decisions made affecting their quality of life and liberty.

Key Competence Area 2: Application of Knowledge: Legislation and Policy

2.1 Appropriate knowledge of and ability to apply in practice –

(a) mental health legislation, related codes of practice and national and local policy guidance, and

(b) relevant parts of other legislation, codes of practice, national and local policy guidance, in particular the Children Act 1989,[6] the Children Act 2004,[7] the Human Rights Act 1998[8] and the Mental Capacity Act 2005;[9]

2.2 Application of knowledge of Welsh language legislation and policy;

2.3 An explicit awareness of the legal position and accountability of AMHPs in relation to the Act, any employing organisation and the authority on whose behalf they are acting;

2.4 The ability to evaluate critically local and national policy and relevant case law to inform AMHP practice;

2.5 The ability to base AMHP practice on a critical evaluation of a range of research relevant to evidence based practice, including that on the impact of the experience of discrimination on mental health.

Key Competence Area 3: Application of Knowledge: Mental Disorder

3.1 Critical and applied understanding of a range of models of mental health and mental disorder, including the contribution of social, physical and development factors;

3.2 Critical and applied understanding of the social perspective on mental disorder and mental health needs in working with patients, relatives, carers and other professionals;

3.3 Critical and applied understanding of the implications of mental disorder for patients, children, families and carers;

3.4 Critical and applied understanding of the implications of a range of relevant treatments and interventions for patients, children, families and carers;

3.5 Critical understanding of the resources that might be available to provide an alternative to admission to hospital.

Key Competence Area 4: Application of Skills: Effective Partnership Working

4.1 The ability to articulate, and demonstrate in practice, the social perspective on mental disorder and mental health needs;

4.2 The ability to communicate appropriately with, and to establish effective relationships with, patients, relatives and carers;

4.3 The ability to articulate the role of the AMHP in the course of contributing to effective inter-agency and inter-professional working;

4.4 The ability to use networks and community groups to influence collaborative working with a range of individuals, agencies and advocates;

4.5 The ability to contribute effectively to planning and implementing options for care, such as alternatives to compulsory admission, discharge and aftercare;

4.6 The ability to recognise, assess and manage effectively risk in the context of the AMHP role;

4.7 The ability to manage effectively difficult situations of anxiety, risk and conflict, reflecting on the potential impact of such situations on patients and others;

4.8 The ability to balance the inherent power in the AMHP role with the objectives of empowering patients;

4.9 The ability to plan, negotiate and, manage, compulsory admission to hospital, reception into guardianship or arrangements for supervised community treatment;

4.10 The ability to manage and co-ordinate effectively the relevant legal and practical processes including the involvement of other professionals as well as patients, relatives and carers;

4.11 The ability to balance and manage the competing requirements of confidentiality and effective information sharing to the benefit of patients and other stakeholders.

Key Competence Area 5: Application of Skills: Professional Decision-Making

5.1 The ability to assert a social perspective in decision-making and to make properly informed, independent decisions;

5.2 The ability to obtain, analyse and share appropriate information from individuals and other resources in order to manage the decision-making process;

5.3 The ability to provide reasoned and clear oral and written reports to promote effective, accountable and independent AMHP decision-making;

5.4 The ability to present a case at a legal hearing;

5.5 The ability to exercise their functions as an AMHP independently, and with authority and autonomy;

5.6 The ability to evaluate the outcomes of interventions with patients, carers and others, including the identification of any unmet need.

Notes

1. 1983 c.20. Section 114 was substituted by section 18 of the Mental Health Act 2007 (c.12). The Secretary of State has issued separate regulations in relation to England.

2. 2000 c.14.

3. SI 2002/253.

4. SI 2002/254.

5. The British Psychological Society is a Royal Charter body, registered as a charity in England and Wales No. 229642 and is at St Andrews House, 48 Princess Road East, Leicester, LE1 7DR.

6. 1989 c.41.

7. 2004 c.31.

8. 1998 c.42.

9. 2005 c.9.

Appendix 5

Forms used in England and Wales

This appendix shows the statutory forms in England and Wales. Not all of the forms in England share the same title as those in Wales, and there are some differences in the content of the forms. Welsh forms are in the left-hand column with English equivalents on the right. To fill in some gaps in the sequence of the right-hand column the English forms are inserted but in italics. Generally these forms then appear again when their place in the Welsh sequence arrives.

Wales	Title of form	England
HO1	Section 2 – application by NR for admission for assessment	A1
HO2	Section 2 – application by an AMHP for admission for assessment	A2
HO3	Section 2 – joint medical recommendation for admission for assessment	A3
HO4	Section 2 – medical recommendation for admission for assessment	A4
HO5	Section 3 – application by NR for admission for treatment	A5
HO6	Section 3 – application by an AMHP for admission for treatment	A6
HO7	Section 3 – joint medical recommendation for admission for treatment	A7
HO8	Section 3 – medical recommendation for admission for treatment	A8
HO9	Section 4 – emergency application by NR for admission for assessment	A9
HO10	Section 4 – emergency application by AMHP for admission for assessment	A10
HO11	Section 4 – medical recommendation for emergency admission for assessment	A11
HO12	Section 5(2) – report on hospital in-patient	H1
HO13	Section 5(4) – record of hospital in-patient	H2
HO14	Sections 2, 3 and 4 – record of detention in hospital	H3
TC1	*Authority for transfer from one hospital to another under different managers*	*(H4)*
HO15	Section 20 – renewal of authority for detention	H5
HO16	Section 21B – authority for detention after AWOL for more than 28 days	H6
HO17	Section 23 – discharge by the responsible clinician or the hospital managers	No form
GUI	Section 7 – guardianship application by NR	G1
GU2	Section 7 – guardianship application by an AMHP	G2
GU3	Section 7 – joint medical recommendation for reception into guardianship	G3
GU4	Section 7 – medical recommendation for reception into guardianship	G4

(Continued)

(Continued)

Wales	Title of form	England
GU5	Section 7 – record of acceptance of guardianship application	G5
TC2	*Section 19 – authority for transfer from hospital to guardianship*	G6
TC3	*Section 19 – authority for transfer of a patient from the guardianship of one guardian to another*	G7
TC4	*Section 19 – authority for transfer from guardianship to hospital*	G8
GU6	Section 20 – renewal of authority for guardianship	G9
GU7	Section 21B – authority for guardianship after AWOL more than 28 days	G10
GU8	Section 23 – discharge by the RC or the responsible LSSA	No form
CP1	Section 17A – CTO	CTO1
CP2	Section 17B – variation of conditions on a CTO	CTO2
CP3	Section 20A – report extending the community treatment period	CTO7
CP4	Section 21B – authority for community treatment after AWOL for more than 28 days	CTO8
CP5	Section 17E – notice of recall to hospital	CTO3
CP6	Section 17E – record of patient's detention in hospital after recall	CTO4
CP7	Section 17F – revocation of CTO	CTO5
TC6	*Section 17F(2) – authority for transfer of recalled community patient to a hospital under different managers*	CTO6
TC8	*Part 6 – transfer of patient subject to compulsion in the community*	CTO9
TC5	*Section 19A – authority for assignment of responsibility for a community patient from one hospital to another under different managers*	CTO10
CP8	Section 23 – discharge by the RC or the hospital managers	No form
TC1	Section 19 – authority for transfer from one hospital to another under different managers	H4
TC2	Section 19 – authority for transfer from hospital to guardianship	G6
TC3	Section 19 – authority for transfer of a patient from the guardianship of one guardian to another	G7
TC4	Section 19 – authority for transfer from guardianship to hospital	G8
TC5	Section 19A – authority for assignment of responsibility for a community patient from one hospital to another under different managers	CTO10
TC6	Section 17F(2) – authority for transfer of recalled community patient to a hospital under different managers	CTO6
TC7	Part 6 – date of reception of a patient to hospital or into guardianship in Wales	M1
TC8	Part 6 – transfer of patient subject to compulsion in the community	CTO9
NR1	Section 25 – report barring discharge by NR	M2
COl	Section 57 – certificate of consent to treatment and second opinion	T1
CO2	Section 58(3)(a) – certificate of consent to treatment	T2
CO3	Section 58(3)(b) – certificate of second opinion	T3
CO4	Section 58A(3)(c) – certificate of consent to treatment (patients at least 18 years of age)	T4
CO5	Section 58A(4)(c) – certificate of consent to treatment and second opinion (patients under 18 years of age)	T5
CO6	Section 58A(5) – certificate of second opinion (patients not capable of understanding nature, purpose and likely effects of the treatment)	T6
CO7	Part 4A – certificate of appropriateness of treatment to be given to a community patient (Part 4A Certificate)	CTO11
CO8	Part 4A – certificate of consent to treatment for community patient (Approved Clinician Part 4A certificate)	CT012

Appendix 6
Tasks for AMHPs involved in MHA assessments (answers)

No.	AMHP task – identify source of words within quotation marks	Source (Act, Code or Guide)
1	To interview the patient in a 'suitable manner'.	S13
2	To have 'regard to any wishes expressed by relatives'.	S13
3	Consider all the circumstances of the case including: 'the past history of the patient's mental disorder, the patient's present condition and the social, familial and personal factors bearing on it, as well as the other options available for supporting the patient, the wishes of the patient and the patient's relatives and carers, and the opinion of other professionals involved in caring for the patient'.	Ref Guide para 8.32
4	'Because a proper assessment cannot be carried out without considering alternative means of providing care and treatment, AMHPs and doctors should, as far as possible in the circumstances, identify and liaise with services which may potentially be able to provide alternatives to admission to hospital. That could include crisis and home treatment teams.'	Code 14.34
5	Decide whether 'detention in a hospital is in all the circumstances of the case the most appropriate way of providing the care and medical treatment of which the patient stands in need'.	S13
6	Ensure that it is 'necessary or proper for the application to be made by' the AMHP.	S13
7	'Take such steps as are practicable' to inform the nearest relative that an application for section 2 has been, or is about to be, made and inform them of their powers of discharge under section 23.	S11
8	If considering section 3 consult NR to ensure that they do not object to the application being made unless 'such consultation is not reasonably practicable or would involve unreasonable delay'.	S11
9	'Take the patient and convey him to hospital' if an application is made by the AMHP.	S6 + Code
10	'If they do not consult or inform the nearest relative, AMHPs should record their reasons. Consultation must not be avoided purely because it is thought that the nearest relative might object to the application.'	Code 14.63
11	If the patient is admitted, the AMHP should make sure that any 'moveable property' of the patient is protected.	Care Act s47

(Continued)

199

(Continued)

No.	AMHP task – identify source of words within quotation marks	Source (Act, Code or Guide)
12	If the nearest relative applies for section 2 or 3, an AMHP must 'interview the patient and provide the [hospital] managers with a report on his social circumstances'.	S14
13	If required to do so by the nearest relative, the SSD must direct an AMHP 'to consider the case with a view to making an application for his admission to hospital'. If AMHP does not apply he must give his reasons in writing to NR.	S13(4)
14	'. . . provide an outline report for the hospital at the time the patient is first admitted or detained, giving reasons for the application and details of any practical matters about the patient's circumstances which the hospital should know.'	Code 14.93

Appendix 7

Practice Direction (First-tier Tribunal) (Health, Education and Social Care Chamber) Statements and Reports in Mental Health Cases

1. This practice direction is made by the Senior President of Tribunals with the agreement of the Lord Chancellor in the exercise of powers conferred by Section 23 of the Tribunals, Courts and Enforcement Act 2007. It applies to a 'mental health case' as defined in rule 1(3) the Tribunal Procedure (First-tier Tribunal) (Health, Education and Social Care Chamber) Rules 2008. Rule 32 requires that certain documents are to be sent or delivered to the tribunal (and, in restricted cases, to the Secretary of State) by the responsible authority, the responsible clinician and any social supervisor (as the case may be). This practice direction specifies the contents of such documents. It replaces the previous Practice Directions on mental health cases dated 30 October 2008 and 6 April 2012, with effect from 28 October 2013.

2. In this practice direction 'the Act' refers to the Mental Health Act 1983 (as amended by the Mental Health Act 2007) . . .

A. In-patients (non-restricted and restricted)

5. For the purposes of this Practice Direction, a patient is an in-patient if they are detained in hospital to be assessed or treated for a mental disorder, whether admitted through civil or criminal justice processes, including a restricted patient (i.e. subject to special restrictions under the Act), and including a patient transferred to hospital from custody. A patient is to be regarded as an in-patient detained in a hospital even if they have been permitted leave of absence, or have gone absent without leave.

6. In the case of a restricted patient detained in hospital, the tribunal may make a provisional decision to order a Conditional Discharge. However, before it finally decides to grant a Conditional Discharge, the tribunal may defer its decision so that satisfactory arrangements can be made. The patient will remain an in-patient unless and until the tribunal finally grants a Conditional Discharge, so this part of the Practice Direction applies.

7. If the patient is an in-patient, the Responsible Authority must send or deliver to the tribunal the following documents containing the specified information in accordance with the relevant paragraphs below:

   - *Statement of Information about the Patient.*

   - *Responsible Clinician's Report, including any relevant forensic history.*

   - *Nursing Report, with the patient's current nursing plan attached.*

   - *Social Circumstances Report including details of any Care Pathway Approach (CPA) and/or Section 117 aftercare plan in full or in embryo and, where appropriate, the additional information required for patients under the age of 18, and any input from a Multi Agency Public Protection Arrangements (MAPPA) agency or meeting.*

8. In all in-patient cases, except where a patient is detained under Section 2 of the Act, the Responsible Authority must send to the tribunal the required documents containing the specified information, so that they are received by the tribunal as soon as practicable and in any event within 3 weeks after the Authority made or received the application or reference. If the patient is a restricted patient, the Authority must also, at the same time, send copies of the documents to the Secretary of State (Ministry of Justice).

9. Where a patient is detained under Section 2 of the Act, the Responsible Authority must prepare the required documents as soon as practicable after receipt of a copy of the application or a request from the tribunal. If specified information has to be omitted because it is not available, then this should be mentioned in the statement or report. These documents must be made available to the tribunal panel and the patient's representative at least one hour before the hearing is due to start.

10. The authors of reports should have personally met and be familiar with the patient. If an existing report becomes out-of-date, or if the status or the circumstances of the patient change after the reports have been written but before the tribunal hearing takes place (e.g. if a patient is discharged, or is recalled), the author of the report should then send to the tribunal an addendum addressing the up-to-date situation and, where necessary, the new applicable statutory criteria.

Statement of Information about the Patient – In-Patients

11. The statement provided to the tribunal must be up-to-date, specifically prepared for the tribunal, signed and dated, and must include:

   (a) the patient's full name, date of birth, and usual place of residence;

   (b) the full official name of the Responsible Authority;

(c) the patient's first language/dialect and, if it is not English, whether an interpreter is required and, if so, in which language/dialect;

(d) if the patient is deaf, whether the patient will require the services of British Sign Language Interpreters and/or a Relay Interpreter;

(e) a chronological table listing:

- the dates of any previous admissions to, discharge from, or recall to hospital, stating whether the admissions were compulsory or voluntary;

- the date when the current period of detention in hospital originally commenced, stating the nature of the application, order or direction that is the authority for the detention of the patient;

- the dates of any subsequent renewal of, or change in, the authority for the patient's detention, and any changes in the patient's status under the Act;

- dates and details of any hospital transfers since the patient's original detention;

- the date of admission or transfer to the hospital where the patient now is;

- the dates and outcomes of any tribunal hearings over the last three years;

(f) the name of the patient's Responsible Clinician and the date when the patient came under the care of that clinician;

(g) the name and contact details of the patient's Care Co-ordinator, Community Psychiatric Nurse, Social Worker/AMHP or Social Supervisor;

(h) where the patient is detained in an independent hospital, details of any NHS body that funds, or will fund, the placement;

(i) the name and address of the local social services authority which, were the patient to leave hospital, would have a duty to provide Section 117 after-care services;

(j) the name and address of the NHS body which, were the patient to leave hospital, would have a duty to provide Section 117 after-care services;

(k) the name and address of any legal representative acting for the patient;

(l) except in the case of a restricted patient, the name and address of the patient's Nearest Relative or of the person exercising that function, whether the patient has made any request that their Nearest Relative should not be consulted or should not be kept informed about the patient's care or treatment and, if so, the details of any such request, whether the Responsible Authority believes that the patient has capacity to make such a request and the reasons for that belief;

(m) the name and address of any other person who plays a significant part in the care of the patient but who is not professionally involved;

(n) details of any legal proceedings or other arrangements relating to the patient's mental capacity, or their ability to make decisions or handle their own affairs.

Responsible Clinician's Report – In-Patients

12. The report must be up-to-date, specifically prepared for the tribunal and have numbered paragraphs and pages. It should be signed and dated. The report should be

written or counter-signed by the patient's Responsible Clinician. The sources of information for the events and incidents described must be made clear. This report should not be an addendum to (or reproduce extensive details from) previous reports, or recite medical records, but must briefly describe the patient's recent relevant medical history and current mental health presentation, and must include:

(a) whether there are any factors that may affect the patient's understanding or ability to cope with a hearing and whether there are any adjustments that the tribunal may consider in order to deal with the case fairly and justly;

(b) details of any index offence(s) and other relevant forensic history;

(c) a chronology listing the patient's previous involvement with mental health services including any admissions to, discharge from and recall to hospital;

(d) reasons for any previous admission or recall to hospital;

(e) the circumstances leading up to the patient's current admission to hospital;

(f) whether the patient is now suffering from a mental disorder and, if so, whether a diagnosis has been made, what the diagnosis is, and why;

(g) whether the patient has a learning disability and, if so, whether that disability is associated with abnormally aggressive or seriously irresponsible conduct;

(h) depending upon the statutory criteria, whether any mental disorder present is of a nature or degree to warrant, or make appropriate, liability to be detained in a hospital for assessment and/or medical treatment;

(i) details of any appropriate and available medical treatment prescribed, provided, offered or planned for the patient's mental disorder;

(j) the strengths or positive factors relating to the patient;

(k) a summary of the patient's current progress, behaviour, capacity and insight;

(l) the patient's understanding of, compliance with, and likely future willingness to accept any prescribed medication or comply with any appropriate medical treatment for mental disorder that is or might be made available;

(m) in the case of an eligible compliant patient who lacks capacity to agree or object to their detention or treatment, whether or not deprivation of liberty under the Mental Capacity Act 2005 (as amended) would be appropriate and less restrictive;

(n) details of any incidents where the patient has harmed themselves or others, or threatened harm, or damaged property, or threatened damage;

(o) whether (in Section 2 cases) detention in hospital, or (in all other cases) the provision of medical treatment in hospital, is justified or necessary in the interests of the patient's health or safety, or for the protection of others;

(p) whether the patient, if discharged from hospital, would be likely to act in a manner dangerous to themselves or others;

(q) whether, and if so how, any risks could be managed effectively in the community, including the use of any lawful conditions or recall powers;

(r) any recommendations to the tribunal, with reasons.

Nursing Report – In-Patients

13. The report must be up-to-date, specifically prepared for the tribunal and have numbered paragraphs and pages. It should be signed and dated. The sources of information for the events and incidents described must be made clear. This report should not recite the details of medical records, or be an addendum to (or reproduce extensive details from) previous reports, although the patient's current nursing plan should be attached. In relation to the patient's current in-patient episode, the report must briefly describe the patient's current mental health presentation, and must include:

   (a) whether there are any factors that might affect the patient's understanding or ability to cope with a hearing, and whether there are any adjustments that the tribunal may consider in order to deal with the case fairly and justly;

   (b) the nature of nursing care and medication currently being made available;

   (c) the level of observation to which the patient is currently subject;

   (d) whether the patient has contact with relatives, friends or other patients, the nature of the interaction, and what community support the patient has;

   (e) strengths or positive factors relating to the patient;

   (f) a summary of the patient's current progress, engagement with nursing staff, behaviour, cooperation, activities, self-care and insight;

   (g) any occasions on which the patient has been absent without leave whilst liable to be detained, or occasions when the patient has failed to return as and when required, after having been granted leave;

   (h) the patient's understanding of, compliance with, and likely future willingness to accept any prescribed medication or treatment for mental disorder that is or might be made available;

   (i) details of any incidents in hospital where the patient has harmed themselves or others, or threatened harm, or damaged property, or threatened damage;

   (j) any occasions on which the patient has been secluded or restrained, including the reasons why such seclusion or restraint was necessary;

   (k) whether (in Section 2 cases) detention in hospital, or (in all other cases) the provision of medical treatment in hospital, is justified or necessary in the interests of the patient's health or safety, or for the protection of others;

   (l) whether the patient, if discharged from hospital, would be likely to act in a manner dangerous to themselves or others;

   (m) whether, and if so how, any risks could be managed effectively in the community, including the use of any lawful conditions or recall powers;

   (n) any recommendations to the tribunal, with reasons.

Social Circumstances Report – In-Patients

14. The report must be up-to-date, specifically prepared for the tribunal and have numbered paragraphs and pages. It should be signed and dated. The sources of information

for the events and incidents described must be made clear. This report should not be an addendum to (or reproduce extensive details from) previous reports, but must briefly describe the patient's recent relevant history and current presentation, and must include:

(a) whether there are any factors that might affect the patient's understanding or ability to cope with a hearing, and whether there are any adjustments that the tribunal may consider in order to deal with the case fairly and justly;

(b) details of any index offence(s) and other relevant forensic history;

(c) a chronology listing the patient's previous involvement with mental health services including any admissions to, discharge from and recall to hospital;

(d) the patient's home and family circumstances;

(e) the housing or accommodation available to the patient if discharged;

(f) the patient's financial position (including benefit entitlements);

(g) any available opportunities for employment;

(h) the patient's previous response to community support or Section 117 aftercare;

(i) so far as is known, details of the care pathway and Section 117 after-care to be made available to the patient, together with details of the proposed care plan;

(j) the likely adequacy and effectiveness of the proposed care plan;

(k) whether there are any issues as to funding the proposed care plan and, if so, the date by which those issues will be resolved;

(l) the strengths or positive factors relating to the patient;

(m) a summary of the patient's current progress, behaviour, compliance and insight;

(n) details of any incidents where the patient has harmed themselves or others, or threatened harm, or damaged property, or threatened damage;

(o) the patient's views, wishes, beliefs, opinions, hopes and concerns;

(p) except in restricted cases, the views of the patient's Nearest Relative unless (having consulted the patient) it would be inappropriate or impractical to consult the Nearest Relative, in which case give reasons for this view and describe any attempts to rectify matters;

(q) the views of any other person who takes a lead role in the care and support of the patient but who is not professionally involved;

(r) whether the patient is known to any MAPPA meeting or agency and, if so, in which area, for what reason, and at what level – together with the name of the Chair of any MAPPA meeting concerned with the patient, and the name of the representative of the lead agency;

(s) in the event that a MAPPA meeting or agency wishes to put forward evidence of its views in relation to the level and management of risk, a summary of those views (or an Executive Summary may be attached to the report); and where relevant, a copy of the Police National Computer record of previous convictions should be attached;

(t) in the case of an eligible compliant patient who lacks capacity to agree or object to their detention or treatment, whether or not deprivation of liberty under the Mental Capacity Act 2005 (as amended) would be appropriate and less restrictive;

(u) whether (in Section 2 cases) detention in hospital, or (in all other cases) the provision of medical treatment in hospital, is justified or necessary in the interests of the patient's health or safety, or for the protection of others;

(v) whether the patient, if discharged from hospital, would be likely to act in a manner dangerous to themselves or others;

(w) whether, and if so how, any risks could be managed effectively in the community, including the use of any lawful conditions or recall powers;

(x) any recommendations to the tribunal, with reasons.

B. Community patients

15. The Responsible Authority must send to the tribunal the following documents, containing the specified information, so that the documents are received by the tribunal as soon as practicable and in any event within 3 weeks after the Authority made or received the application or reference:

- *Statement of Information about the Patient*

- *Responsible Clinician's Report, including any relevant forensic history*

- *Social Circumstances Report including details of any Section 117 aftercare plan and, where appropriate, the additional information required for patients under the age of 18, and any input from a Multi Agency Public Protection Arrangements (MAPPA) agency or meeting.*

16. The authors of reports should have personally met and be familiar with the patient. If an existing report becomes out-of-date, or if the status or the circumstances of the patient change after the reports have been written but before the tribunal hearing takes place (e.g. if a patient is recalled, or again discharged into the community), the author of the report should then send to the tribunal an addendum addressing the up-to-date situation and, where necessary, the new applicable statutory criteria.

Statement of Information about the Patient – Community Patients

17. The statement provided to the tribunal should be up-to-date, signed and dated, specifically prepared for the tribunal, and must include:

(a) the patient's full name, date of birth, and current place of residence;

(b) the full official name of the Responsible Authority;

(c) the patient's first language/dialect and, if it is not English, whether an interpreter is required and, if so, in which language/dialect;

(d) if the patient is deaf, whether the patient will require the services of British Sign Language Interpreters and/or a Relay Interpreter;

(e) a chronological table listing:

- the dates of any previous admissions to, discharge from, or recall to hospital, stating whether the admissions were compulsory or voluntary, and including any previous instances of discharge on to a Community Treatment Order (CTO);

- the date of the underlying order or direction for detention in hospital prior to the patient's discharge onto the current CTO;

- the date of the current CTO;

- the dates of any subsequent renewal of, or change in, the authority for the patient's CTO, and any changes in the patient's status under the Act;

- the dates and outcomes of any tribunal hearings over the last three years;

(f) the name of the patient's Responsible Clinician and the date when the patient came under the care of that clinician;

(g) the name and contact details of the patient's Care Co-ordinator, Community Psychiatric Nurse, and/or Social Worker/AMHP;

(h) the name and address of the local social services authority which has the duty to provide Section 117 after-care services;

(i) the name and address of the NHS body which has the duty to provide Section 117 after-care services;

(j) the name and address of any legal representative acting for the patient;

(k) the name and address of the patient's Nearest Relative or of the person exercising that function, whether the patient has made any request that their Nearest Relative should not be consulted or should not be kept informed about the patient's care or treatment and, if so, the details of any such request, whether the Responsible Authority believes that the patient has capacity to make such a request and the reasons for that belief;

(l) the name and address of any other person who plays a significant part in the care of the patient but who is not professionally involved;

(m) details of any legal proceedings or other arrangements relating to the patient's mental capacity, or their ability to make decisions or handle their own affairs.

Responsible Clinician's Report – Community Patients

18. The report must be up-to-date, specifically prepared for the tribunal and have numbered paragraphs and pages. It should be signed and dated. This report should be written or counter-signed by the patient's Responsible Clinician. The sources of information for the events and incidents described must be made clear. The report should not be an addendum to (or reproduce extensive details from) previous reports, or recite medical records, but must briefly describe the patient's recent relevant medical history and current mental health presentation, and must include:

(a) where the patient is aged 18 or over and the case is a reference to the tribunal, whether the patient has capacity to decide whether or not to attend or be represented at a tribunal hearing;

(b) whether, if there is a hearing, there are any factors that may affect the patient's understanding or ability to cope with it, and whether there are any adjustments that the tribunal may consider in order to deal with the case fairly and justly;

(c) details of any index offence(s) and other relevant forensic history;

(d) a chronology listing the patient's previous involvement with mental health services including any admissions to, discharge from and recall to hospital;

(e) reasons for any previous admission or recall to hospital;

(f) the circumstances leading up to the patient's most recent admission to hospital;

(g) the circumstances leading up to the patient's discharge onto a CTO;

(h) any conditions to which the patient is subject under Section 17B, and details of the patient's compliance;

(i) whether the patient is now suffering from a mental disorder and, if so, what the diagnosis is and why;

(j) whether the patient has a learning disability and, if so, whether that disability is associated with abnormally aggressive or seriously irresponsible conduct;

(k) whether the patient has a mental disorder of a nature or degree such as to make it appropriate for the patient to receive medical treatment;

(l) details of any appropriate and available medical treatment prescribed, provided, offered or planned for the patient's mental disorder;

(m) the strengths or positive factors relating to the patient;

(n) a summary of the patient's current progress, behaviour, capacity and insight;

(o) the patient's understanding of, compliance with, and likely future willingness to accept any prescribed medication or comply with any appropriate medical treatment for mental disorder that is or might be made available;

(p) details of any incidents where the patient has harmed themselves or others, or threatened harm, or damaged property, or threatened damage;

(s) whether it is necessary for the patient's health or safety, or for the protection of others, that the patient should receive medical treatment and, if so, why;

(t) whether the patient, if discharged from the CTO, would be likely to act in a manner dangerous to themselves or others;

(u) whether, and if so how, any risks could be managed effectively in the community;

(v) whether it continues to be necessary that the Responsible Clinician should be able to exercise the power of recall and, if so, why;

(w) any recommendations to the tribunal, with reasons.

Social Circumstances Report – Community Patients

19. The report must be up-to-date, specifically prepared for the tribunal and have numbered paragraphs and pages. It should be signed and dated. The sources of

information for the events and incidents described must be made clear. This report should not be an addendum to (or reproduce extensive details from) previous reports, but must briefly describe the patient's recent relevant history and current presentation, and must include:

(a) whether there are any factors that might affect the patient's understanding or ability to cope with a hearing, and whether there are any adjustments that the tribunal may consider in order to deal with the case fairly and justly;

(b) details of any index offence(s), and other relevant forensic history;

(c) a chronology listing the patient's previous involvement with mental health services including any admissions to, discharge from and recall to hospital;

(d) the patient's home and family circumstances;

(e) the housing or accommodation currently available to the patient;

(f) the patient's financial position (including benefit entitlements);

(g) any employment or available opportunities for employment;

(h) any conditions to which the patient is subject under Section 17B, and details of the patient's compliance;

(i) the patient's previous response to community support or Section 117 aftercare;

(j) details of the community support or Section 117 after-care that is being, or could be made available to the patient, together with details of the current care plan;

(k) whether there are any issues as to funding the current or future care plan and, if so, the date by which those issues will be resolved;

(l) the current adequacy and effectiveness of the care plan;

(m) the strengths or positive factors relating to the patient;

(n) a summary of the patient's current progress, behaviour, compliance and insight;

(o) details of any incidents where the patient has harmed themselves or others, or threatened harm, or damaged property, or threatened damage;

(p) the patient's views, wishes, beliefs, opinions, hopes and concerns;

(q) the views of the patient's Nearest Relative unless (having consulted the patient) it would be inappropriate or impractical to consult the Nearest Relative, in which case give reasons for this view and describe any attempts to rectify matters;

(r) the views of any other person who takes a lead role in the care and support of the patient but who is not professionally involved;

(s) whether the patient is known to any Multi Agency Public Protection Arrangements (MAPPA) meeting or agency and, if so, in which area, for what reason, and at what level – together with the name of the Chair of any MAPPA meeting concerned with the patient, and the name of the representative of the lead agency;

(t) in the event that a MAPPA meeting or agency wishes to put forward evidence of its views in relation to the level and management of risk, a summary of those views (or an Executive Summary may be attached to the report); and where relevant, a copy of the Police National Computer record of previous convictions should be attached;

(u) whether it is necessary for the patient's health or safety, or for the protection of others, that the patient should receive medical treatment and, if so, why;

(v) whether the patient, if discharged from the CTO, would be likely to act in a manner dangerous to themselves or others;

(w) whether, and if so how, any risks could be managed effectively in the community;

(x) whether it continues to be necessary that the Responsible Clinician should be able to exercise the power of recall and, if so, why;

(y) any recommendations to the tribunal, with reasons.

C. Guardianship patients

20. If the patient has been received into guardianship the Responsible Authority must send to the tribunal the following documents, containing the specified information, so that they are received by the tribunal as soon as practicable and in any event within 3 weeks after the Authority made or received a copy of the application or reference:

- *Statement of Information about the Patient*

- *Responsible Clinician's Report, including any relevant forensic history*

- *Social Circumstances Report including details of any Care Pathway Approach (CPA) and, where appropriate, the additional information required for patients under the age of 18, and any input from a Multi Agency Public Protection Arrangements (MAPPA) agency or meeting.*

21. The authors of reports should have personally met and be familiar with the patient. If an existing report becomes out-of-date, or if the status or the circumstances of the patient change after the reports have been written but before the tribunal hearing takes place, the author of the report should then send to the tribunal an addendum addressing the up-to-date situation and, where necessary, the new applicable statutory criteria.

Statement of Information about the Patient – Guardianship Patients

22. The statement provided to the tribunal should be up-to-date, signed and dated, specifically prepared for the tribunal, and must include:

(a) the patient's full name, date of birth, and current place of residence;

(b) the full official name of the Responsible Authority;

(c) the patient's first language/dialect and, if it is not English, whether an interpreter is required and, if so, in which language/dialect;

(d) if the patient is deaf, whether the patient will require the services of British Sign Language Interpreters and/or a Relay Interpreter;

(e) a chronological table listing:

- the dates of any previous admissions to, discharge from or recall to hospital, stating whether the admissions were compulsory or voluntary;

- the dates of any previous instances of reception into guardianship;

- the date of reception into current guardianship, stating the nature of the application, order or direction that constitutes the original authority for the guardianship of the patient;

- the dates and outcomes of any tribunal hearings over the last three years;

(f) the name and address of any private guardian;

(g) the name of the patient's Responsible Clinician and the date when the patient came under the care of that clinician;

(h) the name and contact details of the patient's Care Co-ordinator, Community Psychiatric Nurse, and/or Social Worker/AMHP;

(i) the name and address of any legal representative acting for the patient;

(j) the name and address of the patient's Nearest Relative or of the person exercising that function, whether the patient has made any request that their Nearest Relative should not be consulted or should not be kept informed about the patient's care or treatment and, if so, the details of any such request, whether the Responsible Authority believes that the patient has capacity to make such a request and the reasons for that belief;

(k) the name and address of any other person who plays a significant part in the care of the patient but who is not professionally involved;

(l) details of any legal proceedings or other arrangements relating to the patient's mental capacity, or their ability to make decisions or handle their own affairs.

Responsible Clinician's Report – Guardianship Patients

23. The report must be up-to-date, specifically prepared for the tribunal and have numbered paragraphs and pages. It should be signed and dated. The report should be written or counter-signed by the patient's Responsible Clinician. The sources of information for the events and incidents described must be made clear. This report should not be an addendum to (or reproduce extensive details from) previous reports, or recite medical records, but must briefly describe the patient's recent relevant medical history and current mental health presentation, and must include:

(a) whether there are any factors that may affect the patient's understanding or ability to cope with a hearing, and whether there are any adjustments that the tribunal may consider in order to deal with the case fairly and justly;

(b) details of any index offence(s), and other relevant forensic history;

(c) a chronology listing the patient's previous involvement with mental health services including any admissions to, discharge from and recall to hospital, and any previous instances of reception into guardianship;

(d) the circumstances leading up to the patient's reception into guardianship;

(e) any requirements to which the patient is subject under Section 8(1), and details of the patient's compliance;

(f) whether the patient is now suffering from a mental disorder and, if so, what the diagnosis is and why;

(g) whether the patient has a learning disability and, if so, whether that disability is associated with abnormally aggressive or seriously irresponsible conduct;

h) details of any appropriate and available medical treatment prescribed, provided, offered or planned for the patient's mental disorder;

(i) the strengths or positive factors relating to the patient;

(j) a summary of the patient's current progress, behaviour, capacity and insight;

(k) the patient's understanding of, compliance with, and likely future willingness to accept any prescribed medication or comply with any appropriate medical treatment for mental disorder that is, or might be, made available;

(l) details of any incidents where the patient has harmed themselves or others, or threatened harm, or damaged property, or threatened damage;

(m) whether, and if so how, any risks could be managed effectively in the community;

(n) whether it is necessary for the welfare of the patient, or for the protection of others, that the patient should remain under guardianship and, if so, why;

(o) any recommendations to the tribunal, with reasons.

Social Circumstances Report – Guardianship Patients

24. The report must be up-to-date, specifically prepared for the tribunal and have numbered paragraphs and pages. It should be signed and dated. The sources of information for the events and incidents described should be made clear. This report should not be an addendum to (or reproduce extensive details from) previous reports, but must briefly describe the patient's recent relevant history and current presentation, and must include:

(a) whether there are any factors that might affect the patient's understanding or ability to cope with a hearing, and whether there are any adjustments that the tribunal may consider in order to deal with the case fairly and justly;

(b) details of any index offence(s), and other relevant forensic history;

(c) a chronology listing the patient's previous involvement with mental health services including any admissions to, discharge from and recall to hospital, and any previous instances of reception into guardianship;

(d) the patient's home and family circumstances;

e) the housing or accommodation currently available to the patient;

(f) the patient's financial position (including benefit entitlements);

(g) any employment or available opportunities for employment;

(h) any requirements to which the patient is subject under Section 8(1), and details of the patient's compliance;

(i) the patient's previous response to community support;

(j) details of the community support that is being, or could be, made available to the patient, together with details of the current care plan;

k) the current adequacy and effectiveness of the care plan;

(l) whether there are any issues as to funding the current or future care plan and, if so, the date by which those issues will be resolved;

(m) the strengths or positive factors relating to the patient;

(n) a summary of the patient's current progress, behaviour, compliance and insight;

(o) details of any incidents where the patient has harmed themselves or others, or threatened harm, or damaged property, or threatened damage;

(p) the patient's views, wishes, beliefs, opinions, hopes and concerns;

(q) the views of the guardian;

(r) the views of the patient's Nearest Relative unless (having consulted the patient) it would be inappropriate or impractical to consult the Nearest Relative, in which case give reasons for this view and describe any attempts to rectify matters;

(s) the views of any other person who takes a lead role in the care and support of the patient but who is not professionally involved;

(t) whether the patient is known to any MAPPA meeting or agency and, if so, in which area, for what reason, and at what level – together with the name of the Chair of any MAPPA meeting concerned with the patient, and the name of the representative of the lead agency;

(u) in the event that a MAPPA meeting or agency wishes to put forward evidence of its views in relation to the level and management of risk, a summary of those views (or an Executive Summary may be attached to the report); and where relevant, a copy of the Police National Computer record of previous convictions should be attached;

(v) whether, and if so how, any risks could be managed effectively in the community;

(w) whether it is necessary for the welfare of the patient, or for the protection of others, that the patient should remain under guardianship and, if so, why;

(x) any recommendations to the tribunal, with reasons.

D. Conditionally discharged patients

25. A conditionally discharged patient is a restricted patient who has been discharged from hospital into the community, subject to a condition that the patient will remain liable to be recalled to hospital for further treatment, should it become necessary. Other conditions may, in addition, be imposed by the tribunal, or by the Secretary of State (Ministry of Justice).

26. This part only applies to restricted patients who have actually been granted a Conditional Discharge and who are living in the community. In the case of a restricted patient detained in hospital, the tribunal may make a provisional decision to order

a Conditional Discharge. Before it finally grants a Conditional Discharge, the tribunal may defer its decision so that satisfactory arrangements can be put in place. Unless and until the tribunal finally grants a Conditional Discharge, the patient remains an in-patient, and so the in-patient part of this Practice Direction (and not this part) applies.

27. Upon being notified by the tribunal of an application or reference, the Responsible Clinician must send or deliver the Responsible Clinician's Report, and any Social Supervisor must send or deliver the Social Circumstances Report. If there is no Social Supervisor, the Responsible Clinician's report should also provide the required social circumstances information.

28. The required reports, which must contain the specified information, are:

   • *Responsible Clinician's Report, including any relevant forensic history*

   • *Social Circumstances Report from the patient's Social Supervisor, including details of any Section 117 aftercare plan and, where appropriate, the additional informa-tion required for patients under the age of 18, and any input from a Multi Agency Public Protection Arrangements (MAPPA) agency or meeting.*

29. The reports must be sent or delivered to the tribunal so that they are received by the tribunal as soon as practicable and in any event within 3 weeks after the Responsible Clinician or Social Supervisor (as the case may be) received the notification.

30. The Responsible Clinician and any Social Supervisor must also, at the same time, send copies of their reports to the Secretary of State (Ministry of Justice).

31. The authors of reports should have personally met and be familiar with the patient. If an existing report is more than six weeks old, or if the status or the circumstances of the patient change after the reports have been written but before the tribunal hearing takes place (e.g. if a patient is recalled), the author of the report should then send to the tribunal an addendum addressing the up-to-date situation and, where necessary, the new applicable statutory criteria.

Responsible Clinician's Report – Conditionally Discharged Patients

32. The report must be up-to-date, specifically prepared for the tribunal and have num-bered paragraphs and pages. It should be signed and dated. The report should be written or counter-signed by the patient's Responsible Clinician. If there is no Social Supervisor, the Responsible Clinician's report should also provide the required social circumstances information. The sources of information for the events and incidents described must be made clear. This report should not be an addendum to (or repro-duce extensive details from) previous reports, or recite medical records, but must briefly describe the patient's recent relevant medical history and current mental health presentation, and must include:

   (a) whether there are any factors that might affect the patient's understanding or ability to cope with a hearing, and whether there are any adjustments that the tribunal may consider in order to deal with the case fairly and justly;

(b) details of the patient's index offence(s), and any other relevant forensic history;

(c) details of the patient's relevant forensic history;

(d) a chronology listing the patient's involvement with mental health services including any admissions to, discharge from and recall to hospital;

(e) reasons for any previous recall following a Conditional Discharge and details of any previous failure to comply with conditions;

(f) the circumstances leading up to the current Conditional Discharge;

(g) any conditions currently imposed (whether by the tribunal or the Secretary of State), and the reasons why the conditions were imposed;

(h) details of the patient's compliance with any current conditions;

(i) whether the patient is now suffering from a mental disorder and, if so, what the diagnosis is and why;

(j) whether the patient has a learning disability and, if so, whether that disability is associated with abnormally aggressive or seriously irresponsible conduct;

k) details of any legal proceedings or other arrangements relating to the patient's mental capacity, or their ability to make decisions or handle their own affairs;

(l) details of any appropriate and available medical treatment prescribed, provided, offered or planned for the patient's mental disorder;

(m) the strengths or positive factors relating to the patient;

(n) a summary of the patient's current progress, behaviour, capacity and insight;

(o) the patient's understanding of, compliance with, and likely future willingness to accept any prescribed medication or comply with any appropriate medical treatment for mental disorder;

(p) details of any incidents where the patient has harmed themselves or others, or threatened harm, or damaged property, or threatened damage;

(q) an assessment of the patient's prognosis, including the risk and likelihood of a recurrence or exacerbation of any mental disorder;

(r) the risk and likelihood of the patient re-offending and the degree of harm to which others may be exposed if the patient does re-offend;

(s) whether it is necessary for the patient's health or safety, or for the protection of others, that the patient should receive medical treatment and, if so, why;

(t) whether the patient, if absolutely discharged, would be likely to act in a manner harmful to themselves or others, whether any such risks could be managed effectively in the community and, if so, how;

(u) whether it continues to be appropriate for the patient to remain liable to be recalled for further medical treatment in hospital and, if so, why;

(v) whether, and if so the extent to which, it is desirable to continue, vary and/or add to any conditions currently imposed;

(w) any recommendations to the tribunal, with reasons.

Social Circumstances Report – Conditionally Discharged Patients

33. The report must be up-to-date, specifically prepared for the tribunal and have numbered paragraphs and pages. It should be signed and dated. The sources of information for the events and incidents described should be made clear. This report should not be an addendum to (or reproduce extensive details from) previous reports, but must briefly describe the patient's recent relevant history and current presentation, and must include:

    (a) the patient's full name, date of birth, and current address;

    (b) the full official name of the Responsible Authority;

    (c) whether there are any factors that might affect the patient's understanding or ability to cope with a hearing, and whether there are any adjustments that the tribunal may consider in order to deal with the case fairly and justly;

    (d) details of the patient's index offence(s), and any other relevant forensic history;

    (e) a chronology listing the patient's involvement with mental health services including any admissions to, discharge from and recall to hospital;

    (f) any conditions currently imposed (whether by the tribunal or the Secretary of State), and the reasons why the conditions were imposed;

    (g) details of the patient's compliance with any past or current conditions;

    (h) the patient's home and family circumstances;

    (i) the housing or accommodation currently available to the patient;

    (j) the patient's financial position (including benefit entitlements);

    (k) any employment or available opportunities for employment;

    (l) details of the community support or Section 117 after-care that is being, or could be made available to the patient, together with details of the current care plan;

    (m) whether there are any issues as to funding the current or future care plan and, if so, the date by which those issues will be resolved;

    (n) the current adequacy and effectiveness of the care plan;

    (o) the strengths or positive factors relating to the patient;

    (p) a summary of the patient's current progress, compliance, behaviour and insight;

    (q) details of any incidents where the patient has harmed themselves or others, or threatened harm, or damaged property, or threatened damage;

    (r) the patient's views, wishes, beliefs, opinions, hopes and concerns;

    (s) the views of any partner, family member or close friend who takes a lead role in the care and support of the patient but who is not professionally involved;

    (t) whether the patient is known to any Multi Agency Public Protection Arrangements (MAPPA) meeting or agency and, if so, in which area, for what reason, and at what level – together with the name of the Chair of any MAPPA meeting concerned with the patient, and the name of the representative of the lead agency;

(u) in the event that a MAPPA meeting or agency wishes to put forward evidence of its views in relation to the level and management of risk, a summary of those views (or an Executive Summary may be attached to the report); and where relevant, a copy of the Police National Computer record of previous convictions should be attached;

(v) in the case of an eligible compliant patient who lacks capacity to agree or object to their placement or treatment, whether or not deprivation of liberty under the Mental Capacity Act 2005 (as amended) would be more appropriate;

(w) whether the patient, if absolutely discharged, would be likely to act in a manner harmful to themselves or others, whether any such risks could be managed effectively in the community and, if so, how;

(x) whether it continues to be appropriate for the patient to remain liable to be recalled for further medical treatment in hospital and, if so, why;

(y) whether, and if so the extent to which, it is desirable to continue, vary and/or add to any conditions currently imposed;

(z) any recommendations to the tribunal, with reasons.

E. Patients under the age of 18

34. All the above requirements in respect of statements and reports apply, as appropriate, depending upon the type of case.

35. In addition, *for all patients under the age of 18*, the **Social Circumstances Report** must also state:

(a) the names and addresses of any people with parental responsibility, and how they acquired parental responsibility;

(b) which public bodies either have worked together or need to liaise in relation to after-care services that may be provided under Section 117 of the Act;

(c) the outcome of any liaison that has taken place;

(d) if liaison has not taken place, why not – and when liaison will take place;

(e) the details of any multi-agency care plan in place or proposed;

(f) whether there are any issues as to funding the care plan and, if so, the date by which those issues will be resolved;

(g) the name and contact details of the patient's Care Co-ordinator, Community Psychiatric Nurse, Social Worker/AMHP or Social Supervisor;

(h) whether the patient's needs have been assessed under the Children Act 1989 or the Chronically Sick and Disabled Persons Act 1970 and, if not, the reasons why such an assessment has not been carried out and whether it is proposed to carry out such an assessment;

(i) if there has been such an assessment, what needs or requirements have been identified and how those needs or requirements will be met;

(j) if the patient is subject to or has been the subject of a Care Order or an Interim Care Order:

- the date and duration of any such order;
- the identity of the relevant local authority;
- the identity of any person(s) with whom the local authority shares parental responsibility;
- whether there are any proceedings which have yet to conclude and, if so, the court in which proceedings are taking place and the date of the next hearing;
- whether the patient comes under the Children (Leaving Care) Act 2000;
- whether there has been any liaison between, on the one hand, social workers responsible for mental health services to children and adolescents and, on the other hand, those responsible for such services to adults;
- the name of the social worker within the relevant local authority who is discharging the function of the Nearest Relative under Section 27 of the Act;

(k) if the patient is subject to guardianship under Section 7 of the Act, whether any orders have been made under the Children Act 1989 in respect of the patient, and what consultation there has been with the guardian;

(l) if the patient is a Ward of Court, when the patient was made a ward of court and what steps have been taken to notify the court that made the order of any significant steps taken, or to be taken, in respect of the patient;

(m) whether any other orders under the Children Act 1989 are in existence in respect of the patient and, if so, the details of those orders, together with the date on which such orders were made, and whether they are final or interim orders;

(n) if a patient has been or is a looked after child under Section 20 of the Children Act 1989, when the child became looked after, why the child became looked after, what steps have been taken to discharge the obligations of the local authority under Paragraph 17(1) of Schedule 2 of the Children Act 1989, and what steps are being taken (if required) to discharge the obligations of the local authority under Paragraph 10 (b) of Schedule 2 of the Children Act 1989;

(o) if a patient has been treated by a local authority as a child in need (which includes a child who has a mental disorder) under Section 17(11) of the Children Act 1989, the period or periods for which the child has been so treated, why they were considered to be a child in need, what services were or are being made available to the child by virtue of that status, and details of any assessment of the child;

(p) if a patient has been the subject of a secure accommodation order under Section 25 of the Children Act 1989, the date on which the order was made, the reasons it was made, and the date it expired;

(q) if a patient is a child provided with accommodation under Sections 85 and 86 of the Children Act 1989, what steps have been taken by the accommodating authority or the person carrying on the establishment in question to discharge their notification responsibilities, and what steps have been taken by the local authority to discharge their obligations under Sections 85, 86 and 86A of the Children Act 1989.

Appendix 8

The Conflicts of Interest Regulations for England

The Mental Health (Conflicts of Interest) (England) Regulations 2008 (Statutory Instrument 2008 No. 1205 (England))

The Secretary of State, in exercise of the powers conferred by section 12A of the Mental Health Act 1983, makes the following Regulations:

Citation, commencement and application

1. (1) These Regulations may be cited as the Mental Health (Conflicts of Interest) (England) Regulations 2008 and shall come into force on 3rd November 2008.

   (2) These Regulations apply in relation to England only.

Interpretation

2. (2) In these Regulations –

   'the Act' means the Mental Health Act 1983;

   'AMHP' means an approved mental health professional;

   'application' means an application mentioned in section 11(1) of the Act;

   'assessor' means – (a) an AMHP, or (b) a registered medical practitioner.

General

3. Regulations 4 to 7 set out the circumstances in which there would be a potential conflict of interest within the meaning of section 12A(1) of the Act such that an AMHP shall not make an application or a registered medical practitioner shall not give a medical recommendation.

Potential conflict for financial reasons

4. (1) An assessor shall have a potential conflict of interest for financial reasons if the assessor has a financial interest in the outcome of a decision whether or not to make an application or give a medical recommendation.

   (2) Where an application for the admission of the patient to a hospital which is a registered establishment is being considered, a registered medical practitioner who is on the staff of that hospital shall have a potential conflict of interest for financial reasons where the other medical recommendation is given by a registered medical practitioner who is also on the staff of that hospital.

Potential conflict of interest for business reasons

5. (1) When considering making an application or considering giving a medical recommendation in respect of a patient, an assessor shall have a potential conflict of interest for business reasons if both the assessor and the patient or another assessor are closely involved in the same business venture, including being a partner, director, other office holder or major shareholder of that venture.

   (2) Where the patient's nearest relative is making an application, a registered medical practitioner who is considering giving a medical recommendation in respect of that patient shall have a potential conflict of interest for business reasons if that registered medical practitioner and the nearest relative are both closely involved in the same business venture, including being a partner, director, other office holder or major shareholder of that venture.

Potential conflict of interest for professional reasons

6. (1) When considering making an application or considering giving a medical recommendation in respect of a patient, an assessor shall have a potential conflict of interest for professional reasons if the assessor –

   (a) directs the work of, or employs, the patient or one of the other assessors making that consideration;

   (b) except where paragraph (3) applies, is a member of a team organised to work together for clinical purposes on a routine basis and –

   (i) the patient is a member of the same team, or

   (ii) the other two assessors are members of the same team.

   (2) Where the patient's nearest relative is making an application, a registered medical practitioner who is considering giving a medical recommendation in respect of that patient shall have a potential conflict of interest for professional reasons if that registered medical practitioner –

   (a) directs the work of, or employs, the nearest relative, or

   (b) works under the direction of, or is employed by, the patient's nearest relative.

(3) Paragraph (1)(b) shall not prevent a registered medical practitioner giving a medical recommendation or an AMHP making an application if, in their opinion, it is of urgent necessity for an application to be made and a delay would involve serious risk to the health or safety of the patient or others.

Potential conflict of interest on the basis of a personal relationship

7. (1) An assessor who is considering making an application or considering giving a medical recommendation in respect of a patient, shall have a potential conflict of interest on the basis of a personal relationship if that assessor is –

   (a) related to a relevant person in the first degree;

   (b) related to a relevant person in the second degree;

   (c) related to a relevant person as a half-sister or half-brother;

   (d) the spouse, ex-spouse, civil partner or ex-civil partner of a relevant person; or

   (e) living with a relevant person as if they were a spouse or a civil partner.

   (2) For the purposes of this regulation –

   (a) 'relevant person' means another assessor, the patient, or, if the nearest relative is making the application, the nearest relative;

   (b) 'related in the first degree' means as a parent, sister, brother, son or daughter and includes step relationships;

   (c) 'related in the second degree' means as an uncle, aunt, grandparent, grandchild, first cousin, nephew, niece, parent-in-law, grandparent-in-law, grandchild-in-law, sister-in-law, brother-in-law, son-in-law or daughter-in-law and includes step relationships;

   (d) references to step relationships and in-laws in sub-paragraphs (b) and (c) are to be read in accordance with section 246 of the Civil Partnership Act 2004.

Appendix 9
Multiple choice answers

This appendix gives the answers to the questions that appear at the end of some chapters. The first number gives the chapter number, so 2.1 is the first question at the end of Chapter 2. If the reasons for the answers are not clear, return to the body of the chapter for an explanation.

1.1 For the purposes of an admission under section 3 which of the following could, by themselves, be considered as a form of 'mental disorder'?

   (a) Learning disability ☐

   (b) Dependence on alcohol ☐

   (c) Disorder of mind ☑

   (d) Dependence on drugs ☐

   (e) Disability of mind ☑

   (f) Learning disability associated with abnormally aggressive or seriously irresponsible conduct ☑

1.2 Psychopathic disorder does not appear in the Mental Health Act 1983 as amended.

   (a) True ☑

   (b) False ☐

1.3 Learning disability is defined in the Act as 'a state of arrested or incomplete development of mind which includes significant impairment of intelligence and social functioning'.

   (a) True ☑

   (b) False ☐

2.1 Which of the following criteria are necessary before a doctor can recommend compulsory admission on section 3?

   (a) The patient is suffering from a mental disorder of a nature or degree which makes it appropriate for him to receive medical treatment in a hospital. ☑

   (b) The patient is a danger to himself or others. ☐

(c) Appropriate medical treatment is available to him. ☑

(d) Treatment is likely to alleviate or prevent a deterioration of his condition. ☐

(e) Treatment cannot be provided unless the patient is detained. ☑

(f) Admission is necessary for the health or safety of the patient or for the protection of other persons. ☑

2.2 Sections 135 and 136 allow people to be moved from one place of safety to another.

(a) True ☑

(b) False ☐

2.3 A duly completed application form combined with the necessary medical recommendations provides sufficient authority for the applicant to force their way into the patient's home.

(a) True ☐

(b) False ☑

3.1 Which of the following can make a written order to discharge a patient detained in hospital under Part 2 of the Act?

(a) The hospital managers ☑

(b) The nearest relative ☑

(c) Any relative ☐

(d) An approved mental health professional ☐

(e) The responsible clinician ☑

3.2 Which of these may apply to the county court for the appointment of someone to act as nearest relative?

(a) Any relative of the patient ☑

(b) The hospital managers ☐

(c) Any other person with whom the patient is residing ☑

(d) The patient ☑

(e) An approved clinician ☐

(f) An approved mental health professional ☑

(e) The responsible clinician ☐

4.1 Which of the following may apply to admit a patient to hospital in an emergency under section 4?

(a) Any relative ☐

(b) The nearest relative ☑

(c) An approved mental health professional ☑

4.2 An applicant who conveys a patient to hospital has all the powers that police officers have when they take someone into custody.

   (a) True   ☑

   (b) False   ☐

5.1 A patient remanded to a hospital on an interim hospital order under section 38 may be detained after renewals for a maximum of:

   (a) 28 days   ☐

   (b) 12 weeks   ☐

   (c) six months   ☐

   (d) a year   ☑

5.2 A patient who is subject to a hospital order made by the court under section 37 is first entitled to apply to the mental health review tribunal:

   (a) after six months   ☑

   (b) within six months   ☐

   (c) after one year   ☐

6.1 Key principles of the Mental Capacity Act include:

   (a) A presumption of capacity exists for all those aged 16 or over.   ☑

   (b) All practicable steps should be taken to help a person make a decision before they're considered incapable.   ☑

   (c) An unwise decision implies a lack of capacity.   ☑

   (d) Acts done on behalf of an incapacitated person must be in his/her best interests.   ☑

   (e) All decisions made on behalf of an incapacitated person must be registered with the Court of Protection.   ☐

   (f) Decisions should be the least expensive available in terms of cost to the person.   ☐

   (g) Decisions should seek to be less restrictive in terms of the person's rights and freedom of action.   ☑

6.2 A decision on a person's mental capacity needs to be made in relation to the particular matter at the time when the decision has to be made.

   (a) True   ☑

   (b) False   ☐

6.3 The test for capacity under the Mental Capacity Act is whether the person can:

   (a) understand the relevant information   ☑

   (b) retain the relevant information   ☑

(c) believe the relevant information ☐

(d) use or weigh the relevant information as part of the decision-making process ☑

(e) communicate the decision ☑

(f) read and sign a consent form ☐

7.1 A mental health tribunal can vary the conditions attached to a CTO.

(a) True ☐

(b) False ☑

7.2 A patient who is subject to a section 3 detention is first entitled to apply to the tribunal:

(a) after six months ☐

(b) within six months ☑

(c) after one year ☐

8.1 Which of the following functions might be performed by the Care Quality Commission/Health Inspectorate Wales?

(a) investigating complaints by detained patients ☑

(b) discharging patients from detention ☐

(c) appointing second opinion doctors for consent to treatment provisions ☑

(d) visiting and interviewing detained patients in private ☑

(e) recommending leave of absence with a view to discharge ☐

8.2 The CQC/HIW does not have a remit to see patients subject to community treatment orders.

(a) True ☑

(b) False ☐

9.1 Where a care order is made the local authority becomes the child's nearest relative.

(a) True ☑

(b) False ☐

9.2 With the increasing problem of bed shortages, an AMHP would need to consider the Health and Safety at Work Act when deciding the timing of a visit to a patient as part of a Mental Health Act assessment.

(a) True ☑

(b) False ☐

9.3 Meeting the requirements of section 47 of the Care Act 2014 specifically requires an AMHP to perform the functions.

(a) True ☐

(b) False ☑

10.1 Which rights are *specifically* enshrined in English law as a result of the Human Rights Act?

    (a) Freedom of thought, conscience and religion   ☑

    (b) Freedom of expression   ☑

    (c) Freedom to bear arms   ☐

    (d) Freedom to give advance agreement to medical treatment   ☐

    (e) The right to marry and found a family   ☑

    (f) Freedom to travel without personal identification within Europe   ☐

    (g) Prohibition of discrimination   ☑

10.2 Under Article 3 (prohibition of torture) no one shall be subjected to:

    (a) inhuman or degrading treatment or punishment   ☑

    (b) unwanted psychiatric treatment if detained but mentally capable   ☐

    (c) seclusion for more than eight hours   ☐

    (d) torture   ☑

10.3 Everyone who is deprived of his liberty by arrest or detention shall be entitled to take proceedings by which the lawfulness of his detention shall be decided speedily by a court.

    (a) True   ☑

    (b) False   ☑

11.1 Which of the following assessments form part of the Deprivation of Liberty Safeguards procedures?

    (a) Best interests   ☑

    (b) No refusals (e.g. objection from LPA donee)   ☑

    (c) Age   ☑

    (d) Financial   ☐

    (e) Eligibility   ☑

    (f) Whether receiving MHA section 117 after-care   ☐

    (g) Mental capacity   ☑

    (h) Abnormally aggressive or seriously irresponsible conduct   ☐

    (i) Mental disorder   ☑

11.2 Under the DoLS procedure one professional could carry out all of the required assessments.

    (a) True   ☐

    (b) False   ☑

11.3 Under the DoLS procedure a representative will be appointed for the individual after deprivation of liberty has been authorised.

    (a) True   ☑

    (b) False   ☐

Appendix 10

Supervision Orders under the Criminal Procedures (Insanity) Act 1964

Schedule 1A of the Criminal Procedure (Insanity) Act 1964

Schedule 2 of the Domestic Violence, Crime and Victims Act 2004 under s5A

SCHEDULE 1A

SUPERVISION ORDERS

Part 1

Preliminary

1. (1) In this Schedule 'supervision order' means an order which requires the person in respect of whom it is made ('the supervised person') to be under the supervision of a social worker or an officer of a local probation board ('the supervising officer') for a period specified in the order of not more than two years.

   (2) A supervision order may, in accordance with paragraph 4 or 5 below, require the supervised person to submit, during the whole of that period or such part of it as may be specified in the order, to treatment by or under the direction of a registered medical practitioner.

   (3) The Secretary of State may by order direct that sub-paragraph (1) above shall be amended by substituting, for the period for the time being specified there, such period as may be specified in the order.

(4) An order under sub-paragraph (3) above may make in paragraph 11(2) below any amendment which the Secretary of State thinks necessary in consequence of any substitution made by the order.

(5) The power of the Secretary of State to make orders under sub-paragraph (3) above shall be exercisable by statutory instrument which shall be subject to annulment in pursuance of a resolution of either House of Parliament.

Part 2

Making and effect of orders

Circumstances in which orders may be made

2. (1) The court shall not make a supervision order unless it is satisfied that, having regard to all the circumstances of the case, the making of such an order is the most suitable means of dealing with the accused or appellant.

   (2) The court shall not make a supervision order unless it is also satisfied –

      (a) that the supervising officer intended to be specified in the order is willing to undertake the supervision; and

      (b) that arrangements have been made for the treatment intended to be specified in the order.

Making of orders and general requirements

3. (1) A supervision order shall either –

      (a) specify the local social services authority area in which the supervised person resides or will reside, and require him to be under the supervision of a social worker of the local social services authority for that area; or

      (b) specify the local justice area in which that person resides or will reside, and require him to be under the supervision of an officer of a local probation board appointed for or assigned to that area.

   (2) Before making such an order, the court shall explain to the supervised person in ordinary language –

      (a) the effect of the order (including any requirements proposed to be included in the order in accordance with paragraph 4, 5 or 8 below); and

      (b) that a magistrates' court has power under paragraphs 9 to 11 below to review the order on the application either of the supervised person or of the supervising officer.

   (3) After making such an order, the court shall forthwith give copies of the order to an officer of a local probation board assigned to the court, and he shall give a copy –

      (a) to the supervised person; and

      (b) to the supervising officer.

(4) After making such an order, the court shall also send to the designated officer for the local justice area in which the supervised person resides or will reside ('the local justice area concerned') –

(a) a copy of the order; and

(b) such documents and information relating to the case as it considers likely to be of assistance to a court acting for that area in the exercise of its functions in relation to the order.

(5) Where such an order is made, the supervised person shall keep in touch with the supervising officer in accordance with such instructions as he may from time to time be given by that officer and shall notify him of any change of address.

Requirements as to medical treatment

4. (1) A supervision order may, if the court is satisfied as mentioned in sub-paragraph (2) below, include a requirement that the supervised person shall submit, during the whole of the period specified in the order or during such part of that period as may be so specified, to treatment by or under the direction of a registered medical practitioner with a view to the improvement of his mental condition.

(2) The court may impose such a requirement only if satisfied on the written or oral evidence of two or more registered medical practitioners, at least one of whom is duly registered, that the mental condition of the supervised person –

(a) is such as requires and may be susceptible to treatment; but

(b) is not such as to warrant the making of a hospital order within the meaning of the Mental Health Act 1983.

(3) The treatment required under this paragraph by any such order shall be such one of the following kinds of treatment as may be specified in the order, that is to say –

(a) treatment as a non-resident patient at such institution or place as may be specified in the order; and

(b) treatment by or under the direction of such registered medical practitioner as may be so specified;

but the nature of the treatment shall not be specified in the order except as mentioned in paragraph (a) or (b) above.

Requirements as to medical treatment

5. (1) This paragraph applies where the court is satisfied on the written or oral evidence of two or more registered medical practitioners that –

(a) because of his medical condition, other than his mental condition, the supervised person is likely to pose a risk to himself or others; and

(b) the condition may be susceptible to treatment.

(2) The supervision order may (whether or not it includes a requirement under paragraph 4 above) include a requirement that the supervised person shall submit, during the whole of the period specified in the order or during such part of that period as may be so specified, to treatment by or under the direction of a registered medical practitioner with a view to the improvement of the condition.

(3) The treatment required under this paragraph by any such order shall be such one of the following kinds of treatment as may be specified in the order, that is to say –

    (a) treatment as a non-resident patient at such institution or place as may be specified in the order; and

    (b) treatment by or under the direction of such registered medical practitioner as may be so specified;

but the nature of the treatment shall not be specified in the order except as mentioned in paragraph (a) or (b) above.

Requirements as to medical treatment

6. (1) Where the medical practitioner by whom or under whose direction the supervised person is being treated in pursuance of a requirement under paragraph 4 or 5 above is of the opinion that part of the treatment can be better or more conveniently given in or at an institution or place which –

    (a) is not specified in the order, and

    (b) is one in or at which the treatment of the supervised person will be given by or under the direction of a registered medical practitioner,

he may, with the consent of the supervised person, make arrangements for him to be treated accordingly.

(2) Such arrangements may provide for the supervised person to receive part of his treatment as a resident patient in an institution or place of any description.

(3) Where any such arrangements are made for the treatment of a supervised person –

    (a) the medical practitioner by whom the arrangements are made shall give notice in writing to the supervising officer, specifying the institution or place in or at which the treatment is to be carried out; and

    (b) the treatment provided for by the arrangements shall be deemed to be treatment to which he is required to submit in pursuance of the supervision order.

Requirements as to medical treatment

7. While the supervised person is under treatment as a resident patient in pursuance of arrangements under paragraph 6 above, the supervising officer shall carry out the supervision to such extent only as may be necessary for the purpose of the revocation or amendment of the order.

Requirements as to residence

8. (1) Subject to sub-paragraph (2) below, a supervision order may include requirements as to the residence of the supervised person.

   (2) Before making such an order containing any such requirement, the court shall consider the home surroundings of the supervised person.

Part 3

Revocation and amendment of orders

Revocation of order

9. (1) Where a supervision order is in force in respect of any person and, on the application of the supervised person or the supervising officer, it appears to a magistrates' court acting for the local justice area concerned that, having regard to circumstances which have arisen since the order was made, it would be in the interests of the health or welfare of the supervised person that the order should be revoked, the court may revoke the order.

   (2) The court by which a supervision order was made may of its own motion revoke the order if, having regard to circumstances which have arisen since the order was made, it considers that it would be inappropriate for the order to continue.

Amendment of order by reason of change of residence

10. (1) This paragraph applies where, at any time while a supervision order is in force in respect of any person, a magistrates' court acting for the local justice area concerned is satisfied that the supervised person proposes to change, or has changed, his residence from the area specified in the order to another local social services authority area or local justice area.

   (2) Subject to sub-paragraph (3) below, the court may, and on the application of the supervising officer shall, amend the supervision order by substituting the other area for the area specified in the order.

   (3) The court shall not amend under this paragraph a supervision order which contains requirements which, in the opinion of the court, cannot be complied with unless the supervised person continues to reside in the area specified in the order unless, in accordance with paragraph 11 below, it either –

   (a) cancels those requirements; or

   (b) substitutes for those requirements other requirements which can be complied with if the supervised person ceases to reside in that area.

Amendment of requirements of order

11. (1) Without prejudice to the provisions of paragraph 10 above, but subject to sub-paragraph (2) below, a magistrates' court for the local justice area concerned may, on the application of the supervised person or the supervising officer, by order amend a supervision order –

    (a) by cancelling any of the requirements of the order; or

    (b) by inserting in the order (either in addition to or in substitution for any such requirement) any requirement which the court could include if it were the court by which the order was made and were then making it.

  (2) The power of a magistrates' court under sub-paragraph (1) above shall not include power to amend an order by extending the period specified in it beyond the end of two years from the day of the original order.

Amendment of requirements in pursuance of medical report

12. (1) Where the medical practitioner by whom or under whose direction the supervised person is being treated for his mental condition in pursuance of any requirement of a supervision order –

    (a) is of the opinion mentioned in sub-paragraph (2) below, or

    (b) is for any reason unwilling to continue to treat or direct the treatment of the supervised person,

he shall make a report in writing to that effect to the supervising officer and that officer shall apply under paragraph 11 above to a magistrates' court for the local justice area concerned for the variation or cancellation of the requirement.

  (2) The opinion referred to in sub-paragraph (1) above is –

    (a) that the treatment of the supervised person should be continued beyond the period specified in the supervision order;

    (b) that the supervised person needs different treatment, being treatment of a kind to which he could be required to submit in pursuance of such an order;

    (c) that the supervised person is not susceptible to treatment; or

    (d) that the supervised person does not require further treatment.

Supplemental

13. (1) On the making under paragraph 9 above of an order revoking a supervision order, the designated officer for the local justice area concerned, or (as the case may be) the Crown Court, shall forthwith give copies of the revoking order to the supervising officer.

(2) A supervising officer to whom in accordance with sub-paragraph (1) above copies of a revoking order are given shall give a copy to the supervised person and to the person in charge of any institution in which the supervised person is residing.

Supplemental

14. (1) On the making under paragraph 10 or 11 above of any order amending a supervision order, the designated officer for the local justice area concerned shall forthwith –

(a) if the order amends the supervision order otherwise than by substituting a new area or a new place for the one specified in the supervision order, give copies of the amending order to the supervising officer;

(b) if the order amends the supervision order in the manner excepted by paragraph (a) above, send to the designated officer for the new local justice area concerned –

(i) copies of the amending order; and

(ii) such documents and information relating to the case as he considers likely to be of assistance to a court acting for that area in exercising its functions in relation to the order;

and in a case falling within paragraph (b) above, the designated officer for that area shall give copies of the amending order to the supervising officer.

(2) Where the designated officer for the court making the order is also the designated officer for the new local justice area –

(a) sub-paragraph (1)(b) above does not apply; but

(b) the designated officers shall give copies of the amending order to the supervising officer.

(3) Where in accordance with sub-paragraph (1) or (2) above copies of an order are given to the supervising officer, he shall give a copy to the supervised person and to the person in charge of any institution in which the supervised person is or was residing.

Appendix 11
Suggested documentation for Regulation 24

To use this form you need to be sure that (i) the first person named is indeed the nearest relative, and (ii) they are not incapable of acting as such through reasons of mental disorder or other illness.

Letter from the Nearest Relative under the Mental Health Act 1983 delegating the functions to another person under Regulation 24 of the Mental Health (Hospital, Guardianship and Treatment) (England) Regulations 2008.

I (full name)	....
of (address)	....
	....
(telephone no.)	....
being the nearest relative of	....
(address)	....
as (state relationship to patient)	....

within the meaning of the Mental Health Act 1983, hereby authorise

(full name)	....
of (address)	....
	....
(telephone no.)	....

(state
relationship to
patient) ....

to perform in respect of the patient the functions conferred upon the nearest relative by Part 2 and section 66 of the Mental Health Act 1983.

This authorisation is to last:

(please tick one box only)

until further notice, or

until .... (specify date), or

until the end of the current detention/ guardianship/CTO

and that this should be the case even if I lose capacity with regard to this decision. Otherwise I understand that I may revoke this authority at any time (despite whichever box I have ticked above) by giving notice in writing to the person authorised and

(a) in the case of hospital detention or Community Treatment Order, the hospital managers, or

(b) in the case of guardianship, the local authority and private guardian (if any).

I agree to a copy of this letter being passed to the person authorised, the hospital managers and, in the case of guardianship, the local authority and private guardian, to act as a notice of my delegation of nearest relative functions under the Mental Health Act 1983 and associated Regulations.

(to be signed by donor):

Signed .... Date ....

I acknowledge receipt of this authorisation to exercise the functions of nearest relative.

I understand that this authorisation takes effect on my receipt of this document.

(to be signed and dated by recipient):

Signed .... Date ....

This form may be sent electronically if the delegated person is willing to accept it in this form. It would be advisable for the AMHP to be sent a copy.

References

Barber, P., Brown, R. and Martin, D. (2012) *Mental Health Law in England and Wales,* Sage.

Bartlett, P. and Sandland, R. (2014) *Mental Health Law* (fourth edition), Oxford University Press.

Brown, R. (1999) The Revised Code of Practice to the Mental Health Act 1983: Some Initial Thoughts. *Journal of Mental Health Law*, 48–60.

Brown, R., Adshead, G. and Pollard, A. (2009) *The Approved Mental Health Professional's Guide to Psychiatry and Medication,* Sage.

Brown, R., Barber, P. and Martin, D. (2015) *The Mental Capacity Act 2005: A Guide for Professionals* (third edition), Sage.

Burns, T. et al (2013) Community Treatment Orders for Patients with Psychosis (OCTET): A Randomised Controlled Trial. *The Lancet Online*, March 26, 2013 http://dx.doi.org/10.1016/ S0140-6736(13)60107-5.

Department of Health (2015) *Mental Health Act 1983, Code of Practice,* TSO.

DHSS (1975) (Butler) *Report of Committee on Mentally Abnormal Offenders,* Cmnd 6244, HMSO.

DHSS (1978) *Review of the Mental Health Act 1959,* Cmnd 7320, HMSO.

DHSS (1981) *Reforming Mental Health Legislation,* Cmnd 8405, HMSO.

Fernando, S. and Keating, F. (eds) (2008) *Mental Health in a Multi-Ethnic Society,* Routledge.

Gelder, M., Andreasen, N., Lopez-Ibor, J. and Geddes, J. (eds) (2012) *New Oxford Textbook of Psychiatry,* Oxford University Press.

Goldberg, D. and Huxley, P. (1992) *Common Mental Disorders: A Bio-Social Model,* Tavistock.

Gostin, L. (1977) *A Human Condition,* Vol. 2, MIND.

Hale, B. (2010) *Mental Health Law* (fifth edition), Sweet and Maxwell.

Heller, T., Reynolds, J., Gomm, R., Muston, R. and Pattison, S. (eds) (2000) *Mental Health Matters, A Reader,* Palgrave Macmillan.

Hewitt, D. (2013) Illegitimate Concern. *Solicitors Journal*, 157 (25).

Home Office (2012) *Police and Criminal Evidence Act 1984: Codes of Practice, Code C,* TSO.

House of Lords and House of Commons (2005) *Joint Committee on the Draft Mental Health Bill,* Parliament.

Hudson, J. and Webber, M. (2012) *The National AMHP Survey 2012: Final Report*, King's College London.

Law, J. (ed.) (2015) *Oxford Dictionary of Law* (eighth edition), Oxford University Press.

Leff, J. and Vaughn, C. (1985) *Expressed Emotion in Families,* Guilford.

Ministry of Justice (2009) *Guidance for Social Supervisors*, MoJ.

Montgomery, J. (2002) *Health Care Law*, Oxford University Press.

Mughal, A. and Richards, S. (2015) *The Deprivation of Liberty Safeguards (DoLS) Handbook*, Bookwise.

National Assembly for Wales (2001) *Adult Mental Health Services for Wales*, http://www.wales.nhs.uk/publications/adult-health-e.pdf

National Institute for Mental Health in England (2008) *Mental Health Act 2007: New Roles*, DH.

National Policing Improvement Agency (2010) *Guidance on Responding to People with Mental Ill Health or Learning Disabilities*, Association of Chief Police Officers.

Pilgrim, D. (2002) The Biopsychosocial Model in Anglo-American Psychiatry: Past, Present and Future? *Journal of Mental Health,* 11(6), 585–594.

Puri, B., Brown, R., McKee, H. and Treasaden, I. (2012) *Mental Health Law* (second edition), Hodder Arnold.

Yeates, V. (2005) Death of the Nearest Relative? Carers' and Families' Rights to Challenge Compulsion under Current and Proposed Mental Health Legislation. *Journal of Mental Health Law*, 123–137.

Cases

AM v SLAM [2013] UKUT 0365

B v Barking, Havering and Brentwood Community Healthcare NHS Trust [1999] 1 FLR 106

BB v Cygnet Health Care and London Borough of Lewisham [2008] EWHC 1259

Bibby v Chief Constable of Essex Police [2000] All ER (D) 487

C v Blackburn and Darwen Borough Council (2011) EWHC 3321 (COP)

Cheshire West and Chester Council v P [2011] EWCA Civ 1257

CX v LA [2011] EWHC 1918

DD v (1) Durham County Council (2) Middlesbrough City Council [2012] EWHC 1053 (QB)

GD v Edgware Community Hospital and London Borough of Barnet [2008] EWHC 3572

HL v UK (2004) 40 EHRR 761

JT v UK (2000) 30 EHRR CD 77

KD v Walsall MBC and Others [2015] UKUT 0251

Kimber v Kimber [2000] 1 FLR 383

London Borough of Hillingdon v Neary [2011] EWHC 1377 (COP)

MD v Nottinghamshire Health Care NHS Trust [2010] UKUT 59

NL v Hampshire County Council [2014] UKUT 465

Nottingham City Council v UNISON [2004] EWHC 893

P v Cheshire West and Chester Council and Another; P & Q v Surrey CC [2014] UKSC 19

PCT v LDV (A), CC and B Healthcare Group [2013] EWHC 272 (Fam)

R v Bournewood Community and Mental Health Trust NHS *ex parte* L [1998] 3 WLR 107

R v East London and the City Mental Health NHS Trust and Another (Respondents) *ex parte* von Brandenburg [2003]

R v Manchester City Council *ex parte* Stennett [2002] UKHL 34

R v Mental Health Review Tribunal for West Midlands and North West *ex parte* H [2000] All ER (D) 2189

R v Wilson *ex parte* Williamson [1996] COD 42 (QBD)

R (CS) v MHRT [2004] EWHC 2958 (Admin)

R (DR) v Mersey Care NHS Trust [2002] MHLR 386

R (E) v Bristol City Council [2005] EWHC 74 (Admin)

R (GC) v Managers of the Kingswood Centre (2008) EWHC (CO/7784/2008)

R (H) v London North and East Region Mental Health Review Tribunal [2001] EWCA Civ 415

R (Munjaz) v Mersey Care NHS Trust [2005] UKHL 58

R (Tagoe-Thompson) v The Hospital Managers of the Park Royal Centre [2003] EWCA Civ 330

R (von Brandenburg) v East London and the City Mental Health NHS Trust and Another (Respondents) [2003] UKHL 58

R (Wooder) v Fegetter and the Mental Health Act Commission [2002] EWCA Civ 554

Re D (Mental patient: Habeas corpus) [2000] 2 FLR 848

Re F (Mental Health Act: Guardianship) [2000] 1 FLR 192

Re Whitbread [1997] EWHC 102

Reed (Trainer) v Bronglais Hospital [2001] EWHC 792 (Admin)

TTM v London Borough of Hackney [2010] EWHC 1349 (Admin); [2011] EWCA Civ 4

TW v Enfield Borough Council [2014] EWCA Civ 362

Ward v Commissioner of Police [2005] UKHL 32

Winterwerp v Netherlands (1979) 2 EHRR 387

Some useful websites

Care Council for Wales **www.ccwales.org.uk**

Care Quality Commission **www.cqc.org.uk**

Department of Health **www.dh.gov.uk**

Essex Chambers Newsletters **www.39essex.com**

Health and Care Professions Council **www.hpc-uk.org**

Healthcare Inspectorate Wales **www.hiw.org.uk**

Luke Clements **www.lukeclements.co.uk**

Mental Capacity Law and Policy **www.mentalcapacitylawandpolicy.org.uk**

Mental Health Law Online **www.mentalhealthlaw.co.uk**

Welsh Government **www.wales.gov.uk**

Index

absence without leave 44

acid test 32

Act for regulating private madhouses 1774 3

admission for assessment: in cases of emergency – section 4 25, 160–1; Form A2 164–6; Form A4 167–8; and nearest relative 19, 65; section 2 18–20, 23–4, 120, 157–8

admission for treatment: Form A6 169–71; Form A8 172–3; under section 3 21–4; section 3: checklists for applications/forms 158–60

admission to hospital: compulsory 16, 18, 25–6, 74–5; general points 161

Adult Mental Health Services for Wales 73

advance decisions 114

after-care of patients: defined 128; under section 117 3, 43, 51–2, 128–9; supervised after-care 39, 45

age assessment, DoLS 151

alcohol dependency 9–10, 152

AMHPs: and admission for assessment under section 2 19, 24; and admission for treatment under section 3 21, 22, 24; assessment for compulsory admission/guardianship 74–5; as best interests assessor (BIA) 154; and community treatment orders 46, 47, 48, 49, 50; competences 186–9; consultation 80–2; and CQC/HIW 133–4; and detention under DoLS/Mental Health Act 154–5; and Equality Act 2010 139; functions under the MHA 72–3; guiding principles governing 73–4; independence of 81; legal framework governing 136–40; liability of 77–8; management and supervision of 79–82; and Mental Health Act 1983 72–3, 77, 181–2; and mental health tribunals 79, 120; and nearest relative 54–5, 57, 58, 59, 61–3, 64–5, 66–8, 72, 73, 76–7; professional groups able to become 80; Regulations for England 183–9; Regulations for Wales 190–6; reports for applications under sections 2, 3 or 4 25–6; reports for managers' hearings 123; responsibility for actions and section 139 77–9; role of 1; and section 117 after-care 128–9; and section 3 25–6, 52, 118; and social circumstances reports 123–4, 125–6, 127; as social

supervisors 87; and supervision orders 93–4; tasks for in MHA assessments 83–4, 199–200; and use of interpreters 75–6

AM v SLAM (2013) 34–6

application for detention, and nearest relative 63–4

application in respect of patient already in hospital, section 5 28

appropriate adult (AA), role of 96–9

'appropriate medical treatment' test 12–13

approved clinician (AC): and consent 102; and reviewing treatment 132

approved mental health professional (AMHP) *see* AMHPs

approved social workers (ASWs) 79, 80, 120–1 *see also* AMHP

Asperger's syndrome 12

assessment: for access to resources 127; admission for in cases of emergency – section 4 25, 160–1; admission for under section 2 18–20, 23–4, 120; for compulsory admission or guardianship 74–5; DoLS 151–3; for possible admission to hospital 124–6; for possible reception into guardianship 127; section 136 95; tasks for AMHPs in MHA assessments 83–4, 199–200; two-stage approach to a 20–1

associate managers 121

autistic spectrum disorders 12 *see also* Asperger's syndrome; *Bournewood* case (1993–1998); *HL v UK* (2004)

bad faith, acting in 77–8

Barber *et al.* 10

barring order, section 25 122

Bartlett, P. and Sandland, R. 66

BB v Cygnet Health Care and London Borough of Lewisham (2008) 26

behavioural frameworks, mental disorder 6

behavioural test 12

best interests: assessment DoLS 152–3; Mental Capacity Act 2005 111, 112

best interests assessor (BIA), and DoLS 149, 151–3, 154

Bibby v Chief Constable of Essex Police (2000) 96

Bingham, Lord 78